FAMILY LAW AND GENDER IN THE MIDDLE EAST AND NORTH AFRICA

The volume serves as reference point for anyone interested in the Middle East and North Africa as well as for those interested in women's rights and family law, generally or in the MENA region. It is the only book covering personal status codes of nearly a dozen countries. It covers Muslim family law in the following Middle East/North African countries: Tunisia, Egypt, Morocco, Algeria, Iraq, Lebanon, Jordan, Israel, Palestine, and Qatar. Some of these countries were heavily affected by the Arab Spring, and some were not. With authors from around the world, each chapter of the book provides a history of personal status law both before and after the revolutionary period. Tunisia emerges as the country that made the most significant progress politically and with respect to women's rights. A decade on from the Arab Spring, across the region, there is more evidence of stasis than change.

ADRIEN K. WING is Associate Dean for International and Comparative Programs at the University of Iowa College of Law, where she has taught for over thirty-five years. She is also the Bessie Dutton Murray Professor of Law. Author of over 150 publications, her courses include Law in the Muslim World.

HISHAM A. KASSIM is a seasoned attorney at Kassim Legal, PLLC in Washington DC, who represents a wide range of international and MENA-based clients. Previously, he opened the Amman office of the Kalbian Hagerty law firm after several years based in its Washington, DC office. He holds a Bachelor's degree from the University of Virginia, a JD degree from the University of Iowa College of Law, and an LLM degree from New York University. Kassim is fluent in Arabic and English and is a published scholar in major US law reviews. He has coauthored several publications with Dean Adrien Wing.

T0381537

FAMILY LAW AND GENDER IN THE MIDDLE EAST AND NORTH AFRICA

Change and Stasis since the Arab Spring

Edited by

ADRIEN K. WING

University of Iowa

HISHAM A. KASSIM

Kassim Legal PLLC

CAMBRIDGE
UNIVERSITY PRESS

Shaftesbury Road, Cambridge CB2 8EA, United Kingdom

One Liberty Plaza, 20th Floor, New York, NY 10006, USA

477 Williamstown Road, Port Melbourne, VIC 3207, Australia

314–321, 3rd Floor, Plot 3, Splendor Forum, Jasola District Centre, New Delhi – 110025, India

103 Penang Road, #05-06/07, Visioncrest Commercial, Singapore 238467

Cambridge University Press is part of Cambridge University Press & Assessment, a department of the University of Cambridge.

We share the University's mission to contribute to society through the pursuit of education, learning and research at the highest international levels of excellence.

www.cambridge.org
Information on this title: www.cambridge.org/9781107023529

DOI: 10.1017/9781139151719

© Cambridge University Press & Assessment 2023

This publication is in copyright. Subject to statutory exception and to the provisions of relevant collective licensing agreements, no reproduction of any part may take place without the written permission of Cambridge University Press & Assessment.

First published 2023

A catalogue record for this publication is available from the British Library.

A Cataloging-in-Publication data record for this book is available from the Library of Congress

ISBN 978-1-107-02352-9 Hardback
ISBN 978-1-009-35112-6 Paperback

Cambridge University Press & Assessment has no responsibility for the persistence or accuracy of URLs for external or third-party internet websites referred to in this publication and does not guarantee that any content on such websites is, or will remain, accurate or appropriate.

CONTENTS

CONTRIBUTORS

SARA ABABNEH is a lecturer in International Relations at the University of Sheffield where she teaches modules on Middle Eastern Politics, Gendered Politics of the Arab World and on Race and Racism in International Relations. Prior to that she was an Associate Professor and the Head of the Political and Social Research Unit at the University of Jordan's Center for Strategic Studies. Ababneh earned her DPhil in Politics and International Relations from St. Antony's College, University of Oxford. Ababneh was selected as the Carnegie Centennial Fellow at the Middle East Institute at Columbia University in New York. She also was a Visiting Scholar at the University of Tübingen. Dr. Ababneh has conducted research on Mandate Palestine, gender and Islamism, Muslim family laws, and labor movements. Her research interests include class, gender and struggles for liberation, social justice, post-colonial and feminist IR theory, and economic sovereignty. Currently, Ababneh studies the popular Jordanian protest movement (*al-Hirak al-Sha'bi al-Urduni*).

NADA AMMAR is an immigration lawyer in southern California. She is the recipient of a LLB degree from the Lebanese University-Filière Francophone de Droit, a master's degree in Law, accredited by Pantheon-Assas-Paris II, in Litigation, Arbitration and Alternative Dispute Resolution, and a LLM degree in International and Comparative Law from Chapman School of Law in California. Prior to attending Chapman, she worked as a legal officer at the regional office of the United Nations High Commissioner for Refugees (UNHCR) in Beirut. She managed various legal cases pertaining to refugees with a particular focus on cases of arbitrary detention, extradition, child protection, and statelessness.

NATHALIE BERNARD-MAUGIRON is a senior researcher at the French Institute of Research for Development (IRD) in Paris. She holds a PhD in

Public Law from the University of Paris and a master's degree in International Human Rights Law from the University of Grenoble (France). She supervises doctoral dissertations at the Ecole de droit de la Sorbonne. She was codirector of the Institut d'études de l'Islam et des sociétés du monde musulman (IISMM) at the Ecole des Hautes études en sciences sociales (EHESS) in Paris from 2010 to 2014 where she was also teaching a seminar on contemporary law in the Arab world until 2019. She teaches comparative Middle East constitutional law at SciencesPo Paris. She was a part-time faculty member at the Political Science department of the American University in Cairo from 2001 to 2005, where she taught Egyptian constitutional law and human rights courses. Bernard-Maugiron works on personal status law, the judiciary, and constitutionalism in Egypt and in the Arab world.

STEPHANIE WILLMAN BORDAT is a founding partner at Mobilising for Rights Associates (MRA), an international nonprofit women's rights organization based in Rabat, and is currently working in Morocco, Algeria, Tunisia, and Libya. She earned a BA degree from Swarthmore College and a JD degree from Columbia Law School as well as a Maitrise en Droit from Paris I Sorbonne. She has worked as a human rights lawyer and grassroots activist for over twenty-three years in collaboration with local women's rights groups and lawyers across the Maghreb. Her work involves human rights education, legal accompaniment, strategic litigation, monitoring and documentation, and national and international advocacy. Bordat also consults for international donors as a researcher and teaches several university courses on social change. She was a Fulbright Scholar at the Mohammed V University Law School in Rabat, Morocco.

MOUNIRA M. CHARRAD is an associate professor of Sociology, University of Texas, Austin, and a Non-Resident Fellow at the Baker Institute, Rice University. Her book, *States and Women's Rights: The Making of Postcolonial Tunisia, Algeria and Morocco* won numerous distinguished awards including Best Book in Sociology from the American Sociological Association and Best Book on Politics and History Greenstone Award from the American Political Science Association. Her articles have appeared in major scholarly journals. She has edited or co-edited *Patrimonial Power in the Modern World, Patrimonial Capitalism and Empire, Women Rising: In and Beyond the*

Arab Spring, Women's Agency: Silences and Voices, and *Femmes, Culture et Société au Maghreb*. Her new book, *Forging Feminism: From Autocracy to Revolution in Tunisia* is forthcoming with Columbia University Press. Her work has centered on state formation, colonialism, law, citizenship, kinship, women's rights, social movements and protest. It has been translated into French, Arabic, and Chinese. She received her undergraduate education from the Sorbonne in Paris and her PhD from Harvard University.

HYUN JEONG HA is an assistant professor of Sociology at Duke Kunshan University, China. Her research interests include religion and politics, sectarianism, gender, emotions, the Middle East and North Africa, and ethnography. She has written about religious minorities, the Arab Uprisings, sectarian relations, and Islamic feminism in contemporary Egypt. Her current research examines the question of how ethnic and religious differences manifest in everyday interactions between the Muslim majority and the Christian minority after the 2011 Arab Uprisings in Egypt. Her work has appeared in *Journal of Peace Research, Ethnic and Racial Studies*, and *Research in Social Movements, Conflicts, and Change*, among others and in several edited volumes. She received her B.A. in Arabic from Hankuk University of Foreign studies and M.S. in Sociology from Seoul National University. She earned her Ph.D. in Sociology from the University of Texas at Austin and was a Global Religion Research Initiative Postdoctoral Research Fellow at the University of Notre Dame.

HAIDER ALA HAMOUDI is Interim Dean and a professor of law at the University of Pittsburgh School of Law. He earned his BS degree at MIT as well as his JD and JSD degrees at Columbia Law School. His scholarship focuses primarily on Islamic law and Middle Eastern law. He has written extensively on the Iraqi Personal Status Code, and attempts to repeal it, in various law reviews and book chapters. Hamoudi's books include *Negotiating in Civil Conflict: Imperfect Bargaining and Constitutional Construction in Iraq, Islamic Law in Modern Courts: Cases and Materials*, and the *Nutshell on Islamic Law*. He teaches Contracts, Commercial Law, and Islamic Law.

MICHAEL MOUSA KARAYANNI is the Bruce W. Wayne Professor of Law at the Hebrew University of Jerusalem. He holds graduate degrees from George Washington University National Law Center (LLM), Hebrew

University of Jerusalem (LLD), and University of Pennsylvania (SJD). He has held visiting positions at Georgetown Law Center, Melbourne Law School, Stanford Law School, Yale Law School, University of Chicago Law School, Institute for Advanced Study in Princeton, and Wissenschaftskolleg zu Berlin. His research interests are in private international law and interreligious law, multiculturalism, and civil procedure. Among his recent publications are *Conflicts in Conflict, A Conflict of Laws Case Study of Israel and the Palestinian Territories*, and *A Multicultural Entrapment: Religion & State among the Palestinian Arabs in Israel*.

LINA M. KASSEM holds the position of Visiting Assistant Professor of Government and International Relations at William and Mary. Prior to joining William and Mary in 2021, she taught for three years at the Asian University for Women in Bangladesh and has also taught at institutions such as Qatar University in Qatar, Zayed University in the UAE, and Wilmington College in the US. With a PhD in Political Science from the University of Cincinnati, Lina's research focus is on topics such as race, representation of Arab and Muslim Americans, women in Islamic law, nationalism, and identity construction.

HISHAM A. KASSIM is a seasoned attorney at Kassim Legal PLLC in Washington DC, who represents a wide range of international and MENA-based clients. Previously, he opened the Amman office of the Kalbian Hagerty law firm after several years based in its Washington, DC office. He holds a Bachelor's degree from the University of Virginia, a JD degree from the University of Iowa College of Law, and an LLM degree from New York University. Kassim is fluent in Arabic and English and is a published scholar in major US law reviews. He has coauthored several publications with Dean Adrien Wing.

SAIDA KOUZZI is a founding partner at Mobilising for Rights Associates (MRA), an international nonprofit women's rights organization based in Rabat and is currently working in Morocco, Algeria, Tunisia, and Libya. She holds a LLB degree from Mohammed V University in Rabat. She has worked as a grassroots activist for over twenty-three years in collaboration with diverse local women's rights groups and lawyers across the Maghreb. Her work involves human rights education, legal accompaniment, strategic litigation, monitoring and documentation, and national and international advocacy. Kouzzi also consults for international donors as a researcher. She worked at a leading human rights law firm in Rabat, Morocco, and was a long-time active member of the Association Marocaine des Droits de l'Homme.

JONATHAN KUTTAB is a Palestinian attorney and human rights activist. He is currently the Executive Director of Friends of Sabeel North America (FOSNA). He grew up in Jerusalem, studied in the US, earning his BA degree from Messiah College and JD degree from University of Virginia Law School. He worked a few years at the Wall Street law firm of Mudge Rose Guthrie & Alexander. He is a member of the Bar Associations in New York, Israel, and Palestine. Kuttab founded a number of human rights organizations including Al Haq and the Mandela Institute for Palestinian Prisoners and is the chairman of the board of Bethlehem Bible College and of Holy Land Trust. He was the Head of the Legal Committee negotiating the Cairo Agreement of 1994 between Israel and the PLO. He is a recognized authority on international law, human rights, and Palestinian and Israeli affairs.

ADRIEN K. WING is the Associate Dean for International and Comparative Programs at the University of Iowa College of Law, where she has taught for over thirty-five years. She is also the Bessie Dutton Murray Professor of Law. She received her AB degree from Princeton University, MA degree from UCLA, and JD degree from Stanford Law School. Author of over 150 publications, Wing is the director of the UI Center for Human Rights and France summer abroad program and was the onsite director for the London Law Consortium semester abroad program for three years. She served as the Associate Dean for Faculty Development as well. Her courses include International Human Rights Law and Law in the Muslim World.

ACKNOWLEDGMENTS

I dedicate this book to my dear friends and colleagues from the Middle East and North African region, who have inspired me since my first trip there over 40 years ago. I would like to especially acknowledge my life partner James Sommerville, as well as my seven children, 19 grandchildren, and wonderful daughters and sons-in law. Plus, I must sincerely thank my coeditor Hisham Kassim, who was a great student and has become a dear coauthor, colleague, and friend. I am deeply indebted to all our wonderful contributors as well as many hardworking research assistants from the University of Iowa College of Law.

—Adrien K. Wing

I am deeply grateful to the dedication and hard work of our contributors, research assistants, and many others who toiled away on this book with Dean Wing and me. Without them there would be no book. I would also like to thank Dean Wing, who took a chance on me more than ten years ago when I first joined the University of Iowa. Finally, a special word of thanks to my wife, Kate Touchton-Leonard, to whom I would like to dedicate this book.

—Hisham A. Kassim

∽

Introduction

Family Law and Gender in the Middle East and North Africa: Change and Stasis since the Arab Spring

ADRIEN K. WING AND HISHAM A. KASSIM

I.1 Introduction

Achieving alterations in the status of women's rights is a difficult long-term process around the world. There are many areas that can be subject to change, including in educational attainment, employment participation, health care access, and political representation. A key area remains personal status or family law. Marriage, divorce, and child custody remain at the core of many women's existence and influence possibilities in education, employment, and politics as well. In some nations, family law is secular in nature; and in others, it is based upon customary practices, and/or religion too. The Middle East and North Africa is an area where personal status law is strongly based on religious practices in most countries.

While various upheavals have occurred over the decades,[1] the region is unique in that it experienced the Arab Spring in 2010–2011, which many hoped would lead to substantive political and other change in multiple countries. Additionally, since 2018, people in several countries, including Iraq, Lebanon, Sudan, and Algeria plus Iran, Morocco, Tunisia, and Palestine, to a more limited degree, have protested declining economic conditions, cronyism, and corruption.[2] Now that more than a decade has passed, it is clear that progressive political change did not sustain itself in most nations.[3]

This book focuses on the status of family law. Are most countries still using the rules that originated with Ottoman law? Did any changes occur during or after the Arab Spring? Under what circumstances? Were women's groups or politicians involved? This book covers family law in the following Middle East and North African countries: Tunisia, Egypt, Morocco, Algeria, Iraq, Lebanon, Jordan, Israel, Palestine, and Qatar.

While most countries may be predominantly Muslim, there are some that have Christian or other groups. The volume will focus only on Muslim family law, noting some differences between Sunni and Shi'a branches where relevant. Some of these countries were heavily affected by the Arab Spring, and some were not.

With specialist authors who are professors or practitioners from around the world, the chapters provide coverage of family law both before and up until about one decade after the Arab Spring. While personal status codes include inheritance law, this volume only focuses on marriage, divorce, and custody issues.

It does not appear that major change has occurred in most countries. Tensions between traditionalist/conservative and other more moderate or reformist forces can result in regression in all areas, including family law, rather than progress. Tunisia emerges as the country that made the most significant progress politically and with respect to women's rights.

This introduction will first highlight changes that occurred during the Arab Spring, especially in certain countries, and the status of women at that time. Then, it will provide an overview of the chapters featured. The conclusion will provide some lessons learned.

I.2   The Arab Spring[4]

The world was in shock and awe in the winter of 2010 when Tunisia, a small North African country, was able to remove its twenty-three-year-long leader President Zine El Abedine Ben Ali from power in less than a month – and with relatively little violence.[5] The spark that set off this remarkable event was the self-immolation of a young man, a twenty-six year-old fruit vendor named Mohamed Bouazizi.[6] The local police in his small town prohibited him from selling meager produce as a means to eke out a poor living.[7] Shockingly, rather than passively accepting this fate, Bouazizi set fire to himself. The acts of the Tunisian police had violated Bouazizi's basic human dignity and revealed the hopelessness of a corrupted system in which he could see no future. His bold final act touched off a firestorm of activity throughout the Middle East and North Africa – and ignited global attention.[8]

Tunisia was an unlikely birthplace and catalyst for revolution and change. It was a favorite playground of European tourists, with warm weather, self-contained seaside resorts, fantastic Roman ruins, and the sizzling hot sands made famous by the Star Wars movies. It is not a nation that is immediately associated with warriors on the battlefield. Editor/author Wing has visited this beautiful country several times, and it always brings to mind the smell of jasmine. This national flower is often sold even in small restaurants. Men regularly place it behind their ears and people accept it in the form of fragrant garlands. As homage to this national symbol, the events taking place in Tunisia were referred to in popular media outlets as the Jasmine Revolution.[9]

The Jasmine Revolution ignited with such force that it quickly spread to other parts of the region – most notably, Egypt. This country carries the cultural mantle of the Arab world, with several thousand years of rich history and culture. The fall of thirty-year President Hosni Mubarak marked a truly momentous occasion across the Arab world. Most significantly, the internet activity of the "Facebook generation,"[10] along with the support of the military and massive labor and community organizing, managed to achieve Mubarak's fall in an astonishingly short period of time. Egypt's uprising included the efforts of both men and women, from all different socioeconomic spheres, who held a variety of social and political opinions. This diverse pool of citizens united to achieve a common goal – to remove Mubarak from power and to implement a democracy capable of addressing national issues such as poor education, rising agricultural prices, the growing gap between the rich and the poor, and the inadequate quality of social services and support.[11]

Tunisia's revolution and Mubarak's overthrow fostered the assumption that the rest of the Arab world would follow suit – with dictators and repressive regimes falling like dominos. However, this assumption was premature. Some kingdoms, such as Morocco and Jordan, engaged in limited political reform.[12] Saudi Arabian officials chose to appease Saudi citizenry by preemptively paying millions of dollars to young and unemployed citizens – including fifty-three million dollars to help people understand the Qur'an.[13]

In other countries, such as Syria and Yemen, political leaders resisted being taken down like Mubarak or suffering exile in Saudi Arabia like the former Tunisian President Ben Ali. Syrian President Assad held on despite attacks from multiple forces, internal and external. Yemeni President Ali Abdullah Saleh ultimately had to resign and was assassinated in 2017.[14] Bahrain's Sunni minority was able to continue governing a Shi'a majority, despite protests.[15] Forty-year Libyan leader Colonel Muammar Qaddafi's best efforts to avoid a fate similar to Mubarak and Ben Ali ultimately proved unsuccessful. His bullet-ridden body and that of his son Muatassim were displayed for several days after their deaths.[16]

Despite the dramatic events involving some countries, the "Arab Spring" did not develop its momentum into an "Arab Fall" that could be sustained. For example, in Egypt, the Muslim Brotherhood and the even more conservative Islamist groups known as Salafists won almost two-thirds of the votes,[17] but then were overthrown.

Another prominent example is Tunisia, where the moderate Islamist party Ennahda, which was previously banned under the Ben Ali regime, won the October 2011 election with 40 percent of the vote.[18] Many feared that the Ennahda party would cut back on Tunisia's well-known secularist approach to governance,[19] reversing decades of progress in the field of women's rights. They ended up stepping down in a peaceful manner, and politics have been complicated ever since.

Many people in the region suffer from severe "spirit injuries." This term from Wing's work is a concept to signify psychological and emotional distress on an individual or group wide basis.[20] While nations throughout the Middle East and North Africa achieved political independence in another era, from that moment of political independence until the Arab Spring, many citizens throughout the region have never been able to attach much meaning to that independence. Authoritarian leadership created societies where the concept of self-determination has had little value.[21]

Many citizens in the region may or may not be interested in achieving a form of government similar to Western democracies. A number of these latter societies have been having political difficulties since the era of the Arab Spring. Many Middle East citizens may want the opportunity to speak, think, write, and participate in ways they have never done before, experiencing participation on their own terms.

I.3   Challenges Facing Arab Women

Historically, women in the region have faced a severe backlash when asserting their rights.[22] In the 1950s Algerian Revolution, social equality during social unrest eventually gave way to the status quo with the words: "[Women], you had your moment; now go back to your traditional roles."[23] Women have historically expressed concern on a wide variety of issues, including but not limited to: poor access to education; lack of career opportunities; "domestic" and external violence; restricted participation in public life; and unequal inheritance, marriage, divorce, and custody rights.

Many hoped that any advances from the Arab Spring would include women in the region. The Arab Spring clearly established an opportunity or a revolutionary moment for some women to take up unprecedented public roles alongside men. The international community acknowledged this fact when Yemeni activist Tawakkul Karman became one of three women who won the 2011 Nobel Prize for Peace.[24] Many other women worked visibly at the front lines of the revolution, breaking gendered cultural norms and fighting for the freedom of their fellow citizens.[25]

Events in Tunisia saw the country take positive steps toward increasing women's rights. Politically, new Tunisian election laws required 50 percent of candidates running for office and listed on the ballots to be female.[26] Although women were not at the top of the party lists, they managed to win 24 percent overall for the constituent assembly in Tunisia in 2011.[27] In a positive move, the then-newly elected president, long-time rights activist Moncef Marzouki, promised equal rights for women in Tunisia. Nevertheless, continued incidents of sociopolitical coercion against women with respect to dress, such as forcing female university lecturers to wear a veil, casted uncertainty on the outlook for gender equity in Tunisia.[28]

The Tunisian interim government removed almost all of its reservations to the Convention on the Elimination of All Forms of Discrimination against Women (CEDAW),[29] an amazing decision, in light of the fact that the CEDAW contains the most reservations of any international convention.[30] The majority of these reservations indicate that a treaty binds a government only so far as it does not conflict with local customs and religion – effectively gutting the practical purpose of the document.[31] The Tunisian elimination of most of these reservations is a revolutionary and laudatory act for a country in the region, though it is difficult to gauge its long-term significance at this juncture.

One area of difficulty for Tunisian women may be the fact that the government has retained one general reservation: that Tunisia will not take any legislative action conflicting with Chapter 1 of the Constitution.[32] Chapter 1 includes a statement that the national religion is Islam, which could potentially invite various religious-based arguments against legal reform for women's rights; however, until now, Tunisia has not used Chapter 1 as an excuse for maintaining laws or practices that subvert CEDAW. Perhaps there is a fair chance that Tunisia will be making a serious effort to meet its obligations under CEDAW, providing inspiration for other reforms in the region to follow.[33]

The Tunisian elections placing the conservative Islamist party Ennahda in power sparked controversy, debate, and demonstrations by women throughout the country.[34] Many women viewed the introduction of a socially conservative Islamist party as a threat to the advancements and strides gained through their efforts over many years as the most secular country in the region.[35] Concerns regarding the reinstitution of polygamy and potential changes to currently egalitarian divorce laws sparked a renewed effort by Tunisian women to politically engage themselves and continue the momentum of the Arab Spring to protect their rights.[36] Some Tunisians were worried that the new conservative government would roll back such gains.[37]

Many women in the region experienced a cultural backlash, as well as government-sponsored discrimination and abuse. Human Rights Watch obtained statements from politically active women who described their detention at an Egyptian military base, which included forced virginity tests by the personnel.[38] An official confirmed the military had performed the virginity tests, which constitute unlawful assault under both Egyptian and international law. In a blow to women's rights, many women who were tested were charged with prostitution and the army doctor who performed the tests, was acquitted.[39]

Despite women's active participation in Mubarak's downfall, the spring 2011 revisions to the Egyptian constitution largely ignored women's rights.[40] As human rights activist and physician Dr. Nawal El Saadawi observed, "[t]he blood of the women killed in the revolution is still wet, and we were being betrayed."[41] No women sat on the appointed eight-person Constitutional Committee.[42] Additionally, the 2011 revisions require the president of Egypt to marry an Egyptian wife – effectively limiting the presidency to a man, even in the language delimited by the founding document.[43]

On International Women's Day 2011, a month after the fall of Mubarak, marchers for women's rights in Tahrir Square encountered crowds of men who shouted verbally abusive statements and sexually harassed them. At one stage, men held up a woman in full niqab face-veil and chanted, "this is a real Egyptian woman!" [44]

In December, horrifying images circulated in the mainstream international press showed Egyptian military police dragging a woman wearing traditional Egyptian Islamic dress through the street, beating her and stomping on her stomach; her bright blue bra was exposed as she lay on the street, becoming a symbol for the military oppression.[45] Subsequent protesters held up signs with her images, chanting warnings such as, "This is the army that is protecting us!"[46]

Despite the discouraging events, Egyptian female journalist Bothaina Kamel ran for president as the only female candidate.[47] While some questioned the seriousness of her campaign, Kamel explained that she was interested in asserting and enforcing the rights of both men and women. Unfortunately, however, Kamel did not collect enough signatures to actually achieve placement on the ballot.[48] The fall 2011 Egyptian elections required each party to include a woman on its party list, but women candidates only won 2 percent of the vote.[49]

This disappointing trend continued in Libya, where the government dropped the proposed 10 percent quota for women after negative reaction from many quarters.[50]

Women in Libya had more rights at certain points in history than women in some other Arab countries.[51] Women played various roles as part of the February 17 revolution. As St. John posited, women transitioned from state-serving "feminism" of the nationalist, post-independence regimes to "non-institutional activism on the streets and through cyber-space."[52]

Unfortunately, the National Transitional Council (NTC), a body established by the rebels to give a political face to the revolution, only appointed two women to the forty-person government.[53] In addition, the NTC Chairman Mustafa Abdul-Jalil announced that polygamy would be reintroduced in Libya, and that any laws conflicting with Islam would be null and void.[54]

On a positive note, after two years, the Libyan government officially recognized that pro-Gaddafi forces had used rape as a weapon of war and issued a decree authorizing payment of reparations for sexual violence during the revolution.[55]

There have been various efforts to update the 2011 interim constitution. Unfortunately, the efforts have been unsuccessful. It remains to be seen if the final document will have sufficient protections on paper, much less in reality.

I.4 The Volume

Chapter 1 highlights the most successful Arab country in terms of political and family law reform: Tunisia. It occupies a special place among the countries that have experienced the Arab Spring. Not only was it the cradle of the uprisings, but it was also the only country where the uprisings were followed by a serious effort at democratization. This process may be under threat as President Kais Saied collapsed the government in 2021, consolidating his power. Interestingly, he appointed the first female prime minister, Najla Bouden Romdhane, but it remains to be seen if her presence has any effect on women's rights. In "Sustained Reforms: Family Law in Tunisia," renowned University of Texas Professor Mounira M. Charrad and Duke Kunshan University Professor Hyun Jeong Ha, offer an overview of the sustained reforms of Islamic family law that occurred in Tunisia from the 1950s to 2021. They trace developments during major time periods starting with the end of colonial rule in 1956 and ending with the aftermath of the 2010/11 Arab Spring that ushered a process of democratization in the last decade. They discuss the reforms that placed Tunisia at the vanguard of the Arab world in regard to liberalizing family law and women's rights. They argue that sustained reforms were possible because succeeding regimes found it in their best interests to pursue a reformist policy.

The post-revolution, democratically elected new governments maintained the legislation in place or continued further on the reformist path, possibly in part for their own interests and in part in response to demands from women's and other groups. The authors think that a major tension at the moment separates tendencies among political constituencies: those who defend a conservative Islam and are likely to favor a system of law more faithful to it, those who consider themselves moderate Islamists and are open to reforms, and secularists who tend to prefer a law that is separate from religion.

Chapter 2, "Family Law in Egypt" was written by Dr. Nathalie Bernard-Maugiron, from the French Institute of Research for Development. Egypt was directly affected by the Arab Spring but with a different political result than Tunisia. Egypt adopted a new constitution in 2014 that strengthened the principle of equality between men and women. In spite of its call on the State to achieve equality in all areas, family law continues to establish significant differences between wives and husbands. The chapter examines the reforms introduced in Egyptian personal status law since the beginning of the twentieth century and the differences based on gender that remain in both marriage and divorce rights. It stresses how governments had to present the reforms as taking place within the *Shari'a* in order to avoid rejection by conservative religious circles and society.

Before the removal of Mubarak in 2011, women's groups were hoping to reform personal status laws further. They became fearful under the Muslim Brother President Mohammed Morsi that their rights would be further curtailed after Islamist parties won the 2012 parliamentary and presidential elections. Amendments to personal status laws, dubbed Suzanne laws, after Mubarak's wife, Suzanne Mubarak, were the target of Islamist groups, who attempted to discredit them by associating them with the previous regime, and claiming that they were designed to break up Egyptian families and impose Western values.[56] No amendments were adopted before the 2013 removal of Morsi by the army.

In January 2017, alarmed by a rising divorce rate, President Abdel Fatah al-Sisi demanded that new legislation be enacted to invalidate orally pronounced repudiation and protect the family. The Council of Senior Scholars at al-Azhar University rejected this proposal, stressing that prohibiting orally pronounced divorce would be in contradiction with the consensus among the *Umma* (Islamic faithful) since the age of Prophet Mohamed.

Various proposals to amend family law have been submitted by the government, members of the parliament, the National Council for Women, and even by the Council of Senior al-Azhar scholars, but none of them had been adopted through 2022.

Two chapters concerning Maghreb countries – Morocco and Algeria – were written by Stephanie Willman Bordat and Saida Kouzzi, from the Mobilising for Rights Associates organization. In "Women's Rights in the Moroccan Family Code: Caught between Change and Continuity" (Chapter 3), the authors examine the 2004 Moroccan Family Code. The enactment process was marked by unprecedented public mobilization for and against reforms. In November 2011, national legislative elections brought to power a governmental coalition led by the Islamist Justice and Development Party (PJD) for the first time in Moroccan history. The party was reelected in 2016 elections for an additional five years of a conservative government.

Over the past decade, international human rights bodies and local activists have repeatedly highlighted the need for further revisions to the Family Code to abolish remaining inequality. These include calls to: prohibit polygamy; ban the marriage of minors; give men and women the same access to divorce; ensure equal property rights upon dissolution of marriage; and provide for equality of mothers and fathers in child guardianship.

The PJD government had made it clear that it opposed Family Code reforms. This was made particularly evident during the 2017 United Nations Universal Periodic Review, when Morocco rejected a record number of 44 out of 244 UN Human Rights Council recommendations.

A good number of these rejected recommendations called for eliminating discriminatory provisions in the Family Code.

The 2004 Family Code illustrates the limited capacity of elected political institutions to produce consensus for social reform through a democratic process.[57] The problematic implementation of the Code raises questions about how an independent judiciary could be detrimental for women's rights. The future of the relationship between the Palace and the different branches of government, of the responsiveness of national authorities to international human rights bodies, and of the substance of women's rights in the law, remain to be seen, given the recent change in the ruling party and Royal announcement calling for reforms to the Family Code.

In "Postponing Equality in the Algerian Family Code" (Chapter 4), the authors examine the 1984 Algerian Family Code and 2005 amendments. Both the original Code and the amendments faced substantial challenges in their enactment and were drawn out over decades. Algerian women's groups have had to advocate for reforms in a difficult context involving an entrenched state bureaucracy, military dominance, a decade-long civil war between security forces and armed Islamist groups, discrimination against the Berber ethnic group, and major natural disasters. The Code perpetuates inequality and discrimination against women. Reforms reflect concessions to the Islamists, such as by maintaining the mandatory presence of the male marital guardian (*wali*) for women at marriage.

In February 2012 at its 51st session, the UN Committee on the Elimination of Discrimination against Women expressed its concern at the discrimination against women in the Family Code and made recommendations for additional reforms to bring Algeria into compliance with its international obligations.[58] Those provisions the Committee cited specifically as needing review and amendment include: the requirement of the *wali*; polygamy; women's limited access to divorce; inequality of women in custodial and guardianship rights; and unequal rights to property acquired during marriage upon divorce.

Five years later, the UN Human Rights Council reiterated these same concerns,[59] but Algeria rejected the sentiments. It assured the Council that a working group had been created to examine possible reforms to the Family Code.[60] At the time of publication, no such reforms had been made.

The future of the Family Code and women's rights in Algeria remains to be seen. The *Hirak* (popular protest movement) emerged in Algeria in February 2019. It included a Feminist Square as well as women who were among the protestors. The government subsequently engaged in a severe crackdown.

In "Juristic and Legislative Rulemaking: A History of the Personal Status Code of Iraq, 1959–2020" (Chapter 5) by University of Pittsburgh Interim Dean Haider Ala Hamoudi, the author discusses the 1959 Iraqi Personal Status Code. It was controversial at the time of enactment, and it remains so to this day. Some of the controversy relates to its progressive elements, which include a ban on child marriage, expanded child custody rights granted to mothers, and limitations on polygamy. Another significant dimension to the controversy concerns the extent to which the Iraqi state should have the power to legislate at all with respect to personal status matters, instead of deferring to traditional religious authorities for rulemaking. This chapter highlights some of the key rules of the Personal Status Code, its evolution over time, its treatment in the courts, and the controversies that continue to surround it. The chapter shows that in many ways, the challenges facing the Personal Status Code reflect the cleavages that have posed an existential threat to Iraq since its creation.

The Personal Status Code is the subject of serious contention along two axes. The first, paralleling the Kurdish-Arab divide, concerns the degree to which the Code should adhere to traditional understandings of the *Shari'a*, as opposed to innovating in favor of modern conceptions of women's rights. The Kurds have moved the Personal Status Code as it applies in their region very much in the direction of innovation and change. The Code as applied in Arab-dominated Iraq, is considerably more conservative and, perhaps more significantly, is subject to more pressure from conservative forces than from liberal ones.

The second axis, which reflects the Shi'a-Sunni divide, concerns whether there should be a personal status code at all, with Shi'i Islamist political forces seemingly hostile to the very existence of a uniform code, preferring devolution of the authority to make rules of the family to jurists and clerics. Efforts to achieve wholesale abolition of the Code have to date failed. Since the end of 2019, around the tenth anniversary of the Arab Spring, the repeal efforts have largely abated due to broader popular unrest. The original Arab Spring had failed to ignite the same level of political upheaval in Iraq as it had elsewhere, at least among the Shi'a. With memories still fresh of Ba'ath totalitarianism and the unspeakable repression of Shi'is and Shi'ism, the Shi'i population seemed at that time to be in no mood to threaten a new political order that had established their domination. Ten years later, in a state characterized by rampant corruption, appalling governance, and little by way of legislative accomplishment, Shi'is across Iraq's south clearly felt differently and initiated demonstrations against the ruling elites. Their demands were not merely similar to those of demonstrators in Egypt, Tunisia, Yemen, and elsewhere a decade earlier – they were identical. This has put issues of personal status law on the back burner for the time being.

In the longer term, however, it is hard to believe that the divisions that have long defined Iraq will not result in further episodes of significant instability. It seems inevitable that debates over the substantive provisions of the Personal Status Code, or indeed whether there should be one at all, will at some point in the future reemerge with significant fervor.

Attorney Nada Ammar wrote "The Status of Muslim Women in the Mosaic of Islamic Family Law in Lebanon" (Chapter 6). While there were some protests during the Arab Spring, the moribund sectarian governmental arrangement was more dominant. The Lebanese family law system characterized by legal and judicial pluralism controls major aspects of a woman's rights such as marriage, child custody, and social rights. The relevant laws are the 1962 Judiciary Act regulating the Sunni and Jaafaree judiciaries, and the 1917 Ottoman Family Rights Law. While issues of personal status are exclusively left to religious courts and sectarian legislation, it is undeniable that women in Lebanon are left to the whim of not only an entrenched religious establishment, but also cultural norms of patriarchy. Historical practices of Islamic family law issues find little premise in *Shari'a* but rather in the interpretation and implementation thereof. Thus, opening the door to activism and Islamic jurisprudential approach could bring change on religiously delicate issues. In pursuit of gender equality, efforts to reform laws and break the status quo have in certain instances proved successful. Yet, any transition to a more progressive personal status law does not appear likely in the near future. Thus, another avenue would be for Lebanese Muslim feminists to call for the reading and rethinking of Islamic family law from an egalitarian viewpoint. It does not appear likely in the near future as the country economically and politically struggles, especially since the 2020 Beirut Port explosion.

University of Sheffield Professor Sara Ababneh wrote "In Circles We Go: A Brief Historical Overview of the Jordanian Personal Status Law" (Chapter 7). While there were some Arab Spring protests, King Abdullah was able to retain control and replace various government officials. This chapter examines the development of the Jordanian Personal Status Law (JPSL) from the Ottoman Family Rights Law (1917) to the 2019 reforms. It provides an overview of the main changes which the JSPL has undergone. Centrally, the chapter argues that most changes have not been progressive in terms of leading to greater gender equality or justice. In addition to being discriminatory in terms of sex, the JPSL also enshrines class hierarchies. Where alterations have been made, they have not touched the overall rationale of the law. There were no efforts to revisit the sources of the law, to rethink certain assumptions which were based on seventh-century Arabian society, or stem from conservative colonial European jurisprudence, or to think of alternative "Islamic versions."

What is most striking about the journey of the development of the JPSL is how little the law has changed in over one hundred years. Where alterations have been made, they have not touched the overall rationale of the law. Certainly, important advances have been made. Mothers have been allowed to keep their children for longer periods of time. However, legal reforms have not altered the institution of guardianship as an exclusively male privilege.

In other instances, the current law is more restrictive than earlier laws or social practices. The ability for women to initiate a nofault divorce (khulu') is an example of this. Another example is that during the Ottoman period, women could stipulate that their husbands could not marry another woman. This legally prevented husbands from entering another marriage. At the core of the unequal relations between the sexes and the classes is the notion that men are providers and women are entitled to maintenance. Despite the fact that women now often work and provide for themselves, this basic equation has not been rethought. The logic of obedience in return for maintenance continues to act as the main justification for legislation that is discriminatory in terms of sex and class.

Unlike their Ottoman predecessors, Jordanian legislators have stayed clear from rethinking the JPSL in terms of current times and requirements. In the 2019 discussions of the PSL, any critique of the law was seen as a critique to the *Shari'a*, and Islam itself. [61]

There are two chapters relating to Palestinians. Hebrew University Professor Michael Karayanni wrote "The Palestinian Minority in Israel" (Chapter 8). *Shari'a* jurisdiction among the Palestinian minority in Israel is one of long standing. It goes back to the Ottoman millet system where people had to participate in religious courts and follow norms of their religious sect. However, in light of the geo-constitutional context of the state of Israel as a Jewish nation state, sustaining *Shari'a* jurisdiction was subjected to various policies emanating from state institutions as well as Palestinian internal organizations.

The Muslim minority's family law and gender issues in Israel are a peculiar entanglement between the personal-religious and the secular-territorial. In addition, the case of the Muslim minority is special given the national tension between it as part of a national minority and the State of Israel – a conflict that adds a dimension of its own. In this chapter, the author gives a general survey of governing norms as well as the general policies that dictate their application.

Reforms did not materialize to their full extent, at least in the domain of family law, in light of the crippling effect of the long-standing conflict between the Palestinian minority and the Israeli establishment. Working to reform Palestinian personal law will certainly create cracks from within that will weaken this minority in its major political battles with the Israeli state institutions. Additionally, the Israeli establishment has traditionally benefited from the existing structure of traditional religious law governing in matters of personal status as it suited its control policy of "divide," or rather "define and rule."[62] Some reforms did make it through, among which were reforms that took place in other Arab countries. For example, the practice of appointing informants (*mukhbirin*) by a *Shari'a* court to assess alimony payments for Muslim women was abolished, while citing its abolition in other Arab countries. The appointment of a woman to the position of a *Shari'a* court *qaddi* was also facilitated by the fact that such an appointment already took place in other Arab countries.[63] The author calls this mode of reform "organic transplantation" and hopes that local *Shari'a* reforms will continue to draw on reforms taking place in other Arab countries.

The second chapter on Palestinians, "West Bank and Gaza Personal Status Law" (Chapter 9) was written by attorney Jonathan Kuttab and volume editor Wing. Those living in the West Bank are governed by Jordanian Personal Status Law. Those in Gaza are governed by the Egyptian Law on Family Rights. While there were protests during the Arab Spring in Palestine directed against the Palestinian government, they were within the context of continuing Occupation. Unfortunately, it does not appear that the respective family laws will be unified in the near future given the ongoing political and legislative paralysis in Palestine. The political situation remains bleak. In such conditions, the status quo, that is, the dysfunctional split personal status system that exists today, may remain. Although it seems fairly implausible at this point, the two-state solution could result in some change in personal status law. Perhaps, the Palestinian Authority would be able to function once again and a new Palestinian Legislative Council would be elected. Modern legislation could be passed, and a unified code could occur. Alternatively, perhaps the two parts of Palestine would decide to retain differences, much as states in the United States have done. If one state came about (equally implausible at the moment), each community might decide to retain the millet system as representative of their deeply held beliefs.

Alternatively, under a revitalized two-state or one-state solution, a new possibility could emerge. All the myriad denominations, as well as secular people, would need to learn to coexist together. It may well be possible to dream of a proper, modern civil personal status law that provides an alternative to all who wish to abide by its provisions and escape the religious courts of their respective faith communities. Such a law would solve many problems that are not properly addressed by the millet system.

In many countries, there is a civil law that applies to everyone, yet those who choose a Catholic religious wedding, for example, can get one, and the state will recognize that wedding and its consequences. If they later choose to divorce, they can do so, even if their particular religious community does not recognize their divorce, and would not allow them to remarry in a religious ceremony. Yet their divorce – just like their marriage – is recognized and effective. The authors query whether this could ever be in Palestine's future.

Visiting William & Mary Professor Lina M. Kassem wrote Chapter 10 on a Gulf society: "Qatari Family Law, When Custom Meets *Shari'a*." It provides a summary of recent legal reforms undertaken by the state of Qatar to advance the status of women. While most legal initiatives in Qatar were top-down, started mostly by the state, there is a growing and active civil society that is emerging to press for even more progressive reforms. One of the most important legal reforms was the codification of the Qatari Family Law (QFL) in 2006. This chapter explores the most important articles of the family law, as well as highlighting potential challenges, to women's equality in the state of Qatar.

This close examination of Qatar's efforts to develop a family law code that seeks to ameliorate some of the vulnerabilities faced by women living in traditional Qatari society shows both the extent to which these efforts have been successful, as well as highlighting some of its shortcomings. There is still much work that still needs to be done. Reconciling the need for progressive legal reforms, while upholding long-held customs and traditions has proven difficult. While Qatar has sought to strengthen the rights of women through the ratification of international conventions such as CEDAW, it continues to have reservations. Perhaps more telling is the extended clarification from the state that argues that the state of Qatar considers legislation that is mostly meant to be "conducive to the interest of promoting social solidarity." The emphasis is placed on the collective right of the family at the expense of the individual rights of women.

While government attempts at promoting real and progressive legal reform cannot be completely dismissed, there needs to be a parallel movement among civil society groups to further encourage the government in the direction of more progressive reforms.

I.5   Conclusion

What are the lessons we can learn from the personal status law experiences of the Middle Eastern and North African countries featured? First, these laws remain deeply rooted in the ancient customs intertwined with the religious practices of the various societies. Most of the practices date back to the Ottoman Empire. They are rarely modified, even if other laws are being altered.

Second, the practices are resistant to changes based on more modern laws adopted after independence or various regime changes. Other priorities may have existed that emphasized economic development or various issues. Elite consolidation or monopolies on power were more important than general uplift of more than half the population.

Third, the practices are resistant to Western influences and may be viewed by some as a clash of civilizations between the West and the Islamic world.[64] The Western elements definitely include Western liberal feminism, which may be perceived as part of alien attempts to change or dominate local societies. Traditional feminism continues to be disliked even in Western societies by minority group women and others, who feel it is another form of prioritizing the needs of middle or upper class white women on the backs of women of color.

Fourth, it may be that one cannot essentialize and assume all the women or all the men in any country want any particular type of change in the family laws. There is a wide range of views influenced by class, geography, education, politics, religion, and other factors.

Fifth, it is uncertain what might be the difference if women were better represented in the various legislatures. Would it affect who might be more motivated to push for change? It would be interesting to see if countries like Rwanda, which have a female parliamentary majority,[65] have made a difference in the family law area and what that difference has been.

Sixth, societal upheaval such as the Arab Spring may mean the populace prefers to prioritize other issues such as political stability, the economy, or health care during a pandemic, over changing deeply seated doctrines such as family law.

Seventh, traditionalist forces may have been stronger and more ascendant over the last century. Conservative values may be even more entrenched since the Arab Spring. Studies in the region show that the majority of people are resistant to gender equality.[66] There is strong support for Islamic family law. Change may be cyclical, with ebbs and flows, whether it be initiated by the Muslim Brotherhood, Al Qaeda, Isis, or less well-known political forces. These traditionalist elements are global in nature and can be found in all Western countries as well.

Eighth, it is impossible to essentialize the region. Tunisia may continue to be at the forefront compared to most other countries. Any potential reformist efforts would have to work well within the specific political, religious, and cultural context of a particular nation.

In conclusion, any type of change in family law in the region may occur at a glacial pace in most countries. It will be up to the women and men, whether within civil society or within the governmental branches – whether conservative or reformist – to decide what works best in the short and long term in their respective nations.

Notes

1 Andrea Dessi, "Popular Mobilisation and Authoritarian Reconstitution in the Middle East and North Africa: Ten Years of Arab Uprisings," in S. Colombo and D. Huber (eds.). *Ten Years of Protests in the Middle East and North Africa: Dynamics of Mobilisation in a Complex (Geo) political Environment* (Peter Lang, 2022), pp. 199–201. The many revolts/revolutions include the 1979 Iran revolution; 1990s Algerian civil war; 1975–90 Lebanon civil war; 1979 Afghan-Soviet war; 1980s Syrian Muslim Brotherhood clashes; 1987 and 2000 Palestinian Intifada; 1980s Iraq Shia-Kurdish clash; Iran-Iraq war; 1990s Gulf war; 1990s Egypt Islamic insurgency; 2000 US Afghan invasion; Iraq war; 2005 Lebanon Cedar revolution; and 2006 Hamas electoral victory.

2 Dessi, "Popular Mobilisation and Authoritarian Reconstitution in the Middle East and North Africa," p. 191.

3 See, e.g., Asef Bayat, *Revolution without Revolutionaries: Making Sense of the Arab Spring* (Stanford University Press, 2017); Asef Bayat, *Revolutionary Life: The Everyday of the Arab Spring* (Harvard University Press, 2021).

4 This part drawn from Adrien K. Wing, "The Arab fall: The Future of Women's Rights" (2012) 18 *University of California Davis Journal of International Law and*

Policy, 445; Adrien K. Wing and Peter Nadimi, "Muslim Women's Rights in the Age of Obama" (2011) 20 *Transnational Law and Contemporary Problems*, 431; Adrien K. Wing and Hisham Kassim, "After the Last Judgment: The Future of the Egyptian Constitution" (2011) 52 *Harvard Journal of International Law* online, 301, www.harvardilj.org/2011/04/online_52_wing_kassim.

5 Mona Eltahawy, "Tunisia's Jasmine Revolution," *Washington Post*, January 15, 2011, www.washingtonpost.com/wp-dyn/content/article/2011/01/14/AR2011011405084 .html.

6 "Tunisia Suicide Protester Mohammed Bouazizi Dies," BBC World News, January 5, 2011, www.bbc.co.uk/news/world-africa-12120228.

7 "Tunisia Suicide Protester Mohammed Bouazizi Dies."

8 Yasmine Ryan, "The Tragic Life of a Street Vendor," *Aljazeera*, January 20, 2011, http://english.aljazeera.net/indepth/features/2011/01/201111684242518839.html.

9 Elizabeth Arrott, Lisa Bryant, and Henry Ridgwell, "Tunisians Mourn Losses in Jasmine Revolution," *Voice of America*, January 21, 2011, www.voanews.com/lear ningenglish/home/world/Tunisians-Mourn-Loses-in-Jasmine-Revolution- 114390324.html.

10 John D. Sutter, "The Faces of Egypt's 'Revolution 2.0,'" *CNN World*, February 21, 2011, www.cnn.com/2011/TECH/innovation/02/21/egypt.internet.revolution/index .html.

11 Cengiz Gunay, "Mubarak's Egypt: Bad Paternalism, and the Army's Interest in Managed Transition," *OpenDemocracy*, February 3, 2011, www.opendemocracy .net/cengiz-g%C3%BCnay/mubaraks-egypt-bad-paternalism-and-armys-interest- in-managed transition.

12 Alan Greenblatt, "In Arab States, It's Good to Be the King," *NPR*, November 12, 2011,
www.npr.org/2011/11/10/142218146/in-arab-states-its-good-to-be-the-king.

13 Mary Phillips Sandy, "Saudi Arabia Giving Citizens a 15 Percent Raise to Avoid Becoming the Next Libya," *AOL NEWS*, February 23, 2011, www.aolnews .com/2011/02/23/saudi arabia giving citizens a 15 percent raise to avoid becomi/. Saudi Arabia permitted women to vote and run in municipal elections as of 2015, and the right to drive took place in 2018. Neil MacFarquhar, "Saudi Monarch Grants Women Right to Vote," *New York Times*, September 26, 2011, www.nytimes .com/2011/09/26/world/middleeast/women-to-vote-in-saudi-arabia-king-says .html?pagewanted=all; Rita Stephan and Mounira Charrad, "Introduction: Advancing Women's Rights in the Arab world," Rita Stephan and Mounira Charrad (eds.), *Women Rising: In and beyond the Arab Spring* (New York University Press, 2020), p. 1. Even the Omanis engaged in mild protests, and the Sultan did make some limited reforms. James Worrall, "Protest and Reform: The Arab Spring in Oman," Larbi Sadiki (ed.), *Routledge Handbook of the Arab Spring* (Routledge, 2015), p. 480.

14 Aminah Ali Kandar, "Refusing the Backseat: Women as Drivers of the Yemeni Uprisings," Stephan and Charrad (eds.), *Women Rising*, p. 68.

15 Kristian Ulrichsen, "The Uprising in Bahrain: Regional Dimensions and International Consequences," Sadiki (ed.), *Routledge Handbook*, p. 133.

16 "Gaddafi Dead: Bodies of Leader, Son, Aide Taken from Misrata Freezer," *Huffington Post*, October 24, 2011, www.huffingtonpost.com/2011/10/24/gaddafi- dead-body_n_1029418.html.

17 Sarah Lynch, "Muslim Brotherhood Top Winner in Egypt," *USA Today*, November 4, 2011, www.usatoday.com/news/world/story/2011-12-04/israel-egypt-elections/51641978/1.

18 "Tunisia's Islamist Ennahda Party Wins Historic Poll," BBC, October 27, 2011, www.bbc.co.uk/news/world-africa-15487647.

19 "Tunisia's Islamist Ennahda Party Wins Historic Poll."

20 Adrien K. Wing and Sylke Merchan, "Rape, Ethnicity and Culture: Spirit Injury from Bosnia to Black America" (1993) 25 *Columbia Human Rights Law Review*, 1.

21 Robert Fisk, "Bonfire of the dictator," *The Independent*, December 31, 2011, www.independent.co.uk/news/world/middle-east/bonfire-of-the-dictators-6283351.html.

22 Isobel Coleman, "Are the Mideast Revolutions Bad for Women's Rights?," *Washington Post*, February 20, 2011, www.washingtonpost.com/wpdyn/content/article/2011/02/18/AR2011021806962.html.

23 Salima Ghezali, Louisa Hanoune, and Khalida Messaoudi, "Engendering or endangering politics in Algeria?" (Spring 2006) 2(2) *Journal of Middle East Woman Studies*, 64.

24 "Tawakkul Karman Says Yemenis Will Continue with Their Peaceful Revolution," *Al Arabiya*, November 10, 2011, http://english.alarabiya.net/articles/2011/11/10/176398.html.

25 Even Bahraini women protested for improvements in their status. Marwa Shalaby and Ariana Marnicio, "Women's Political Participation in Bahrain," Stephan and Charrad (eds.), *Women Rising*, 321.

26 Eileen Byrne, "The Women MPs Tipped to Play Leading Roles in Tunisia's New Assembly," *The Guardian*, October 28, 2011, www.guardian.co.uk/world/2011/oct/29/women-mps-tunisia-government.

27 International Civil Society Action Network, "What Women Say: The Arab Spring and Implications for Women," Brief One, December 2011, www.icanpeacework.org/wp-content/uploads/2011/12/ICAN17.pdf.

28 Or Avi-Guy, "New Order, Same Rules," *Sydney Morning Herald*, December 27, 2011, www.smh.com.au/opinion/politics/new-order-same-rules-20111226-1paf2.html#ixzz1kx11wnXn.

29 Convention on the Elimination of All Forms of Discrimination against Women, G.A. Res. 34/180, U.N. GAOR, 34th Session 107th plenary meeting, U.N. Doc. A/Res/34/180 (December 18, 1979) [hereinafter CEDAW].

30 Brian Whitaker, "Tunisia Is Leading the Way on Women's Rights in the Middle East," *The Guardian*, September 20, 2011, www.guardian.co.uk/commentisfree/2011/sep/10/tunisia-un-human-rights-women.

31 Whitaker, "Tunisia Is Leading the Way on Women's Rights in the Middle East."

32 Whitaker, "Tunisia Is Leading the Way on Women's Rights in the Middle East."

33 Whitaker, "Tunisia Is Leading the Way on Women's Rights in the Middle East."

34 Bouazza Ben Bouazza, "Tunisian Women Demonstrate to Protect Their Rights," *Associated Press*, November 2, 2011, www.google.com/hostednews/ap/article/ALeqM5iBwopsJzONk0IPtzGReBdjjCK9PA?docId=3b92f6a715784eccb490d4a50e24b7be; Hassene Dridi, "Tunisian Women Demonstrate to Preserve Their Rights Following Islamist Election Victory," *Associated Press*, November 2, 2011, www.washingtonpost.com/world/africa/tunisian-women-demonstrate-to-preserve-their-rights-following-islamist-election-victory/2011/11/02/gIQAJnh4fM_story.html; Yasmine Ryan, "Tunisia's Election through the Eyes of Women," *AlJazeera*, October

23, 2011, http://english.aljazeera.net/indepth/spotlight/2011tunisiaelection/2011/10/
20111022104341755235.html; Karem Yehia, "On Tunisia's Elections," *Al Ahram*,
http://weekly.ahram.org.eg/2011/1071/re4.htm.

35 Ryan, "Tunisia's Election through the Eyes of Women."

36 Polygamy for Tunisia? The Islamic Revolution Calls for Multiple Wives, Albawaba,
September 1, 2012, www.albawaba.com/editorchoice/tunisia-polygamy-islamist-
440281.

37 Nadya Khalife, "Tunisia on Board with Women's Rights," *Huffington Post*,
September 29, 2011, www.huffingtonpost.com/nadya-khalife/tunisia-on-board-
with-wom_b_981689.html.

38 "EGYPT: Government Defends Military Trials, 'Virginity Tests' to Human Rights
Advocates," *Los Angeles Times*, June 7, 2011, http://latimesblogs.latimes.com/babylon
beyond/2011/06/egypt-government-justifies-military-trials-virginity-tests-to-human-
rights-advocates.html.

39 "EGYPT"; Abdel-Rahman Hussein, "Egyptian Army Doctor Cleared over 'Virginity
Tests' on Women Activists," *GuardianUK*, March 20, 2012, www.guardian.co.uk/
world/2012/mar/11/egypt-doctor-cleared-virginity-tests.

40 Yasmine Saleh, "Rewrite Egypt Constitution from Scratch, Say Critics," *Reuters*,
February 16, 2011, http://af.reuters.com/article/topNews/idAFJOE71F0N620110216.

41 Jenna Krajeski, "Rebellion," *The New Yorker*, March 14, 2012, www.newyorker
.com/talk/2011/03/14/110314ta_talk_krajeski.

42 Richard Spencer, "Egypt: Islamist Judge to Head New Constitution Committee,"
Telegraph, February 15, 2011, www.telegraph.co.uk/news/worldnews/africaandindia
nocean/egypt/8326469/Egypt-Islamist-judge-to-head-new-constitution-committee
.html.

43 Nathan Brown and Michele Dunne, "Egypt's Draft Constitutional Amendments
Answer Some Questions and Raise Others," *Carnegie*, http://egyptelections
.carnegieendowment.org/2011/03/03/egypt%E2%80%99s-draft-constitutional-amend
ments-answer-some-questions-and-raise-others.

44 "Egypt's Quiet Gender Revolution," *Think Africa Press*, August 24, 2011, http://
thinkafricapress.com/egypt/egypt-quiet-gender-revolution.

45 Isobel Coleman, "'Blue Bra Girl' Rallies Egypt's Women vs. Oppression," *CNN*,
December 22, 2011, www.cnn.com/2011/12/22/opinion/coleman-women-egypt-
protest/index.html.

46 Inderdeep Bains, "Day of Shame in the Middle East: Female Protesters Beaten with
Metal Poles as Vicious Soldiers Drag Girls through Streets," *Daily Mail Online*,
December 19, 2011, www.dailymail.co.uk/news/article-2075683/Egypt-violence-
Female-protesters-brutally-beaten-metal-poles-vicious-soldiers.html.

47 Catriona Davies, "The Woman Who Wants to Be Egypt's First Female President,"
CNN, September 16, 2011, www.cnn.com/2011/09/13/world/meast/egypt-bothaina-
kamel/index.html.

48 "Bothaina Kamel Says She Has No Regrets on Dropping Out of Race," *Egypt
Independent*, April 8, 2012, www.egyptindependent.com/news/bothaina-kamel-
says-she-has-no-regrets-over-dropping-out-race.

49 Heather Moore, "Experts Weigh in on Low Female Representation in Parliament,"
The Daily News Egypt, January 27, 2012, www.thedailynewsegypt.com/experts-
weigh-in-on-low-female-representation-in-parliament.html.

50 "Libya Drops Election Quota for Women; New Assembly to Be Elected in June," *Al Arabiya*, January 20, 2012, http://english.alarabiya.net/articles/2012/01/20/189513 .html.

51 Zahra Langhi, "Gender and State-Building in Libya: Towards a Politics of Inclusion," in Andrea Khalil (ed.), *Gender, Women and the Arab Spring* (Routledge, 2015), p. 70 (Women had the right to khul divorce, women married to non-Libyans could give their kids Libyan citizenship, polygamy only with permission); Ronald Bruce St. John, "Libya's Gender Wars: The Revolution within the Revolution" (2017) 22(5) *Journal of North African Studies*, 889.

52 St. John, "Libya's Gender Wars," 892; Amanda Rogers, "Revolutionary Nuns or Totalitarian Pawns: Evaluating Libyan State Feminism after Mu'ammar al-Gaddafi," in Fatima Sadiqi (ed.), *Women's Movements in Post-"Arab Spring" North Africa* (Palgrave, 2016), p. 177.

53 St. John, "Libya's Gender Wars," p. 892.

54 Adam Nossiter, "Hinting at an End to a Curb on Polygamy, Interim Libyan Leader Stirs Anger," *New York Times*, October 29, 2011, www.nytimes.com/2011/10/30/ world/africa/libyan-leaders-remark-favoring-polygamy-stirs-anger.html?pagewan-ted=all. It should be noted that there are many women who support polygamy, and both authors have friends in Europe and the Middle East who are in favor of the practice. There are numbers of websites supporting women seeking polygamous marriages as well: www.2wives.com/; http://pro-polygamy.com. In February 2013, the Libyan Supreme Court overturned Law 10, a Qaddafi-era marriage act that called for a husband to secure the approval of his first wife before he took a second or seek court permission to marry additional wives if he failed to gain his first wife's approval. St. John, "Libya's Gender Wars," p. 894.

55 St. John, "Libya's Gender Wars."

56 Hebah Saleh, "Egyptian Women Fear Regression on Rights," *Financial Times*, October 1, 2012, www.ft.com/content/b203c126-06f5-11e2-92ef-00144feabdc0.

57 Jean-Philippe Bras, "La réforme du code de la famille au Maroc et en Algérie: quelles avancées pour la démocratie?" (2007) 37*Critique Internationale*, 93–125.

58 UN Committee on the Elimination of Discrimination against Women, Concluding Observations of the Committee, 51st session, 13 February–2 March 2012, CEDAW/ C/DZA/CO/3–4.

59 Human Rights Council, Report of the Working Group on the Universal Periodic Review, Algeria, 19 July 2017, A/HRC/36/13.

60 Conseil des droits de l'homme, Rapport du groupe de travail sur l'examen périodique universel Algérie, Additif observations sur les conclusions et/ou recom-mandations, engagements et réponses de l'État examine, 19 September 2017, A/HRC/36/13/Add.1.

61 Taylor Luck, "Across the Arab World, a Women's Spring Comes into View," *Christian Science Monitor*, August 9, 2017, www.csmonitor.com/World/Middle-East/2017/0809/Across-the-Arab-world-a-Women-s-Spring-comes-into-view.

62 Mahmood Mamdani, *Define and Rule, Native as Political Identity* (Harvard University Press, 2012). On this issue and the whole religion and state configuration in Israel, see Michael Karayanni, *A Multicultural Entrapment, Religion and State among the Palestinian-Arabs in Israel* (Cambridge University Press, 2020).

63 Karayanni, *A Multicultural Entrapment*, chapter 6.

64 Samuel Huntington, *Class of Civilizations and Remaking of the World Order* (Simon & Shuster, 1996).

65 UNWomen, "Revisiting Rwanda Five Years after Record-Breaking Parliamentary Elections," August 13, 2018, www.unwomen.org/en/news/stories/2018/8/feature-rwanda-women-in-parliament.

66 Polls were done in Egypt, Iraq, Jordan, Libya, Morocco, and Tunisia. Pamela Abbott and Andrea Teti, "Why Women's Rights Have Made Little Progress since the Arab Spring," *Newsweek*, April 21, 2017, www.newsweek.com/arab-spring-gender-equality-women-rights-progress-egypt-tunisia-587317.

1

Sustained Reforms

Family Law in Tunisia

MOUNIRA M. CHARRAD AND HYUN JEONG HA

What the Arab Spring uprisings of 2011 have meant for women's rights is the key question addressed in this chapter. Tunisia occupies a special place among the countries that have experienced the Arab Spring. Not only was it the cradle of the uprisings, but it is also the only country where the uprisings were followed by a process of democratization for a decade rather than a quick return to authoritarianism or the establishment of a fragmented state as in other countries. The political system changed again in 2021 with power concentrated in the executive. Democratization lasted an entire decade. Uncertainty currently reigns, however, about the future of politics in the country. Historically, with reforms spanning over more than a half-century, Tunisia has been a leading country in the Middle East and North Africa (MENA) in regard to family law and women's rights.[1] Today, it continues to stand at the forefront of the modern Muslim Middle East in this respect.

To understand the current standing of Tunisia in regard to family law requires close attention to the history of the country and especially to its Code of Personal Status (CPS), a pioneer reform promulgated in the 1950s. Called the *Majalla* in Arabic, the CPS expanded women's rights in marriage, polygamy, divorce, alimony, and custody.[2] Several amendments in the same vein followed in the ensuing decades. Although inequities persist, notably in regard to inheritance,[3] the CPS is the most "woman friendly" legislation in the region. The initial reform and subsequent amendments enhanced the protection of the nuclear family, women, and children.

This chapter discusses the sustained reforms that revamped family law in Tunisia from the 1950s to 2021. It stops in 2021 because at the time of this writing, in early 2023, the political situation in general and gender politics in particular are highly volatile. We suggest that political motivations have shaped the policy on family law and women's rights. We argue that sustained reforms were possible because succeeding regimes found it in their best interests to pursue a reformist policy. This was clearly the case in the 1950s, but it was also true later. It is only in the 1980s that women's activism emerged in earnest in Tunisia. From then on and throughout the 1990s until the Jasmine Revolution of the Arab Spring in 2010/11, the political interests of the regime aligned with demands voiced by women's rights advocates, although the regime discouraged or punished activism. The 1950s to 2010 represent a time when reforms of family law resulted primarily from what we refer to as "politics from above," in contrast with "politics from below" by grassroots movements as after the Arab Spring.[4] The political opening that followed the Arab Spring in 2010/11 generated new policies and debates about family law and women's rights. In the period that witnessed a process of democratization and a more open political system from 2011 to 2021, women's rights activists became vocal in pressing for new reforms.

The sociological literature usually sees pressures from women's movements on the state as the driving force for the expansion of women's rights because it draws heavily on the history of the United States where women's activism played a critical role.[5] The case of Tunisia, however, calls into question this dominant model. It offers an example of authoritarian regimes making reforms for reasons of their own interests and thus creating a platform on which further regimes could build later, when democratization occurred (in flux but real nevertheless for a decade). After providing an overview of the history and legal system of Tunisia, we outline the substance of the reforms and their significance. Methodologically, we use primarily legal texts, commentaries of legal scholars or social science analysts, and newspaper articles for the most recent period.[6]

The chapter proceeds with a brief comparison of Tunisia with other countries in the Middle East and North Africa at the time of the Arab Spring so as to place the Tunisian case in perspective, followed by an overview of legal systems in the history of the country. It then moves on with a discussion of family law in the critical period of the 1950s/1960s, the changes from the 1980s to 2010, and the most recent policies and debates since the Jasmine Revolution of the Arab Spring in 2010/11 until 2021. Given how dynamic family law has been in Tunisia, we suggest that this historical framework going from the postcolonial period to the interruption of democratization in 2021 is the most appropriate for the analysis.

1.1 Tunisia in Context and History

1.1.1 International Context

In an extensive survey comparing countries of the Arab world on gender equity, published in 2010 at the eve of the Arab Spring, Freedom House

Table 1.1 Country ratings chart[a]

	Non-discrimination and access to justice	Autonomy, security, and freedom of the person	Economic rights and equal opportunity	Political rights and civic voice	Social and cultural rights
ALGERIA	3.1	3.0	3.0	3.0	3.0
BAHRAIN	2.2	2.6	3.1	2.3	2.9
EGYPT	3.0	2.9	2.9	2.7	2.6
IRAN	1.9	2.1	2.7	2.1	2.5
IRAQ	2.7	1.9	2.6	2.6	2.3
JORDAN	2.7	2.7	2.9	2.9	2.8
KUWAIT	2.2	2.4	3.1	2.4	2.9
LEBANON	2.9	3.0	3.0	2.9	3.1
LIBYA	2.4	2.6	2.8	1.8	2.5
MOROCCO	3.1	3.2	2.8	3.1	2.9
OMAN	2.1	2.1	2.9	1.8	2.5
PALESTINE	2.6	2.4	2.9	2.7	2.6
QATAR	2.1	2.3	2.9	1.8	2.5
SAUDI ARABIA	1.4	1.3	1.7	1.2	1.6
SYRIA	2.7	2.3	2.9	2.2	2.5
TUNISIA	3.6	3.4	3.2	3.1	3.3
UAE	2.0	2.3	3.1	2.0	2.5
YEMEN	1.9	1.9	1.9	2.0	2.0

[a] Kelly and Breslin (eds.), *Women's Rights*, p. 23.

ranked Tunisia first regarding women's legal rights.[7] Table 1.1 shows that Tunisia ranked highest with a score of 3.6 out of 5 in the categories of nondiscrimination and access to justice for women and 3.4 in autonomy, security, and freedom of the person for women. These two categories touch on the issues of family law that constitute the focus of this chapter and the second – autonomy, security and freedom – concerns them directly. The same study conducted in 2005 showed similar results for Tunisia, again with scores of 3.6 and 3.4 for the same categories.[8]

1.1.2   Historical Overview and Legal System

A brief consideration of geopolitics and history should help place the reforms in their national context. The overwhelming majority, or 98 percent, of the Tunisian population, estimated at over 11 million, is of Arab descent, Arabic-speaking, and Sunni Muslim. Only approximately 2 percent consist of Europeans and members of other minorities such as Berbers or Jews. Given its relatively homogeneous ethnic and religious population, Tunisia has been spared some of the conflicts experienced by Arab states with sizeable minorities. As of 2016, the urban population represented 67 percent of the total.[9] The total adult literacy rate was 79.1 percent as of 2012 and education was mandatory for all Tunisians aged six to sixteen. The country successfully achieved economic growth from the 1970s to the early 2010s, with a steadily growing GDP.[10]

Historically, Tunisia was under the influence of the Ottoman Empire from the seventeenth to the nineteenth centuries and later under French colonial rule from 1881 until 1956. From 1956 to the Arab Spring in 2011, sovereign Tunisia had two presidents: Habib Bourguiba for thirty years (1957–1987) and Zine al Abidine Ben Ali for twenty-four years (1987–2011). Both leaders adhered to a de facto one-party system and resorted to repressive policies against religious and political challengers. Although exhibiting patrimonial politics and an absence of democracy in its postcolonial history,[11] Tunisia nevertheless experienced relative political stability compared to other MENA countries. Habib Bourguiba prioritized a modernization and secularization project by undermining the power base of tribal and Islamic conservative groups. Ben Ali continued to strictly ban political activities including those of the Nahda Party, a moderate Islamist party, which operated underground or in exile most of the time.[12]

The first postcolonial Constitution of Tunisia was adopted in 1959, three years after independence from French colonial rule. It defined Tunisia as an independent republic with Islam as its religion and Arabic as its official language. It was amended several times, in 1988, 1999, 2002, 2003, and 2008,[13] and the 1988 amendment, in particular, reinforced the authority of the president in allowing for three five-year terms.[14] Following the Jasmine Revolution, a new constitution was ratified in 2014. It reaffirmed Islam as the religion of Tunisia and Arabic as its language. The legal system was put in place in the early phase of the postcolonial state. Bourguiba's government created a single and unified system for all Tunisians by abolishing Islamic and Jewish courts in an effort to place Tunisian citizens under the jurisdiction of the same courts organized under a single, national system, regardless of religious affiliation.[15] Citizenship rather than religion thus became the basis of access to the law and the courts.

Since the collapse of Ben Ali's authoritarian regime in 2011, Tunisia has undergone key institutional and political changes. A general election for a National Constituent Assembly was held in October and a presidential election in December 2011. A High Committee for Political Reform was formed and played a major role in laying new foundations for the constitution and laws related to elections and political parties, with an eye for the rule of law.[16] The Nahda Party, the Islamist party, won the largest number of votes in the general election, more than 40 percent of the seats in parliament.[17] Moncef Marzouki, previously a human rights activist living in exile in Europe, was elected as interim president. Importantly for family law and women's rights, in March 2012, the Nahda Party declared that it would not support making Shari'a, or Islamic stipulations based on original texts of Islam, the main source of legislation in the new Constitution, thus maintaining family law as enacted in the CPS of 1956 and its amendments.

In December 2014, Beji Caid Essebsi, the former prime minister, was elected the new president. He won the first regular presidential election following the Jasmine Revolution, becoming Tunisia's first freely elected president. Essebsi is the founder of the Nidaa Tounes political party, a coalition party with a secularist bent, which won a plurality in the 2004 parliamentary election. With over 100 legally recognized political parties in existence since the revolution, Tunisia was considered by many as the country with the most democratic political system in North Africa and, some would argue, in the Muslim Middle East from the Arab Uprisings of 2011 to the interruption of democracy in 2021.[18]

1.2   Foundational Reforms of the 1950s–1960s: The Code of Personal Status[19]

Any discussion of family law in Tunisia inevitably focuses on the CPS, a pioneer piece of legislation and the most progressive legal code in Muslim majority countries in North Africa and the Muslim Middle East. In order to appreciate the magnitude of the reforms introduced by the CPS in 1956, however, it is useful to briefly consider family law before the promulgation of the CPS.

1.2.1   Family Law Untouched under Colonial Rule

During colonization, although it changed other parts of the law such as commercial law (important for economic purposes), the French colonial state maintained the *shari'a* or Islamic stipulations as the law applying to the Muslim population in regard to family matters. The French were able to exert colonial domination while keeping family law untouched and adopting a hands-off policy, especially since they feared violent reactions if they did reform it. The Muslim population saw family law as the cornerstone of Islam and the ultimate symbol of its identity separate from the French. Heterogeneity in Islamic family law was a major characteristic in the country, due to diverse interpretations and inclinations of different courts and communities. With regional and even local variations inherent to a legal system based on the particular interpretations of religious courts, family law under colonial rule was drawn from original religious scriptures and anchored in the Maliki school of law, which historically predominated throughout the Maghreb, supplemented by local interpretations.[20]

While discussions of Islamic family law often emphasize the influence of religion and religious forces on the formulation of the law, we argue in this chapter that, in order to understand the presence or on the contrary, the absence of reforms, we need to deconstruct Islamic family law. Only such a deconstruction allows us to perceive the kind of family structure that it helps perpetuate. In a nutshell, as a patriarchal legal system, family law enshrined an extended family structure based on agnatic ties (or male ties on the paternal side) and favored men over women.

There was no set minimum legal age for marriage, which in principle could occur after puberty. A matrimonial guardian represented the bride at the marriage ceremony and expressed consent to the union on her behalf. With a right to polygamy, men could have up to four wives. In regard to divorce, a man had the unilateral right of repudiation and thus could terminate a marriage at will. A woman wishing a divorce had to appeal to a religious judge and prove that she had been harmed in the marriage. The grounds on which she could do so were limited and carefully defined, thus making divorce highly unequal between husbands and wives. Although custody was often in favor of the mother when children were young, a woman could lose custody rights later, especially in the case of sons, if the father insisted on having custody over them. In actuality, different courts and judges were more or less lenient and allowed room for negotiation by women. Nevertheless, on the whole, the legislation in effect could be used to the detriment of vulnerable women or children.

1.2.2 Reasons behind the Promulgation of the CPS

A few months after achieving independence, the newly formed government promulgated the CPS on August 13, 1956. The rapid action reflected policy choices made by the leadership of the nationalist movement early on, even before colonial rule ended. The reasons behind the promulgation of the Code in the 1950s are complex and beyond the scope of this chapter. Charrad has argued elsewhere that the bold move represented by the CPS was part and parcel of a broader project to build a nation-state in which patriarchal and tribal networks became marginalized.[21] Members of the new leadership saw Islamic family law as it had been applied in Tunisia, with its decentralized nature and the autonomy of diverse communities, as antithetical to a unified nation. They considered a unified body of legislation a must in the new nation-state. Furthermore, members of the new leadership, based primarily in urban areas, saw their power threatened by clans and tribes. They aggressively engaged in an array of policies aimed at weakening their perceived enemies. They read Maliki family law as favoring extended kinship networks, clans, and tribes and thus to be modified.

Two important questions should be raised concerning the CPS of the 1950s: How much was it motivated by a concern for women and how Islamic versus secular was it in its content? Feminism as organized ideology or mass movement was not part of the public discourse in Tunisia in the mid-1950s. Although some individual women engaged in public debates, they voiced a nationalist, anticolonial rather than a feminist ideology. Postcolonial state agents, for their part, were intent on creating citizens with allegiance to the state more than on liberating women as such. The CPS clearly benefited women, however, in expanding their rights and freedom of choice in family matters. This is because the CPS brought about a new form of citizenship in which individuals, male and female, had more autonomy from extended kin.

Neither fully Islamic nor secular, the content of the CPS departed considerably from the Maliki school of law then in effect at the same time as it retained significant elements of it. It is fair to describe it, however, as an unambiguous reform that redefines the rights and responsibilities of men and women in the family and an innovative interpretation of Islam, rather than a rejection of it.[22] It is important to recall that the CPS applied to all Tunisian citizens, regardless of religion. The following analysis highlights the major points of the initial reforms embodied in the CPS of the 1950s and 1960s.

1.2.3   Marriage and Abolition of Polygamy

In reforming marriage, the CPS made the consent of the bride and groom mandatory. "Marriage is formed only by the consent of the two spouses," stated the Majalla, which required that the bride be present at the marriage contract and directly express her consent to the union.[23] The principle of a matrimonial guardian was abolished. Moreover, the CPS indicated that marriage could be concluded only before two notaries or an officer of the civil registry. Marriage also had to be registered with civil authorities. A certificate delivered by the civil registry, or by two notaries after they performed the marriage, became the only valid proof of marriage. A medical certificate attesting to the good health of the spouses-to-be was also made mandatory. Marriages performed in ways other than those specified had no validity before the law, which now rejected the notion of marriage as a private matter. In requiring that a marriage be performed and recorded by civil authority, the CPS presented a new conception of a marital union, one in which the state had a say.

The Majalla outlawed polygamy altogether. It stated unequivocally, "[P]olygamy is forbidden."[24] An attempt at marrying again, while one was still married, was now punished with imprisonment of one year and a fine of approximately 500 US dollars, which represented the equivalent of a year's income for many Tunisians in 1956. Additional paragraphs annexed to Article 18 in 1964 indicated that, if a man and woman resumed conjugal life after their polygamous marriage had been declared null and void, they would both be subject to imprisonment and a fine, the man for having broken the law on polygamy and the woman as his accomplice.[25] In all matters of polygamy, the judge was urged to apply the maximum sentence.

Concise on the rights and responsibilities of each spouse, the CPS maintained a conservative tone in stating that the wife owed obedience to her husband.[26] This further suggests that feminist concerns were not prominent in the formulation of the CPS. The husband was expected to treat his wife with kindness and provide for her and their children. A new element introduced in the Majalla concerned the financial responsibility of the woman to her husband and children. Whereas in Islamic law a woman's property remained her own without becoming part of the household assets, the Majalla required the wife to contribute to the expenses of the household, if she had the means to do so, thus placing the division of responsibilities between the spouses on a new plane.

The minimum age for marriage was set at fifteen for a woman and eighteen for a man in the initial text of the Majalla, although the general age of legal majority was set at twenty for both men and women.[27] Statistics on marriage revealed, however, that in 1960 and 1961, 48.5 percent of the women who got married did so between the ages of fifteen and nineteen, and 3.8 percent of the men between the ages of eighteen and nineteen.[28] Believing that Tunisians were still marrying too young, the lawmakers issued a new law in 1964, changing the minimum age for marriage to seventeen for a woman and twenty for a man.

1.2.4   Divorce[29]

The CPS changed regulations on divorce in fundamental ways revealing a concern to strengthen the nuclear family on the part of lawmakers. It abolished repudiation (a term that appeared nowhere in the text of the CPS) and a divorce could now take place only in court. The wife and husband were equally entitled to file for divorce, and they could do so by mutual consent. One of them could also file alone, in which case the judge would determine whether one spouse should give compensation to the other – regardless of gender – and what the amount ought to be. An attempt at reconciliation, to be performed by the court, became mandatory.[30]

The Majalla made the father and mother both responsible for the care of a child, as long as they lived together.[31] If the father was no longer able to provide for the child, either in case of death or for any other reason, the next person called upon to assume responsibility was the mother, who now came before other relatives in the order of responsibility. In case of divorce, the CPS initially stipulated that the son would remain with the mother until the age of seven, and the daughter until the age of nine, at which point the father could request custody of his children. However, a new law brought an end to the right of the father to request custody of his children at a given age, stating that there would be no limit on the duration of custody granted to the mother.[32] The judge was to decide to whom to grant custody, without considering degrees or types of kin relations and by focusing exclusively the interest of the child. Thus, rather than basing custody on the nature of the kinship tie between the child and a hierarchy of relatives, the Majalla made the well-being of the child the determining factor. By the same token, it abolished the automatic transfer of children to the father or the paternal kin group.

1.3   Changes from the 1980s to 2010

Little happened in the 1970s in regard to family law. Reforms resumed in the early 1980s and continued in the following decades. The situation in regard to women's issues changed starting in the 1980s when women's associations developed in Tunisia and made demands on behalf of women. The country had invested heavily in education, including the education of women, thus creating a new segment of educated women in the population. Partly as a result of increasing investments in women's education, a women's movement developed increasingly in the 1980s.[33] Whereas the state leadership led the innovative legal changes of the 1950s, women expressed demands in the 1980s and 1990s. Although women activists remained cautious in facing the authoritarian regime then in place, they nevertheless managed to create a climate in which women's rights and women's issues found a place in public discourse.[34] Moreover, identifying with the West and opposing Islamic tendencies, Ben Ali's regime supported women's rights and further reforms of family law.[35] This was a period when the regime faced a growing Islamic fundamentalist threat, engaged in repression against it, and found it advantageous to present to the world an image of woman-friendliness.

1.3.1   The 1980s

A major change concerning divorce occurred in 1981. Article 31 introduced an additional dimension: if either the husband or wife insisted on divorce, compensation was to be allocated to the spouse who incurred material or moral damages resulting from the divorce, and this legal stipulation applied to husbands and wives.[36] Another new regulation stated that a wife should receive a "life allowance" as remedy for material and emotional damage inflicted by the husband. This is an important addition as it introduced the notion of financial compensation for inflicting injury on the wife. This financial compensation was to be paid to the wife either at once or regularly "until she dies, gets remarried or lives with someone who cares for her."[37] The amount of money could change depending on the husband's economic conditions, but it had to be sufficient to support the standard of living the woman enjoyed during her marriage.

1.3.2 The 1990s

Changes in family law made in the 1990s presented a new phase in regard to gender relations. The clause according to which a wife shall obey her husband was dropped from Article 23 of the CPS, although the qualification of the husband as head of the family remained. Instead of the focus on respective duties of the spouses, the emphasis in Article 23 was now on the cooperation between husband and wife to address family affairs, the education of children, and financial decisions, and not to inflict harm or injury.[38] Ben Salem, a Tunisian scholar, considers this amendment as one of the most significant changes in that it established "the equality of spouses with regard to reciprocal family obligations, cooperation in household management, and assistance in childcare."[39]

Another revised stipulation applied to custody. Recognizing the mother's role, this change weakened patriarchal norms and the extended family structure. The revised Article 6 required both the guardian's (usually the father) and mother's consent (instead of only the guardian's consent) in allowing the marriage of a minor below the legal marriage age.[40] This clause constituted a shift from paternal to parental guardianship. The clause, however, did not mean that the marriage of a minor should be determined only by parental agreement. The minor to be married also had to agree, as Article 3 required the consent of both spouses to the marriage. In case of disagreements, the judge had final authority on the matter and his/her decision could not be appealed.

The new Article 67 recognized the mother's right to custody and guardianship in case of the father's death by giving her priority over the husband's close relatives. The father was automatically the holder of guardianship rights over children, but the mother could be granted guardianship if the husband's inability to take care of his child was proven.[41]

Another important revision in the 1990s created the position of family judge.[42] The 1993 amendment of Article 32 stipulated that family judges should be appointed by the president of the Court of First Instance, a process that gave them prominence. The CPS of 1956 had required the judge to attempt reconciliation of a husband and wife. However, the 1993 amendment more forcefully defined the obligations of the family judge, who now had an explicit responsibility to reconcile the couple. The family judge also had authority to determine all the rulings concerning the housing of the spouses, alimony, custody of the children, visitation rights to the children, and life allowance. This change strengthened the "enforcement of laws related to divorce"[43] and brought a more systematic and professionalized approach to family issues.

1.3.3   The 2000s

In 2006, further changes were made, this time mainly with the goal of protecting children and of maintaining the bond between child and parent. A clause was added to Article 66 endowing the family judge with the authority to make decisions on visitation rights. The parent who had custody could not prevent the other parent from seeing their children.[44] A separate clause was also added to extend visitation rights to grandparents in case of a parent's death.[45]

In 2007, the minimum age for marriage was set at eighteen for both women and men.[46] Such ages had previously been fifteen for women and eighteen for men in 1956 and seventeen for women and twenty for men in 1964. The new provision thus raised the age for women and placed the same requirements on men and women.

Other amendments increased the protection of children and mothers by reinforcing the father's financial responsibilities for mother and child after divorce. Extensive amendments on custody were added to Article 56 in 2008[47] and a separate Article 56bis was included. The father was required to provide accommodation to the child and the custodian (usually the mother) or to pay an "accommodation allowance" based on his income and the child's needs. Emphasis was placed on the accountability of the father in regard to providing a dwelling. In case he intentionally did not fulfill his responsibility in this regard, a father faced a three-month to one-year imprisonment with a fine from 100 to 1,000 Tunisian dinars (about $80 to $800) and possibly further punishments.[48]

1.4 Reforms since the Jasmine Revolution: 2011–2021

The period from the collapse of the Ben Ali regime and the Jasmine Revolution of 2010/11 to 2021 represented a new era in the history of the country, where complex social and political forces were unleashed. The governments that came to power since the Jasmine Revolution maintained the CPS and some built on it by further expanding women's rights. Like their predecessors, they took important steps in reforming family law.

President Caid Essebsi (December 2014–July 2019) declared that he wanted to create "total, actual equality between men and women citizens in a progressive way."[49] Critics have questioned his and other power holders' motivations, suggesting that the new governments, as their predecessors had done, were using women's rights as a cover for the lack of true democracy in the country. For example, Guellali of Human Rights Watch said: "For a long time, the old regime used progress on women's rights as a fig leaf to distract from its repressive policies .... By championing women's rights while at the same time expanding impunity for acts of corruption, the Tunisian government is reminding us of how these two contrasted realities worked in the past."[50] It seems clear, however, that this new era involved women's voices, which were now making themselves heard in political debates and discussions of policies by their presence in political parties and through newly created women's associations of various ideological persuasions.

Two developments were remarkable in regard to gender: the repeal of reservations to the United Nations Convention on the Elimination of All Forms of Discrimination against Women (CEDAW) in 2014 and the wording of the new Constitution of 2014. These were followed by major changes in family law between 2015 and 2017: (1) the removal of a travel ban for mothers with their children, (2) the criminalization of domestic violence and increased penalty for marital rape, and (3) the removal of the ban on interreligious marriage of Muslim women. Despite these changes in favor of women's rights and greater gender equity in family law, points of contention remain as with respect to inheritance and custody.

Having ratified CEDAW in 1985 with reservations that rejected any aspect of CEDAW in contradiction with Tunisian law, Tunisia still had a way to go to come in compliance with CEDAW. The Tunisian government announced the lifting of restrictions on CEDAW on October 24,

2011, and notified the General Secretariat of the United Nations on April 23, 2014, which thus marked the official date of the new Tunisian position on the matter and a date that women's rights advocates saw as a marker. However, although all other reservations in regard to Tunisian legislation such as family law were lifted in 2014, Tunisia still maintained a general declaration stating that the country "shall not take any organizational or legislative decision in conformity with the requirements of this Convention where such a decision would conflict with the provisions of Chapter I of the Tunisian Constitution."[51] Chapter I of the constitution states that the religion of the country is Islam; but at the same time, it protects freedom of belief.[52] It is too early to tell how this stipulation, which leaves an opening to challenges of CEDAW, will be interpreted in practice. To place Tunisia in its regional context, it is useful to note that states in the Middle East and North Africa, except Iran, have ratified CEDAW, but all have included reservations (with the exception of Palestine which acceded without reservations).

In the same vein, and called a breakthrough for women's rights by UN Women, the 2014 Tunisian Constitution[53] captured international attention. Adopted on January 27, 2014, after much debate, it enshrines the principle of gender equality.[54] It includes strong protection for women's rights, as stated in article 46, according to which "T[t]he state commits to protect women's established rights and works to strengthen and develop those rights," and guarantees "equality of opportunities between women and men to have access to all levels of responsibility and in all domains."[55] The Constitution of 2014 set an important tone for specific policies and laws that immediately followed.

Shortly after these assertions of women's rights in the position in regard to international law, as with CEDAW, and in the foundational text of the 2014 Constitution, Tunisia continued with reforms of family law. In November 2015, the Tunisian parliament passed a bill, proposed by the Women and Family Affairs Ministry, allowing women to travel with their children without their husbands' approval. A long-established practice, a mother previously had to get permission from the father in order to travel outside Tunisia with her children, while the same restriction did not apply to a father. The lifting of the travel ban endowed women with equal rights in making decisions about their children.[56]

In July 2017, the Tunisian parliament passed a bill that criminalized marital rape. Labeled a landmark, the law aimed to protect women from marital rape and domestic violence and to provide legal grounds to penalize perpetrators.[57] Before this new law, judges did not recognize marital rape as a rape. Another change considered as a major step in reforming family law was the removal of the CPS clause that granted immunity to a rapist when he married the victim.[58] Women's rights organizations had long debated article 227 or the "marry-your-rapist" stipulation previously in effect, which helped the rapist escape prosecution through marriage. The offender could get rid of the sentence or could leave prison if he married the woman whom he raped. In practice, families often arranged marriage in order to protect the family honor and avoid shame. The repeal of the clause not only now prevented rapists from escaping penalization but it could also change the perception of rape at the societal level in the long run. Other countries in the MENA region including Jordan and Lebanon also repealed the same legal stipulation about "marry-your-rapist."[59]

Then, in September 2017, Tunisian women gained the legal right to marry a non-Muslim man. In 1973, a ministerial decree modifying the CPS had stipulated that public authorities could not perform the marriage of a Tunisian Muslim woman with a non-Muslim man. This in effect restricted Tunisian women's freedom to marry someone of their choice and had been an important concern of women's rights advocates. While the 1973 decree was in effect, a marriage between a Tunisian Muslim woman and a non-Muslim man was legally recognized in Tunisia only if the man converted to Islam and provided a certificate of his religious conversion to court.[60] The same restriction did not apply to Tunisian men who were allowed to marry a woman of a religion other than Islam and would have their marriage recognized as valid under Tunisian law. The 2017 removal of the 1973 ban constituted a major step in implementing greater gender equity in regard to marriage.[61]

A contentious issue that remains at the center of debates in regard to family law is that of inheritance. A detailed analysis of the history of inheritance law is outside the scope of this chapter. Following Islamic stipulations as articulated in religious texts, and despite some adjustments over time since the promulgation of the CPS, Tunisian women continue to inherit half as much as men in the same kinship relation to the deceased.[62] Although women's rights advocates have demanded fundamental reforms of inheritance law, none has yet occurred. Another issue concerns custody, which is treated differently for men and women. Article 58 of the CPS advises judges to grant custody to either the mother or the father based on the best interests of the child but prohibits allowing a mother to have her children live with her if she remarries, while no such restriction applies to fathers.[63]

1.5   Conclusion

The above analysis has discussed phases of reforms that revamped family law in the history of Tunisia from the postcolonial period to the aftermath of the Arab Spring. Considering the history from the end of colonial rule in 1956 to 2021, it has shown how each phase provided a platform on which further changes could be implemented. Coming from the top, as "politics from above," multiple reforms expanded women's rights. They opened the door to further reforms when "politics from below" appeared on the scene, as a result of changes in systems of governance.

This chapter has suggested reasons for the different waves of reforms ranging from the initial period of the 1950s, the 1980s, the 1990s and 2000s, and to the post-revolutionary period of the 2010s. The major argument offered is that the political dynamics shaped the policy on family law. Reforms occurred when they were in the best interest of power holders within the state, sometimes under pressure from women's rights activists but at other times not. For several decades under consideration, Tunisia experienced authoritarian regimes that had the upper hand in initiating reforms. The sustained reforms either contributed to the consolidation of power or at least did not jeopardize it, while they served other purposes such as protecting potentially vulnerable women and children. The post-revolution, democratically elected new governments maintained the legislation in place or continued further on the reformist path, possibly in part for their own interests and in part in response to demands from women's and other groups.

The fate of family law in Tunisia now depends once again on politics. The Tunisian Revolution of 2010/11 that sparked the Arab Spring opened an era filled with uncertainty but also with hope. For the first time in its history, Tunisia experienced a form of governance in which the government was more representative of the citizenry than previously, despite limitations. New upheavals occurred again in July 2021 when an emergency declaration froze the work of parliament and placed executive powers in the hands of the president. Where political dynamics will take the country is open to question at this time. In regard to family law, we believe it fair to say that a major tension at the moment separates major tendencies among political constituencies: those who defend a conservative Islam and are likely to favour a system of law more faithful to it, those who consider themselves moderate Islamists and are open to reforms, and secularists who tend to prefer a law that is separate from religion. The tendencies appear in the international context, in Tunisian society at large, and among contenders for power in national politics. Only the future will tell how the tension plays out. All we can venture at this time is that family law will remain high on the list of political stakes.

Notes

1 M. M. Charrad, "Tunisia at the Forefront of the Arab World: Two Waves of Gender Legislation" (2007) 64 *Washington and Lee Law Review*, 1513–1527, 1514.

2 We use the terms *Majalla* and Code of Personal Status (CPS) interchangeably.

3 Inheritance is not discussed in this chapter.

4 M. M. Charrad and A. Zarrugh, "Equal or Complementary? Women in the New Tunisian Constitution after the Arab Spring" (2014) 19(2) *The Journal of North African Studies*, 230–243.

5 J. Freeman, *The Politics of Women's Liberation: A Case Study of an Emerging Social Movement and Its Relation to the Policy Process* (McKay, 1975); S. M. Evans, *Tidal Wave: How Women Changed America at Century's End* (Free Press, 2004); C. Baker, *The Women's Movement against Sexual Harassment* (Cambridge University Press, 2007).

6 We use George N. Sfeir's English translation for the initial CPS promulgated in 1956. See G. N. Sfeir, "The Tunisian Code of Personal Status" (1957) 11 *Middle East Journal*, 309–318. For the most recent changes, we refer to F. Ben Maḥmūd, H. Ben Sulaymah, and S. Dawlah, *Majallat al-aḥwāl al-shakhṣīyah* (Markaz al-Dirāsāt al-Qānūnīyah wa al-Qaḍāʾīyah, 2010) (in Arabic, English, and French).

7 S. Kelly and J. Breslin (eds.), *Women's Rights in the Middle East and North Africa: Progress amid Resistance* (Freedom House, 2010), p. 23. On gender in MENA, see also M. M. Charrad, "Gender in the Middle East: Islam, States, Agency" (2011a) 37 *Annual Review of Sociology*, 417–437.

8 S. Nazir and L. Tomppert (eds.), *Women's Rights in the Middle East and North Africa: Citizenship and Justice* (Freedom House, 2005), p. 25.

9 The World Bank Group, "Urban Population" (2016), https://data.worldbank.org/indicator/SP.URB.TOTL.IN.ZS?end=2016&start=1960.

10 UNICEF, "Tunisia: Statistics" (2013), www.unicef.org/infobycountry/Tunisia_statistics.html.

11 M. M. Charrad, "Central and Local Patrimonialism: State-Building in Kin-Based Societies" (2011b) 636 *The Annals of the American Academy of Political and Social Science*, 50–68.

12 M. S. Gordon, "Ben Ali, Zayn al-Abidine," in P. Mattar (ed.), *Encyclopedia of the Modern Middle East and North Africa*, 2nd ed. (Macmillan Reference USA, 2004), vol. 1, p. 439.

13 World Intellectual Property Organization (WIPO: the UN agency dedicated to the use of intellectual property), "Tunisia: the Constitution of Tunisia, 1959" (2011), www.wipo.int/wipolex/en/details.jsp?id=7201.

14 D. Touchent, "Features: A Guide to the Tunisian Legal System," *Legal and Technology Resources for Legal Professionals* (2002), www.llrx.com/node/870/print.

15 M. M. Charrad, *States and Women's Rights: The Making of Postcolonial Tunisia, Algeria, and Morocco* (University of California Press, 2001), p. 214.

16 M. C. Paciello, "Tunisia: Changes and Challenges of Political Transition," Mediterranean Prospects Technical Report No. 3, The Center for European Studies 14 (2011), www.ceps.eu/ceps/download/5632.

17 Y. Ryan, "Ennahda Claims Victory in Tunisia Poll," *Aljazeera English*, October 26, 2011, www.aljazeera.com/news/africa/2011/10/2011102421511587304.html.

18 S. Kostas, "Tunisia, Political Participation and Ideology," *Mediterranean Affairs*, February 22, 2016, http://mediterraneanaffairs.com/tunisia-political-participation-and-ideological-compromise/.

19 The discussion on the substance and significance of the CPS in the 1950s draws in part on Charrad, *States and Women's Rights*, pp. 201–232.

20 Charrad, *States and Women's Rights*, pp. 31–45.

21 See Charrad, *States and Women's Rights* and "Tunisia at the Forefront."

22 On Islam versus secularism, see S. Bostanji, "Turbulence in the Legal Application of the Tunisian Code of the Personal Status: Conflict in Reference Frames in Work" (2009) 61 *Revue Internationale de Droit Comparé*, 7–47 (in French).

23 See Article 3 in Sfeir, "The Tunisian CPS," 309.

24 See Article 18 in Sfeir, "The Tunisian CPS," 310.

25 Ben Maḥmūd et al., *Majallat*, pp. 138–140.

26 See Article 23 in Sfeir, "The Tunisian CPS," 310.

27 See Article 5 in Sfeir, "The Tunisian CPS," 309. See also République Tunisienne, *Code de la nationalité tunisienne, Code of Tunisian Citizenship* (Imprimerie Officielle, 1983), Article 4.

28 M. Borrmans, *Statut personnel et famille au Maghreb: De 1940 à nos jours* (Mouton, 1977), p. 335 (in French).

29 See Articles 29–33 in Sfeir, "The Tunisian CPS," 310.

30 See Article 32 in Sfeir, "The Tunisian CPS," 310.

31 See Article 47 in Sfeir, "The Tunisian CPS," 311.

32 See Law of 3 June 1966, in Borrmans, *Statut Personnel*, pp. 343–345.

33 Charrad, "Tunisia at the forefront," 1524–1526.

34 L. A. Brand, *Women, the State and Political Liberalization: Middle Eastern and North African Experiences* (Columbia University Press, 1998), pp. 220–246.

35 A. K. Wing and H. Kassim. "The Future of Palestinian Women's Rights: Lessons from a Half-Century of Tunisian Progress," *Washington and Lee Law Review* (2007) 64, 1557.

36 See Article 31 in Ben Maḥmūd et al., *Majallat*, p. 216.

37 See Article 31 in Ben Maḥmūd et al., *Majallat*, p. 216.

38 See Article 23 in Ben Maḥmūd et al., *Majallat*, pp. 167–168.

39 L. Ben Salem, "Tunisia," in Kelly and Breslin (eds.), *Women's Rights in the Middle East and North Africa*, p. 494.

40 See Article 6 in Ben Maḥmūd et al., pp. 89–91.

41 Ben Salem, "Tunisia," p. 496.

42 See Article 32 in Ben Maḥmūd et al., pp. 255–256.

43 Ben Salem, "Tunisia," p. 495.

44 See Article 66 in Ben Maḥmūd et al., p. 409.

45 See Article 66bis in Ben Maḥmūd et al., p. 412.

46 See Article 5 in Ben Maḥmūd et al., pp. 79–80.

47 See Article 56 in Ben Maḥmūd et al., pp. 355–358.

48 See Article 56bis in Ben Maḥmūd et al., pp. 365–367.

49 H. Sally, "Tunisian Muslim Women Allowed to Marry Non-Muslims for First Time in Decades', *Independent*, September 15, 2017. Retrieved November 2, 2017, www .independent.co.uk/news/world/africa/tunisia-muslim-women-marry-non-muslims-first-time-decades-islamic-sharia-religion-a7948916.html.

50 P. Schemm, "This Arab Country Is Allowing Muslim Women to Marry Non-Muslim Men. That's the Good News," *The Washington Post*, September 22, 2017. Retrieved November 2, 2017, www.washingtonpost.com/news/worldviews/wp/2017/09/22/this-arab-country-is-allowing-muslim-women-to-marry-non-muslim-men-thats-the-good-news/?utm_term=.d419c4c60f58.

51 Human Rights Watch, "Tunisia: Landmark Action on Women's Rights: First in Region to Lift Key Restrictions on International Treaty," *Human Rights Watch* (2014), Retrieved November 2, 2017, www.hrw.org/news/2014/04/30/tunisia-land mark-action-womens-rights.

52 T. Amara, "Arab Spring beacon Tunisia signs new constitution," *Reuters*, January 27, 2014. Retrieved November 9, 2017, www.reuters.com/article/us-tunisia-consti tution/arab-spring-beacon-tunisia-signs-new-constitution-idUSBREA0Q0OU20140127.

53 UN Women, "Tunisia's New Constitution: A Breakthrough for Women's Rights," UN Women, February 11, 2014. Retrieved November 9, 2017, www.unwomen.org/en/news/stories/2014/2/tunisias-new-constitution.

54 Charrad and Zarrugh. "Equal or complementary," pp. 230–243.

55 Human Rights Watch, "Tunisia: Landmark Action."

56 Human Rights Watch, "Tunisia: A Step Forward for Women's Rights: Free to Travel with Their Children," *Human Rights Watch* (2015). Retrieved November 2, 2017, www.hrw.org/news/2015/11/12/tunisia-step-forward-womens-rights.

57 R. Roberts, "Tunisia: 'Landmark' New Law Gives Women Protection from Rape and Domestic Violence: 'We Hope That This Precedent That Tunisia Is Setting Will Be Followed by Others (in the Arab world)," *Independent* (2017), July 28, 2017. Retrieved November 2, 2017, www.independent.co.uk/news/world/tunisia-law-women-protect-rape-domestic-violence-north-africa-landmark-rights-abuse-sexual-a7864846.html.

58 Roberts, "Tunisia."

59 E. Dehnert, "As Lebanon, Jordan, Tunisia End 'Marry-Your-Rapist' Laws, Where Next?," *Huffingtonpost* (2017), September 1, 2017. Retrieved November 3, 2017, www.huffingtonpost.com/entry/as-lebanon-jordan-tunisia-end-marry-your-rapist-laws-where-next_us_59a986c8e4b0b5e530fe49e1.

60 P. Schemm, "This Arab Country Is Allowing Muslim Women to Marry Non-Muslim Men. That's the Good News," *The Washington Post* (2017), September 22, 2017. Retrieved November 2, 2017, www.washingtonpost.com/news/worldviews/wp/2017/09/22/this-arab-country-is-allowing-muslim-women-to-marry-non-muslim-men-thats-the-good-news/?utm_term=.d419c4c60f58.

61 S. Hayden, "Tunisian Muslim Women Allowed to Marry Non-Muslims for First Time in Decades," *Independent* (2017), September 15, 2017. Retrieved Nov 2, 2017, www.independent.co.uk/news/world/africa/tunisia-muslim-women-marry-non-muslims-first-time-decades-islamic-sharia-religion-a7948916.html.

62 V. Chambers and C. Cummings, "Building Momentum: Women's Empowerment in Tunisia," Case Study Report (2014). London: Overseas Development Institute.

63 Human Rights Watch, "Tunisia: A Step Forward."

2

Family Law in Egypt

NATHALIE BERNARD-MAUGIRON

2.1 Introduction

The Egyptian government announced in October 2019 that a new personal status law was being prepared by the Ministry of Justice and that the draft bill should be referred to parliament in the beginning of 2020. By December 2022, however, no draft bill had been submitted, though heated debates around possible reforms were dividing the society.

After the 2011 uprisings, Egypt adopted a new constitution in 2014. It strengthened the principle of equality between men and women by declaring that the state shall ensure the achievement of equality between women and men in all civil, political, economic, social, and cultural rights (Art. 11). Despite this call to achieve equality in all areas, family law continues to establish significant differences between women and men, in terms of both marriage and divorce rights.

Discussions around amending Egypt's current corpus of women's rights and personal status legislation have been going on since 2011, both inside and outside parliament, but they have led so far only to superficial changes. In 2017, an amendment to the 1943 inheritance law made it a crime to deprive a woman of her inheritance rights;[1] and in 2014, a law criminalizing sexual harassment was adopted. However, the personal status laws have not yet been revised.

2.2 Egyptian Personal Status Law: An Overview

2.2.1 Egyptian Legal System

Egypt's legal system is influenced by French and Islamic conceptions of law. By the nineteenth century, most civil and criminal laws were secularized, following the French legal tradition; personal status laws, however, remained in the exclusive domain of *shari'a*, in particular, to the dominant view of the Hanafi school, the official school of the Ottoman Empire. In 1875, a codification of *shari'a* rules regarding family law on the basis of the Hanafi doctrine was prepared by Qadri Pasha, future Minister of Justice (1879–1882). It advocated a particularly patriarchal structure for the family. The code, made up of more than 600 provisions, was never promulgated and did not acquire binding legal force. However, it resulted in a concise and accessible account of the Hanafi doctrine and became a standard manual for teaching Hanafi law.[2] Egyptian personal status laws began being codified in the beginning of the twentieth century.

Until 1955, *shari'a* courts had exclusive jurisdiction over personal status matters between Muslim litigants as well as between Muslims and non-Muslims. Community councils were dealing with the personal status of members of the Orthodox Churches, Catholics, Protestants, and Jews.[3] *Shari'a* courts and community councils were abolished by Laws No. 461 and 462 in 1955; and jurisdiction over personal status matters was transferred to ordinary civil courts.[4] While the courts were unified, the law that applied to disputes was still determined by the religion of the parties involved.[5] If two non-Muslim parties belong to the same community and denomination, the personal status law of their common denomination applies. As long as one of the litigants is a Muslim, the personal status law for Muslims, as codified by the Egyptian legislator, applies to the dispute. The personal status law for Muslims is also applied whenever the litigants are from different non-Muslim denominations or belong to a non-Muslim denomination not officially recognized.

2.2.2   Main Laws Dealing with Personal Status

In Egypt, substantive rules of Muslim personal status law have not been codified in a comprehensive and exhaustive code. The policy of the state has been to codify these laws step by step and to take the opportunity of the codification process to introduce reforms and improve women's status within the family. Sadat adopted in 1979 a far-reaching reform that considered polygamy as a sufficient ground to grant a divorce to the first wife. However, the reform, adopted by decree-law, was declared unconstitutional a few years later as an abuse of power.[6]

The first codifications of personal status law began in 1920 and 1929. They enlarged the grounds upon which a woman could initiate divorce.[7] The laws also codified the husband's obligation to provide his wife maintenance during marriage and alimony after divorce and regulated the length of *'idda* (the waiting period following divorce or widowhood during which a woman may not remarry) and put conditions for a repudiation to be considered valid. These laws are still in force, though they were amended in 1985 by Law No. 100.

A 1976 law on alimony established a system whereby wives who were unable to have court rulings for maintenance enforced could get financial support from a fund at Nasser Bank, which was to collect payments from husbands, ex-husbands, and fathers. This system, however, did not work because Nasser Bank had too much trouble collecting funds from debtors. Similar provisions were included in Law No. 1 of 2000 and spelled out in Law No. 11 of 2004, with little more success.

Law No. 100 of 1985 amended the 1920 and 1929 laws, allowing divorced women to receive financial compensation (mut'a) and to keep the marital home until the end of child custody; extended child custody by the mother until 12 for the girls and 10 for the boys. The 1985 law also required that the first wife be informed officially of the new marriage of her husband and allowed husbands to stop spending on their wife if she violated her duty of obedience.

If no specific reference in the laws can be found on a particular point, the judge must follow the most authoritative opinion within the Hanafi school. This means that non-codified Islamic rules (fiqh) will apply only to matters where the law is silent. If a legal provision exists, the judge has to apply the law even if he personally disagrees with its content.

A law of procedure was adopted as early as 1880 to organize the procedure before shari'a courts. The law currently in force is Law No. 1 of 2000 organizing certain Conditions and Procedures of Litigation in Matters of Personal Status. This law abrogated all previous procedural laws dealing with personal status[8] and was intended to facilitate and speed up litigation in these matters. The Code of Civil and Commercial Procedure as well as the Proof Law and the provisions of the Civil Code dealing with the administration and liquidation of successions apply whenever no specific provision is provided.

Law No. 1 of 2000 suppressed fees at all stages of litigation in suits regarding maintenance matters. All personal status cases must first be submitted to a Family Dispute Resolution office. Though formally a "procedural" law, Law No. 1 of 2000 included some "substantive" provisions like an article providing for khul' divorce and one allowing wives married following a "customary marriage" ('urfi) to get a judicial dissolution of their marriage.[9] These two provisions were hidden in this procedural law in an effort to ensure adoption and to avoid the passionate debates a proper substantive law would have generated in the parliament and in society. The provision regarding *khul'*, however, sparked heated debates in parliament and divided public opinion.

In 2004, Law No. 10 was adopted, establishing family courts to bring relief to an over-burdened judicial system and to speed up the legal process. All family disputes (alimony, custody, divorce, etc.) are now consolidated into a single case heard by one court, potentially reducing delays, instead of being examined by different courts in different places.[10] The law decreed that rulings on family law issues would no longer be challengeable before the Court of Cassation. Only the public prosecution is allowed to challenge a ruling before that court on certain conditions.

2.2.3   An Internal Renovation Process of Reform

Personal status law reform has been limited in its scope and constrained by the political context, the survival of patriarchy, and the role played by conservative and religious opposition. Experience has shown that it is not easy to amend these laws because of the resistance of the society and conservative religious groups. Governments, who often resorted to authoritarian means to pass the laws, have always been keen on presenting their reforms as consistent with *shari'a* law and supported and endorsed by eminent religious authorities.

Some laws are preceded by an "explanatory note" that sums up the history of the provisions and tries to legitimate the most innovative revisions. They show how lawmakers did not hesitate to refer to other schools of law, in particular the Maliki school, to bypass the often rigid rules of the Hanafi school, using the *takhayyur* process.[11] Reformers also made eclectic choices of rules, selecting from a wide variety of opinions advocated by eminent jurists of the past within the four Sunnite schools of law and combining them to produce new solutions (*talfiq* process). This allowed the reforms to be presented as taking place within the *shari'a* and avoided strenuous attacks from the conservative religious circles.

For instance, the Hanafi school of law hardly acknowledges the husband's impotency or castration as reasons for legal dissolution of spousal bonds. According to the explanatory note to Law No. 25 of 1929, "the welfare commands to adopt Imam Malik's doctrine in case of discord between spouses," meaning the law granted women the right to divorce for harm for humanitarian reasons. In the same text, the legislature justified recourse to the Maliki doctrine to authorize women to petition for divorce in case of the husband's extended absence, out of fear for the abandoned wife's honor and chastity. The 1920 law made maintenance a recoverable debt from the moment the husband fails to provide it and not, as under Hanafi law, from the moment the wife demands maintenance in court, on the basis of the Maliki and Shafi'i schools.

According to Islamic law, the ruler has the right to confine and define the jurisdiction of his courts. As a result, reformers introduced a procedural device precluding judges from reviewing certain kinds of claims. This expedient, which left the substantive law intact, excluded certain matters from the jurisdiction of the courts and therefore denied judicial relief. For instance, courts were prevented from examining claims pertaining to unregistered marriage contracts or those concluded by minor children. Underage marriages were not forbidden, nor were unregistered ('urfi) marriages, but such marriages could not give rise to judicial claims before the courts in case of denial by the parties, which had a deterrent effect.

With the increasing Islamization trend, reform of personal status law became the field for conflicting interpretations of the sacred law, each group referring to the same body of religious rules but adopting different readings of them. Even feminists and women's rights NGOs have begun to challenge Islamic doctrine from within and call for a distinction to be established between patriarchal tradition and authentic Islam. They choose more and more to refer to new interpretations of the *shari'a* to legitimize their call for additional legal reforms rather than emphasizing human rights and international conventions to avoid accusations of importing Western cultural and imperialist values.[12]

2.3 Salient Highlights of the Personal Status Code[13]

2.3.1 Conclusion of the Marriage Contract

The marriage contract should be concluded by the two future spouses in front of two witnesses and registered. The legal age for marriage is eighteen for men and women. A Muslim man can marry a Christian or a Jewish wife but a Muslim woman can only marry a Muslim husband. A non-Egyptian seeking to marry an Egyptian woman is required to buy LE50,000 worth of investment certificates drawn on the National Bank in her name, if the age difference between them exceeds twenty-five years.

The wife shall express her consent directly and not through a matrimonial guardian. Consummation of the marriage is not to take place until payment by the groom to his bride of the dowry. The custom is to divide the dowry into two shares and to pay the prompt portion upon marriage and the deferred dowry upon divorce or death of the husband.

Unregistered or customary (*'urfi*) marriages are not forbidden but are granted a status inferior to that of registered marriages: No claim concerning such a marriage will be heard by the courts when it is denied by one of the parties, unless it is supported by an official marriage document.[14] Since 2000, the wife can petition for a judicial dissolution of her marriage on the same grounds as those recognized for registered marriages.[15] She can use any written document to prove the existence of the marriage, which will then serve as the basis for her subsequent request for divorce. The divorced wife will not be able to require any financial right for herself. However, the father will have to support his children if his paternity is proven.

Spouses have the right to stipulate conditions in their marriage contract regarding their respective rights and duties. About a third of a page of the contract is left empty to add the conditions the partners may want to include. For instance, they may decide to specify that the wife will be allowed to use *'isma* (she will be able to end the marriage on her own will); that the husband will not be allowed to conclude subsequent marriages without the written approval of his wife; that in case her husband gets married again, the wife will be allowed to dissolve her marriage; that she will be allowed to work and/or to continue her education; or that the mother will have the right to choose the children's schools. The conditions are registered by the *ma'dhun* before the signature of the contract, on the request of the spouses.

Polygamy has been restricted but is not outlawed. The Muslim husband can marry up to four wives simultaneously without having to request the first wife (wives)' agreement unless so stipulated in the marriage contract. The *ma'dhun* shall inform the previous wife of the new marriage of her husband. She will be able to file a judicial action for divorce if she can prove that her husband's subsequent marriage caused her material or mental harm that made continuing with matrimonial life impossible. If the new wife did not know that her husband was already married, she too can petition for divorce.

If the first wife was not informed of the new marriage of her husband, the husband can be condemned to jail and/or receive a penalty, and the *ma'dhun* can be condemned to a financial penalty and may lose his job. The new marriage, however, remains valid.

2.3.2 Effects of the Marriage

The husband has a maintenance obligation toward his wife for the entire duration of the marriage, even if the wife has personal resources and even if she is of a different religion. He must provide her with food, clothing, housing, medical expenses, and other expenses that are required by the law. A court order for maintenance shall be executed on the husband's property if he refuses to comply. Maintenance is a debt from the moment the husband fails to provide and not from the day of the ruling of the judge condemning him to pay. The amount of spousal support is determined on the basis of the husband's level of wealth.[16] The wife does not need to make financial contributions toward family expenses, although in practice many women do. In case of disagreement on the amount of spousal maintenance, or if the husband stops providing, the wife may petition the court to force payment or file for divorce due to the husband's noncompliance with his duty of maintenance.

The marriage relationship is based on agreement between the spouses that the husband provides support and that the wife pledges obedience to her husband. She loses her right to maintenance if she leaves the marital home and refuses to return after her husband has required her to do so via a bailiff's notification.[17] However, she can object to this summons before a court within thirty days from the date of notification by indicating the grounds on which she justifies her disobedience.[18] The court must try to reconcile the two spouses. In case of failure, the wife can initiate a divorce procedure. If she does not object within the time limit, she forfeits her right to maintenance.

The wife does not lose her right to maintenance if she leaves the domicile in cases permitted by the legislature on the grounds of custom or necessity.[19] For example, she has the right to leave her home for a lawful job, provided she does not misuse this right – meaning that it does not conflict with the family's interest, and her husband has not asked her to abstain from going out to work. However, if the husband knew and accepted at the time of contracting the marriage that his wife held a job, he cannot, after the marriage was concluded, request that she does not work.

The default matrimonial regime is separation of property. Each spouse retains individual ownership of assets brought into the marriage and assets obtained during the marriage are registered in their individual name. Women and men have equal rights to acquire, manage, and own their property. If the wife has assets of her own when entering into the marriage, she can subsequently administer and manage them freely and independently.

Parentage of a child is established through marriage. Paternity cannot be established for an illegitimate offspring. Parentage in customary marriages can be established if the father recognizes his child and if marriage can be proven. The mother can bring a case to family court to have paternity established. Paternity disputes and filing for divorce are the only grounds on which courts are allowed to rule (since 2000) on customary marriages in case of denegation by one of the parties.

The father has a personal obligation to provide his minor children with maintenance if they have no personal resources.[20] Maintenance is due until the boy reaches the age of fifteen and until the girl marries or is able to earn an income sufficient for her expenses. The term can also be extended if the boy is incapable of earning due to a physical or mental handicap or is a student. Maintenance must be provided according to the father's means and the child's needs. However, if the child has personal resources, he must cover his own needs.

Guardianship belongs exclusively to the father, who is allowed to make the most important decisions for his children (i.e., manage their money, choose their school, etc.). In the event of the death or incapacity of the father, guardianship is awarded to the closest male relative.

2.3.3   Dissolution of the Marriage

There are different procedures for dissolving a marriage. The husband may terminate the marriage contract at any time and for any reason, while the wife normally needs to bring a case before the judge.

2.3.3.1   Divorce for Prejudice[21]

The wife may petition for divorce on several grounds. Divorce is allowed in case of absence of the husband for more than one year without a valid reason[22] or his condemnation to jail for more than three years.[23] In that case, however, the wife shall wait for a year after his imprisonment to file her action. Divorce is also allowed in case of failure by the husband to provide maintenance.[24] However, such a divorce is revocable: the husband may resume the marriage if he proves his solvency and pays the arrears of maintenance in a delay not exceeding one month. The wife can also file for divorce if her husband is afflicted with a serious or incurable defect or mental disorder.[25] It must be impossible for the wife to continue life with her husband without suffering from harm. The husband must have suffered from this disease before the marriage and without the knowledge of his wife. If the disease appeared after the marriage and the wife, implicitly or explicitly, accepted it after having knowledge of the disease, then she cannot file for divorce on these grounds.

Harm is also a ground for divorce, on the condition that it be such that the continuation of matrimonial life be impossible between two persons of their social standing.[26] The judge will appreciate the prejudice on the basis of his discretionary power. In case of polygamous remarriage of her husband, his wife can petition for divorce if she can prove that his new marriage caused her a moral or material harm that makes the continuation of matrimonial life between persons of their social standing difficult.[27] She should apply within a year after she was informed of the new marriage, except if she agreed explicitly or implicitly. Here again, the judge enjoys discretionary power.

2.3.3.2 Husband Initiated Rupture: Repudiation

The Muslim husband can repudiate his wife. He only needs to go to the *ma'dhun* with two witnesses and declare that his wife is repudiated. He does not need to justify his decision, and his wife does not need to be present. Since 1985, oral repudiation must be registered by the *ma'dhun* within thirty days following the declaration and he shall inform the wife that she has been repudiated.[28] The repudiation takes effect from the date of its occurrence, though in terms of inheritance and other financial rights it becomes effective only from the date of the notification to the wife. Criminal sanctions are provided in case of nonobservance of these procedures.

Repudiation is null and void if performed in a state of inebriation or under duress; it cannot be conditional and its wording shall not be ambiguous.[29] If the wife is repudiated three times, the dissolution becomes irrevocable and the husband will not be able to marry her again unless she gets married to another man, consummates the marriage, and divorces him. To be considered irrevocable, triple repudiation must be done in three separate pronouncements, not in one sitting.[30]

The husband can decide to take his spouse back during the three months following the repudiation (*'idda* period). During this time, the spouses continue to live together and the husband can decide to end the separation with or without the agreement of his wife, explicitly or implicitly, by resuming marital relations and common life. If he uses this possibility, he does not need to conclude a new marriage contract or to pay a new dower. Marital relations are considered as only suspended, but not broken, after the repudiation of the wife by her husband, until the end of the *'idda* period. At the end of the *'idda* period, the marital bond is definitively broken and repudiation becomes irrevocable. If the husband wishes to marry his former wife again, he has to conclude a new marriage contract and pay a new dower.

Law No 100 of 1985 allowed a divorced wife to get financial compensation (*mut'a*) if she was repudiated by her husband without her consent and not for a cause proceeding from her. The amount of the compensation shall not be less than the maintenance of two years with due consideration given to the condition of the husband, the circumstances of the repudiation, and the duration of the marriage.

2.3.3.3   Divorce by Mutual Consent

If the repudiation takes place before the *ma'dhun* in the presence of the wife and with her consent, the husband declares that he repudiates his wife with her consent. This kind of repudiation is an assented or requested dissolution of the marriage, where the wife gives up all or part of her financial rights and may even offer financial compensation to her husband. However, she will keep her right to custody over her children and the father will have to pay them alimony. The marriage will be immediately and definitely terminated.

2.3.4   *"Self-Repudiation"*: 'Isma

'Isma is the right of the married wife to repudiate herself. This option can be stipulated in the marriage contract by the spouses at the time of marriage. The wife will then be allowed to end her marriage unilaterally by going to the *ma'dhun* with two witnesses and asking him to register her self-repudiation. This option given to the wife does not deprive her husband of the right to repudiate her of his own will.

If this condition is not included in the marriage contract and her husband refuses to repudiate her even in return for financial compensation, the wife can only end her marriage through judicial divorce. The procedure will take years instead of a few minutes, and the wife will have to prove she suffered prejudice.

2.3.4.1   Divorce without Fault: *Khul'*

Khul' was introduced by Law 1/2000.[31] It is the procedure whereby a wife can divorce her husband without cause, whether or not he agrees, by returning the dower received from him at the time of the marriage and forfeiting her own financial rights (but not the rights of her children). She only needs to declare to the judge that she detests life with her husband, that continuation of married life between them is impossible, and that she fears she may transgress the "limits of God" due to this detestation. The judge cannot refuse to grant her divorce. *Khul'* takes the form of irrevocable divorce. The ruling is not subject to appeal. This kind of dissolution of the marriage takes less time to obtain than a judicial divorce, but its financial consequences are heavier to bear for the wife.

In exchange of her release, the wife must forfeit all her financial rights and give back the dower (bride-price) she received at the time of the wedding. She has to give up both alimony (*nafaqa al-'idda*) and compensation (*mut'a*) and must renounce the delayed portion of the dower. However, she does not forfeit her nonfinancial rights, that is, the right to children's custody. *Khul'* also does not affect the right of the children to receive alimony from their father.[32]

2.3.5   Effects of the Divorce

After the dissolution of the marriage, the divorced wife shall introduce a separate legal action before the courts to collect her alimony and that of her children. Divorced women do not get a share in their husband's wealth even after a long married life. They are entitled to maintenance during their *'idda* (waiting period) for a period between three months and a year after the divorce and to compensation (*mut'a*) if the marriage has been consummated and the divorce occurred without their agreement and was not due to any cause on their part.[33] The amount of the compensation should not be less than two years of maintenance and is evaluated according to the husband's financial means, the circumstances of the divorce, and the length of the marriage. The judge will decide whether the wife is entitled to such compensation and will set the amount. Fathers have to support their minor children after divorce as they did during marriage, except if the children have their own resources.[34] As enforcement of the court decisions is often difficult, women can turn to a guarantee fund to obtain funding. The fund stands in for the husband before seeking redress against him to obtain the reimbursement of the amounts paid out.

The mother who has been granted custody over her minor children can stay in the rented matrimonial domicile with them for the duration of the custody or until she remarries.[35] The husband cannot stay in the marital home unless he offers another independent and decent housing option before the end of the waiting-period. If the marital home is not rented, the husband is entitled to live in it independently, on the condition that he provides his former wife and their children alternative appropriate accommodation. At the end of the legal period of custody, the father has the right to return to the domicile house even if the judge has extended the period of custody. The wife will then have to find a new accommodation for her and her children.

Since 2005,[36] children (boys and girls) are under the legal custody of the mother until they reach the age of fifteen. Custody can be extended after this age if the judge considers it is in the interest of the children. According to Law No. 4 of 2005, the judge allows the children upon their reaching age fifteen to make a choice regarding which parent they wish to be their custodian.

The law does not make a difference between Muslim and Christian mothers. Some recent court rulings, however, deprived the Christian mother of the custody of her Muslim children after the age of seven, stating that after the age of "religious maturity" children should be raised according to the principles of the Muslim religion and that a Christian mother would not be able to give them such a religious upbringing.

Divorced fathers almost never retain custody of their children and are granted visitation rights only three hours a week, in a public place. They have no right to residential visits of their children, who cannot stay overnight during weekends or holidays without the agreement of the mother. In case of lack of agreement between the father and the mother, the judge determines a public place (garden, park, club, etc.) where the right of visitation will take place. Relatives of the children of divorced parents, including grandparents, aunts, and uncles have no visitation rights.

The divorced (or widowed) mother who remarries loses custody over her children, who will be given to her mother or to the mother of her former husband. The mother can also lose custody, on the request of the father, if the judge considers that the interest of the child requires such a decision (e.g., she abuses them, neglects them, etc.).

2.4   Conclusion

Before the removal of Mubarak in 2011, women's groups were hoping to reform personal status laws further. Among the proposed reforms were to consider customary (*'urfi*) marriages illegal to avoid paternity disputes, to abolish the wife's duty of obedience, to forbid polygamy or at least require its authorization by a judge, to forbid repudiation or at least require that it take place before a judge and be justified, or that divorced spouses split in half assets accumulated during marriage. There were also proposals to allow divorced mothers who remarry to keep custody over their children or to replace paternal guardianship with parental responsibility and to criminalize domestic violence.

While many women's groups were emboldened before the fall of Mubarak to pursue greater equality in family life, they became fearful that under the Muslim Brother President Mohammed Morsi their rights would be further curtailed after Islamist parties won the 2012 parliamentary and presidential elections. Amendments to personal status laws, dubbed Suzanne laws, after Mubarak's wife, Suzanne Mubarak, were the target of Islamist groups, who attempted to discredit them by associating them with the previous regime and claiming that they were designed to break up Egyptian families and impose Western values.[37] Attacks were launched in particular against the 2000 *khul'* law, the 2005 amendments to the custody law that gave divorced women the right to keep their children until they reach the age of fifteen, and the amendment to the Child Law that raised the age of marriage of girls to eighteen. Though no amendment was adopted before the removal of Mohammed Morsi by the army in July 2013, this shows however the limits of empowering women in the family by authoritarian means, which creates resentment toward women's struggles.

In January 2017, alarmed by a rising divorce rate, President Abdel Fatah al-Sisi demanded that new legislation be enacted to invalidate orally pronounced repudiation and protect the family. A few weeks later, the Council of Senior Scholars at al-Azhar rejected this proposal, stressing that prohibiting orally pronounced divorce would be in contradiction with the consensus that has reigned among the Umma since the age of Prophet Mohammed.

Several proposals to amend family law were submitted by members of the parliament, the National Council for Women or even by the Council of Senior Scholars of al-Azhar in 2019, but none of them were adopted. Among the most controversial topics were child custody and access conditions of the noncustodial parent (the father in almost all cases), which have not been changed despite the tabling of several bills suggesting more visitation rights for the noncustodial parent after a divorce, polygamy, customary marriages, wife's obedience, *khul'*, and oral divorce. A draft law submitted by the government in May 2018 to enforce new punishments on parents who force their children into early marriage was not adopted either. A draft unified codification of family law was submitted to parliament in 2020, before being withdrawn in 2021 in the face of protests from feminist movements opposed in particular to the expanded powers it was giving to the guardian to cancel the marriage entered into by a woman without his consent, to the absence of limits to polygamy, and to the reinforcement of the powers of the father as guardian of his children. In June 2022, a family law reform committee was established by the Minister of Justice and instructed to submit a report on possible reforms of family law.

Notes

1 According to this amendment (Art. 49), anyone who deliberately denies the heir, be it a man or a woman, their legal share of the inheritance or confiscates a document confirming this share shall be jailed for six months at least and be subject to a fine ranging between 20,000 Egyptian pounds at least and 100,000 pounds at most. In case of recidivism, the prison sentence shall be no less than one year.

2 K. M. Cuno, *Modernizing Marriage: Family, Ideology, and Law in Nineteenth- and Early Twentieth-Century Egypt* (Syracuse University Press, 2015).

3 Fourteen non-Muslim communities are recognized in Egypt. Most of them are Christian: Orthodox (four different denominations), Catholic (seven different rites), and Protestants. The Jewish community is divided into two sects. Each community still enjoys the right to legislate its own personal status law.

4 Law No. 462/1955 on the Abolition of *Shari'a* Courts and Community Councils and Transferring Pending Cases to the National Courts.

5 The new constitution adopted in January 2014 allows non-Muslims to follow their own religious laws in matters pertaining to personal status (Art. 3).

6 The decree-law had been adopted by the president in application of the emergency powers granted by the constitution, though no genuine necessity required that such measures be taken without delay.

7 Law No. 25 of 1920 regarding Maintenance and Some Questions of Personal Status and Law No 25 of 1929 regarding certain Personal Status Provisions.

8 The 1931 Regulations for *shari'a* courts, Part 4 of the Code of Civil and Criminal Procedure that was dealing with personal status cases and Law No. 462/1955 on the Abolition of *Shari'a* Courts and Community Councils and Transferring Pending Cases to the National Courts.

9 For the meaning of *'urfi* marriages, see Section 2.3.1.

10 M. Al-Sharmani, *Recent Reforms in Personal Status Laws and Women's Empowerment: Family Courts in Egypt* (AUC Social Research Center, 2008), www

.pathwaysofempowerment.org/Familycourts.pdf. See also M. Al-Sharmani, *Gender Justice and Legal Reform in Egypt: Negotiating Muslim Family Law* (American University in Cairo, 2017).

11 The Maliki school, one of the four Sunnite schools, is followed mostly in North Africa, West Africa, the United Arab Emirates, Kuwait, and Oman.

12 See, for instance, M. Zulficar, "The Islamic Marriage Contract in Egypt," in A. Quraishi and F. E. Vogel (eds.), *The Islamic Marriage Contract: Case Studies in Islamic Family Law*, Harvard Series in Islamic Law, 6 (Harvard University Press, 2008), 231–274; D. Singerman, "Rewriting Divorce in Egypt: Reclaiming Islam, Legal Activism and Coalition Politics," in R. Hefner (ed.), *Remaking Muslim Politics: Pluralism, Contestation Democratization* (Princeton University Press, 2005), 161–188; L. Abu-Odeh, "Egyptian Feminism: Trapped in the Identity Debate" (2004) 16(2) *Yale Journal of Law and Feminism*, 145–191; M. Lindbekk, "Inscribing Islamic Shari'a in Egyptian Divorce" (2016) 3(2) *Oslo Law Review*, 103–135; L. E. Fawzy, "Muslim Personal Status Law in Egypt: The Current Situation and Possibilities of Reform through Internal Initiative," in L. Welchman (ed.), *Women's Rights and Islamic Family Law: Perspectives on Reform* (Zed Books, 2004), 17–94.

13 L. Abu-Odeh. "Modernizing Muslim Family Law: The Case of Egypt" (2004) 37 *Vanderbiilt Journal of Transnational Law*, 1043–1146; N. Bernard-Maugiron, "Egyptian Family Law Reform: Between Law in the Books and Law in Action," in N. Nassari (ed.), *Changing God's Law: The Dynamics of Middle Eastern Family Law* (Ashgate, 2016), 181–203; N. Bernard-Maugiron and B. Dupret, "From Jihan to Suzanne: Twenty Years of Personal Status in Egypt" (2002) 19 *Recht van de Islam*, 1–19; D. S. El Alami, "Law No. 100 of 1985 Amending Certain Provisions of Egypt's Personal Status Laws" (1994) 1(1) *Islamic Law and Society*, 116–130; E. Fawzy, "Muslim Personal Status Law in Egypt: The Current Situation and Possibilities of Reform through Internal Initiatives," in L. Welchman (ed.), *Women's Rights and Islamic Family Law: Perspectives on Reform* (Zed Books, 2004), 15–94; N. Sonneveld, "Divorce Reform in Egypt and Morocco: Men and Women Navigating Rights and Duties," (2019) 26 *Islamic Law and Society*, 149–178; N. Sonneveld, "From the Liberation of Women to the Liberation of Men? A Century of Family Law Reform in Egypt" (2017) 7(1) *Religion and Gender*, 88–104, doi.org/10.18352/rg.10197.

14 For a comparison between formal and informal marriages, see N. Sonneveld, "Rethinking the Difference between Formal and Informal Marriages in Egypt," in M. Voorhoeve (ed.), *Family Law in Islam: Divorce, Marriage and Women in the Muslim World*, New Middle Eastern Studies 5 (I. B. Tauris, 2012), 77–108.

15 Article 20 of Law 1/2000 organizing certain Conditions and Procedures of Litigation in Matters of Personal Status.

16 Article 16 of Law 25/1929 as amended by Law 100/1985.

17 Article 11bis (2) of Law 100/1985.

18 Article 11bis (2) of Law 100/1985.

19 Article 7 of Law 100/1985.

20 Article 18bis (2).4 of Law 100/1985 amending Laws No. 25 of 1920 and 1929.

21 A. Chemais, "Divorced from Justice: Women's Unequal Access to Divorce in Egypt," *Human Rights Watch Report* (vol. 16, December 2004); and

N. Bernard-Maugiron and B. Dupret. "Breaking-off the Family: Divorce in Egyptian Law and Practice" (2008) *Hawwa*, 52–74.

22 Articles 12 and 13 of Law 25/1929.

23 Article 14 of Law 25/1929.

24 Article 4 of Law 25/1920.

25 Article 9 of Law 25/1920.

26 Article 6 of Law 25/1929.

27 Article 11bis (1) Law 25/1929, added by Law 100/1985.

28 Article 5bis of Law 25/1929, added by Law 100/1985.

29 Articles 1 and 2 of Law 25/1929.

30 Article 3 of Law 25/1929.

31 Article 20 of Law 1/2000.

32 N. Sonneveld, *Khul' Divorce in Egypt. Public Debates, Judicial Practices, and Everyday Life* (The American University in Cairo Press, 2012); and N. Bernard-Maugiron, "The Judicial Construction of the Facts and the Law: The Egyptian Supreme Constitutional Court and the Constitutionality of the Law on the Khul'" in B. Dupret et al. (eds.), *Narratives of Truth in Islamic Law* (CEDEJ-I.B. Tauris, 2007), 243–264.

33 Articles 17 and 18 of Law 25/1929 and Article 18bis (1) added to Law 25/1929 by Law 1/1985.

34 Article 18bis (2) of Law 25/1929, added to Law 25/1929 by Law 1/1985.

35 Article 18bis (3) of Law 25/1929, added to Law 25/1929 by Law 1/1985.

36 Law 4/2005 amending Article 20 of Law 25 /1929 amended by Law 100/1985.

37 N. Sonneveld and M. Lindbekk, "A Revolution in Muslim Family Law? Egypt's Pre and Post-Revolutionary Period (2011–2013) Compared" (2015) 5 *New Middle Eastern Studies*, www.brismes.ac.uk/nmes/archives/1409.

Women's Rights in the Moroccan Family Code

Caught between Change and Continuity

STEPHANIE WILLMAN BORDAT AND SAIDA KOUZZI

3.1 Introduction[1]

The Moroccan Family Code[2] governs marriage, divorce, marital property, child custody and guardianship, parentage, and inheritance. Its content raises issues of equality between men and women, national identity, changing socioeconomic realities, and the role of religion in law. The process by which the code was enacted and its subsequent implementation illustrate challenges for the relationship between democracy and women's rights.

3.2 Legal Framework

Morocco is a constitutional monarchy with an elected bicameral Parliament. The king is both head of state and commander of the faithful who ensures the respect of Islam.[3] His role as the ultimate political and religious leader is pivotal to understanding the Family Code.

The constitution's preamble provides that duly ratified international conventions have primacy over domestic law, an assertion the Moroccan government often repeats to treaty monitoring bodies.[4] This supremacy is qualified as "within the framework of Constitutional provisions and laws of the Kingdom, in respect of immutable national identity."[5]

Men and women are deemed to have equal civil, political, economic, cultural, social, and environmental rights, although this is conditioned on "respect of Constitutional provisions, and permanent characteristics and laws of the Kingdom."[6]

Articles establishing Islam as the State religion and defining the family as the basis of society provide an opt-out to broader declarations on international human rights and gender equality.[7]

The 2004 Family Code preamble combines multiple references, including *Shari'a*, "Islamic principles of tolerance," *ijtihad* (juridical reasoning), and development of internationally recognized human rights. Its enactment is situated within a process of modernization, progress, justice, equality for women, and democratization.

The Family Code is the only law in Morocco based on religious precepts; "for all issues not addressed by a text in the present code, reference may be made to the *Malikite* School of Jurisprudence and to *ijtihad*."[8] Judges thus have significant power and discretion based on their own interpretation of religious texts, in contrast to the positivist approach used to apply the other, purely civil codes.

3.3   Enactment

The original Personal Status Code, or *Moudawana*, was issued by Royal Decrees in 1957–1958,[9] upon independence from France and Spain. Following campaigns by women's rights groups, the late King Hassan II made minor amendments to the code in September 1993, again through Royal Decree based on the work of a Royal Commission composed of all-male *oulemas*. At that time, Islamist groups, including the Réforme et Renouveau movement of Abdel-Ilah Benkiran, later the head of the government from 2011–2017, mobilized actively against reform.

The family rights component of a 1999 National Plan of Action for the Integration of Women in Development to improve the status of women was met with opposition from both within the government, notably the minister of Habous and Islamic affairs, along with *oulema* and *adoul*, as well as from unrecognized politico-religious groups. The entire Plan, which also focused on increasing women's access to health, education, and employment, was ultimately tabled. King Mohammed VI intervened in his capacity as commander of the faithful to establish a Royal Commission in April 2001. After two and a half years of deliberations, the Commission submitted proposed reforms to the *Moudawana*. King Mohammed VI presented draft legislation in person at the opening of the October 2003 parliamentary session. The Parliament unanimously adopted the final text, and the Family Code was promulgated on February 3, 2004.

Several features of the Family Code's adoption distinguish it from previous versions. First, the Royal Commission was composed of not only *oulemas* but also experts from other fields including law, sociology, and medicine. The Commission's sixteen members included three women. Second, it went into effect immediately upon publication, even though laws generally are not applicable until at least one month following publication. Third, the Royal Decree enacted both the original 1957 Moudawana and the minor reforms made in 1993 without parliamentary debate. In contrast, the final code includes amendments proposed by different parliamentary groups.

The 2004 Family Code was initially applauded, especially internationally. This chapter will analyze the text of the law, distinguishing between provisions where women's rights are protected versus those where the text is unclear and others that remain discriminatory. It will also assess its implementation and describe reform initiatives.

3.4   Marriage

The 2004 Family Code increased the role of judicial authorities in family affairs. The public prosecutor is party to all cases implementing the Code[10] and judicial oversight of marriage was increased.[11] This further reduced the role of the notaries known as *adoul*,[12] who do marital contracts in family affairs.

The marriage of minors remains controversial among decision makers, women's rights activists, and public authorities. The 2004 Code increased the minimum age of marriage for women from fifteen to eighteen, the same as for men. The marriage of minors was intended to be exceptional, only authorized when "justified" and after substantial review by the Family Affairs judge.[13]

Despite these reforms, both the number of petitions for authorization to marry minors and the approval rate are high. In 2018, there were 32,104 petitions to marry a minor, up from 30,312 in 2006. Between 2011 and 2018, 85 percent of such petitions were granted. The overwhelming majority of the minor spouses from 2007–2018, 99 percent, were girls.[14]

The lack of a threshold minimum age below which authorization to marry may never be granted is a "deficiency in the wording of the Code itself."[15] Local NGOs report marriages of girls as young as thirteen, fourteen, and fifteen.[16] In 2018, 1.7 percent of brides were children under the age of fifteen.[17]

The Family Affairs judge must determine whether the minor has "the maturity and physical aptitude to assume the responsibilities of marriage and the discernment to consent to marriage."[18] Judges are supposed to base their decision on medical expertise and a social assessment.[19]

However, they often issue authorizations based on a cursory visual examination of the minor girl's physical appearance and determination that she is capable of assuming "marital responsibilities," rather than resorting to the required outside expertise.[20]

Reasons advanced by judges for authorizing underage marriage include saving family honor, as a solution to poverty, protecting the girl's chastity, and preventing her from debauchery, as sexual relations outside of marriage are illegal.[21] Corruption among public actors and the ease of obtaining medical certificates attesting to the minor girl's "maturity" also facilitate circumvention of the law.[22]

The 2004 Family Code made the *wali* – the bride's marital guardian – optional. Previously, the *wali*'s presence was mandatory, and the law listed male relatives in order of priority (son, father, brother, etc.).[23] Now a woman of legal age may conclude her marriage contract herself, and if she delegates this power to a *wali*, she may choose any male relative.[24] However, only 20.47 percent of marriages were contracted without a *wali* in 2011.[25]

The 2004 Family Code reaffirms the contractual nature of marriage[26] and provides that spouses may stipulate negotiated conditions on personal or financial rights into the marriage contract, provided that they do not contradict the inherent nature of marriage. Violation of a clause is a breach of contract for which the wronged spouse may seek a remedy, including compensation and divorce.[27]

The percentage of marriage contracts with stipulated conditions is extremely limited. Out of 75,173 marriage contracts reviewed from 2006 to 2010 (Morocco Marriage Contract Survey), only 822 – 1.09 percent – included additional clauses. The reasons for a scarcity of additional clauses in marriage contracts include lack of awareness among future couples of their rights, the omnipresence of families in the marriage process, patriarchal and conservative attitudes among *adoul* responsible for drawing up marriage contracts, the lack of legal provisions to compel local authorities to notify future spouses of this possibility, and the absence of obligatory standard marriage contract forms.[28]

The 2004 Family Code sought to eliminate the practice of *fatiha* or *orfi* marriages, most commonly found in rural areas. Concluded without a written contract, these verbal marriages place women in vulnerable situations when the "husband" abandons them and their children leaving them with no enforceable rights. Couples without a written marriage contract initially had a five-year grace period to petition for recognition of their marriage,[29] a deadline later extended to ten years,[30] and again to fifteen years.[31]

Statistics indicate that from 2004 to 2011, the number of judicial recognitions of verbal marriage rose from 6,918 to 38,952, increasing proportionally from 2.84 percent to 10.7 percent of all marriages.[32] In 2018, there were 15,199 such cases.[33] This increase must be read in light of the polygamy reforms, described below.

The Family Code preamble affirms that polygamy is "quasi impossible under *Shari'a*" and is permitted only under "compelling circumstances and stringent restrictions." One justification advanced in defense of polygamy is that it reduces illicit sexual relations outside of marriage, which would occur if it were banned.

Polygamy is not allowed when there is the risk that the husband will treat his wives unequally or when the wife has stipulated a monogamy clause into the marriage contract.[34] However, the Morocco Marriage Contract Survey found that only 0.1 percent contained a monogamy clause.[35]

Absent such a clause, the judge may only authorize polygamy if the husband proves that he has an exceptional and objective justification for taking another wife and has sufficient resources to support both families and guarantee equality in all aspects of life. Once the husband petitions for authorization to take another wife, the judge must summon the current wife to obtain her consent. If she does not agree and the husband insists on marrying the second wife, the judge will initiate an irreconcilable differences divorce (*chiqaq*). The judge must notify the future wife that the petitioner husband is already married, and she must expressly consent to this before the marriage.[36]

Several of these mechanisms existed previously, notably the possibility to insert a monogamy clause in the marriage contract[37] and the requirement that both the current and future wives be notified.[38] Reforms reinforced judicial control over the authorization and notification procedures. One study indicated that over half of men surveyed opposed how the reforms transformed polygamy from a sacred right to dependent on judicial authorization. They perceived this as a restriction on their autonomy and power, even if merely symbolic.[39]

Jurisprudence under the previous law allowed men to marry up to four wives at one time.[40] Legal analysts interpret the reforms as de facto limiting men to two wives. The "exceptional" reason requirement suggests that a man may plausibly be authorized only once to take another wife. Furthermore, the law specifies that the husband must be able to support and guarantee equality between "two" families.[41]

Public discussions before the 2004 Family Code claimed that polygamy was socially obsolete and argued that such a relatively rare phenomenon was not worth the backlash that would result in trying to forbid it entirely. Only 0.38 percent of marriages contracted in 2016 were polygamous.[42] However, the approval rate of petitions for authorization to take another wife has been high; 43.41 percent of such petitions were granted in 2010, up from 40.36 percent in 2009.[43] NGO reports describe how rather than requiring the petitioner husband to prove an exceptional and objective reason, judges often grant authorizations based on his financial status alone.[44]

In practice, provisions on recognizing verbal marriages were used during the fifteen-year legal grace period to circumvent polygamy restrictions. Rather than petition for authorization to take another wife, men instead "recognized" a purportedly preexisting but unregistered verbal marriage. Statistics thus likely reflect a higher rate of verbal marriages and a lower rate of polygamy than occurred in reality.

Under the old Personal Status Code "men committed their finances and women committed their persons."[45] Marriage was based on unequal and asymmetric power relations in the family, with distinct rights and obligations. Previously, men were the head of household[46] and women had a duty of obedience to their husbands.[47] According to the Ministry of Justice, the Family Code's innovation is that spouses have mutual rights and duties, equality in both personal and financial matters relating to the management of family affairs and protection of children, and consultation in decision-making.[48] Both spouses are now jointly responsible for the household.[49] These provisions contradict subsequent articles that still hold the husband responsible for financially supporting his wife and children. It is also worth noting conflicting Penal Code provisions, which, until their repeal in 2013, had maintained the concept of a husband's legal "authority" over his wife.[50]

When either spouse evicts the other from the marital home without justification, the public prosecutor is supposed to intervene to return the evicted person, usually the wife and children, to the house.[51] This has proven problematic in practice, given the length of time it takes law enforcement personnel to intervene, the inability to guarantee her safety upon return in cases of domestic abuse, and the absence of any "marital home" when the couple lives with in-laws and extended family. In 2018, there were 7,913 such cases in front of courts.[52]

3.5 Divorce

Men and women still have unequal access to divorce. While the 2004 Family Code introduced new grounds for divorce based on irreconcilable differences (*chiqaq*), it kept the previous forms of divorce. Divorce provisions reflect "change within continuity" or "déjà vu," privileging "equilibrium" over equality.[53]

According to the Ministry of Justice, dissolution of marriage should be exceptional and only when there is a compelling necessity.[54] Nonetheless, in 2010, one divorce was pronounced for every ten marriages.[55]

The Code has three sections on dissolution of marriage (other than by annulment or death of a spouse): repudiation,[56] divorce,[57] and mutual consent or divorce in exchange for compensation.[58] However, the Ministry of Justice brochures distinguish two categories – "divorce" (which this chapter translates as repudiation) and "divorce judiciaire" (judicial divorce).

Both the previous Personal Status Code and the 2004 Family Code use the same word in Arabic – *talaq*. However, in the official French translation of the former, it was "répudiation" and in the latter translation, it is now "divorce (under judicial control)." When the Family Code was promulgated, the government announced it with much pomp and continues to claim that repudiation was eliminated, creating confusion and disagreement over this point.

Repudiation is the husband's right to unilaterally divorce his wife without justification. Under the old Personal Status Code, it was extrajudicial – the act was drawn up by two *adoul*, and the wife did not have to be present.[59] The 2004 Family Code still allows the husband to divorce without justification and without the wife's assent, although it increased judicial control over the process and reinforced procedural mechanisms. The husband must make all payments due to his wife and children as fixed by the court before the judge may authorize the repudiation. If the husband does not pay within thirty days of the court order, he is deemed to have renounced the repudiation. The husband can still revoke the repudiation and take his wife back before expiry of the *idda* waiting period to ascertain that she is not pregnant.[60]

A wife may repudiate herself (*tamlik*) if her husband has granted her that right in the marriage contract.[61] The vast majority of women are unaware of this possibility,[62] and the Morocco Marriage Contract Survey found only thirteen instances with such a clause.[63]

Spouses may mutually agree to divorce and petition the court separately or jointly.[64] Issues arise as to whether or not there really is mutual consent, and if the divorce was negotiated between equal parties.

In *khol'* the wife compensates her husband for agreeing to repudiate her. Unlike Algeria, Moroccan law still requires the husband's consent to the *khol'*.[65] Blackmail, threats, and forced bargaining by husbands compel women to renounce their rights in exchange for his agreement to divorce, basically turning mutual consent into *khol'*.[66]

Either spouse may seek a judicial divorce on the grounds of irreconcilable differences. Called *chiqaq*, this major innovation of the 2004 Family Code gave women access to divorce that they did not have previously. If reconciliation attempts fail, the judge grants the divorce and makes any financial award based on an assessment of each spouse's responsibility for the separation.[67]

For *chiqaq*, the petitioner spouse must give reasons for seeking divorce but is not obligated to provide evidence of harm or fault. In practice, judges often require proof of the motive for seeking divorce, holding *chiqaq* to the same standard of evidence as fault-based divorce. Alternatively, cases are often decided as *chiqaq* when they would be more appropriate for a fault-based divorce.[68]

Women may also petition for judicial divorce for one of the following causes: (1) violation of a clause in the marriage contract, (2) harm, (3) husband's failure to support her, (4) husband's absence or imprisonment, (5) hidden "flaw" or disease, or (6) husband's oath of abstinence towards his wife.[69]

Violation of a clause in the marriage contract is now an independent ground justifying divorce. The other five forms of divorce available to women existed previously.

The Family Code specifies that "harm" may be either material or moral. The Ministry of Justice provides an expansive definition of harm, citing physical violence, insults, or immoral behavior by the husband.[70] However, conjugal violence cases are often adjudicated as *chiqaq*, either because women cannot meet the high standard of proof required for a fault-based divorce, or prefer the relatively faster *chiqaq* procedure, or because judges wrongly classify the case. While both fault-based divorces and *chiqaq* are supposed to be decided in six months,[71] proceedings frequently take much longer in the former.[72]

All repudiations and judicial divorces except those based on absence must go through a reconciliation attempt, conducted by the judge, two arbitrators, or a family council.[73] The Ministry of Justice, in collaboration with some international and local NGOs, tends to privilege reconciliation over the law and formal justice system in family conflicts.[74] Reconciliation is criticized for lack of adequate facilities and qualified personnel.

The Family Code continues to distinguish between irrevocable and revocable divorces, the latter allowing the husband to "take his wife back" during the *idda* waiting period following repudiation pronounced by him or a judicial divorce for absence or non-maintenance.[75] Now divorce decrees are not subject to appeal, an amendment that speeds up the divorce process relatively speaking and frees up wives.[76]

Statistics show a net increase of all forms of divorce combined, from 34,127 instances in 2004 to 76,450 in 2017. Divorces "under judicial control" – repudiation, *khol'*, mutual consent – represent 32 percent of divorces.[77]

The vast majority of judicial divorces in 2017 were *chiqaq* (98.8 percent), with fault-based divorces quite rare: absence (0.78 percent), harm or violation of a clause in the marriage contract (0.08 percent), lack of financial support (0.21 percent), oath of abstinence (0.01 percent), and illness (0.05 percent).[78]

Mutual consent divorces have increased steadily between and comprised 72.27 percent of nonjudicial divorces in 2017. Among the other forms of repudiation, in 2017 *khol'* was the most prevalent (11.60 percent), followed by repudiation by the husband before (11.46 percent) and after (4.6 percent) consummation. Only *Tamlik* divorces are extremely rare, with only nine total instances reported.[79]

3.6   Property and Financial Relations between Spouses

Payment of the dower – money or property given to the wife by the husband – is a mandatory condition for the marriage contract's validity. The dower's amount should be modest and is the wife's property to manage and dispose of as she wishes. It can be paid in full immediately or deferred but vests fully upon consummation of the marriage.[80]

The wife maintains ownership over all possessions she owned prior to marriage. Disputes arising over household furnishing are decided according "to general rules of evidence," or lacking proof, according to gender habitual use upon oath of the concerned spouse.[81] Proof of ownership of movable property is problematic in reality considering that spouses rarely keep receipts of purchases.

Husbands are legally obligated to financially support their wives, including food, clothing, and medical care. The wife loses her right to maintenance if she has been ordered to return to the conjugal home and refuses. After divorce, husbands have no financial obligations to their ex-wives beyond housing and maintenance expenses during the limited *idda* period.[82]

Upon dissolution of the marriage, the judge may award the wife *muta'a* (consolation gift). The *muta'a* is based on the marriage's duration, husband's financial situation, motives for divorce, and husband's abuse in the exercise of his right to end the marriage.[83] While *muta'a* may be awarded in all forms of marital dissolution, in *chiqaq*, the court takes into account "each spouse's responsibility for the cause of the separation," leading in some instances to a wife being ordered to pay *muta'a* to her husband.[84] In addition to *muta'a*, women who obtain a fault-based divorce may also sue for damages for the harm caused. The judge has significant discretionary power to fix the amounts.

Article 49 maintains the principle of separate marital property. Each spouse retains ownership of assets she or he acquired during marriage, and there is normally no division or sharing of property upon dissolution of marriage. The government presents separate marital property as positive for women's rights, since "marriage has no effect" on women's capacity to own and manage property, and does not "entail the merging of the parties' respective assets."[85]

The 2004 Family Code created the option for spouses to conclude a written property agreement for managing and sharing assets acquired during the marriage. However, statistics revealed that in 2011 there were only 609 marital property contracts for 364,367 marriages,[86] and only 537 in 2017.[87] The Morocco Marriage Contract Survey only found 36 instances, or .05 percent, where the couple had concluded a separate property agreement.[88] The Moroccan government attributes this to romantic notions held by couples and reluctance to think about divorce at the time of marriage.[89]

The last paragraph of Article 49 provides that:

> In the absence of such an agreement, recourse is made to general standards of evidence, while taking into consideration the work of each spouse, the efforts made as well as the responsibilities assumed in the development of the family assets.

There are significant differences of opinion on this provision's interpretation, and its application is problematic. The law is unclear as to whether spouses must prove that they participated financially to an acquisition or if efforts such as housework also justify a share of assets.

A 2016 national survey found that among people who knew about the marital property contract, 57.9 percent think that the *adoul* do not fulfil systematically or at all their obligation to inform future spouses of this possibility; 25.7 percent felt that *adoul* do not think it is important and 41.5 percent that the *adoul* do not want to talk about financial matters when drawing up a marriage contract.[90]

In some regions, local customary law can be more beneficial to women than the Code. Under the *al kad oua ssiâya* system practiced and applied by courts in the Souss region, the wife is entitled to a share of property that she constitutes and establishes with her husband in compensation for her moral and physical efforts during marriage.[91]

3.7 Children

The Family Code only recognizes legitimate paternal filiation – children are attributed to a father if he is legally married or engaged to the mother at the time of conception.[92] "Illegitimate" or "natural" paternity does not exist in Moroccan law. Children born to unwed mothers have no rights from their biological fathers, such as to bear his name, receive financial support, or inherit from him. In contrast, biological mothers whether married or not, are always legally affiliated to and responsible for their children.[93]

The law provides for DNA testing to establish paternity but only to prove or contest the parentage of a child conceived during a legal marriage.[94] Reforms to the Family Code recognized legitimate paternity to a child conceived during the parents' "engagement period," taking steps to protect children's rights and acknowledging that in reality couples frequently have sexual relations before marriage.[95] However, the law does not provide for court-ordered paternity testing of biological fathers against their will upon the request of the single mother or her child.

As a result, the only way for children to benefit from "legitimate" paternity if their parents are not legally married is to file a recognition of marriage petition or to claim that the couple was engaged at the time of conception. This can require evidence of an engagement such as photos, videos, sworn statements by family and neighbors, and the biological father's consent.[96]

The Code maintains inequality between fathers and mothers in legal guardianship of their children. Fathers are legal guardians of their children, even after divorce. Mothers only exercise legal guardianship upon the father's death, absence, or incapacity. She may also manage their children's urgent affairs, if the father is prevented from doing so.[97] It is unclear whether or not the custodial mother may travel abroad with her children without the prior agreement of the legal guardian.[98] These articles limit the more egalitarian provisions under which both spouses assume the responsibility of managing the children's education and consult on decisions concerning the management of family affairs and children.[99]

Child custody is shared by both parents as long as they are married. After divorce, once they turn fifteen, children may choose to live with either their mother or father. Before then, child custody is granted according to a fixed order of priority. First, the mother is awarded custody of her children, but if she is disqualified, custody is awarded to the father, then the maternal grandmother, and then the most qualified of the child's relatives according to a court assessment. Mothers who remarry risk losing custody of their children. However, moving away from the legal guardian to another locality in Morocco is no longer automatic grounds for losing custody.[100]

Fathers are required to support their children financially until they reach legal majority, or age twenty-five for those pursuing higher education. Daughters are the financial responsibility of their fathers until they marry or can support themselves. Mothers must support their children if the father is unable to and if the mother has the means to do so.[101] This is another example where the code places additional responsibilities upon women without granting them corresponding rights.

Upon divorce, children's housing expenses are now assessed separately from and in addition to child support. The father must provide accommodation for his children or rent costs, as determined by the court, and until he does, the children cannot be evicted from the conjugal home.[102]

The one month accelerated procedure in child support cases is difficult to apply and rare in reality. Women have difficulties proving their husband's income and assets, and there is no system for garnishing wages.[103] Child support amounts awarded are generally quite low. Even when courts grant support, problems arise executing judgments, as husbands disappear or give false addresses.[104] Fathers' lack of ability to pay, and corruption and inertia of public authorities also prevent women from receiving child support awards.[105] In 2018, there were 37,953 financial support cases (maintenance to the wife and child support combined) in front of courts.[106] The Family Solidarity Fund to cover unpaid awards for poor women and their children was not established until 2011, and despite amendments made in 2018 to expand the eligibility criteria,[107] that same year a mere 4,542 women benefitted from the Fund.[108]

3.8 Future Directions

As the above descriptions illustrate, and as observers have noted, the 2004 Code addresses women's rights within the framework of the traditional family, to the exclusion of many categories of women. The Code is based on complementarity and reciprocity between male and female relatives and embodies a concept of rights as dependent on fulfilling duties.[109]

Nonetheless, the Moroccan government actively promotes the Family Code as eliminating discrimination against women and establishing gender equality. It identifies challenges to implementing the Code as ignorance among the population, conservative mentalities, lack of trained officials, and inadequate infrastructure.[110] Women's rights groups likewise point to law enforcement shortcomings, including lengthy proceedings, corruption, and the low number of family courts and insufficient personnel.[111]

Multiple references in the law to international human rights standards, positive law, and religious principles lead to inconsistent decisions across jurisdictions. The latitude given to judges frequently results in conservative interpretations of the law, to the detriment of women's rights.

Over the past decade, international human rights bodies and local activists have repeatedly highlighted the need for further revisions to the Family Code to abolish remaining inequality. These include calls to prohibit polygamy, ban the marriage of minors, give men and women the same access to divorce, ensure equal property rights upon dissolution of marriage, provide for equality of mothers and fathers in child guardianship, and establish equality in inheritance.[112] Several MP-sponsored bills propose reforms to Family Code articles related to the marriage of minors and parentage; some of these have been stalled in committee for review in the lower house of Parliament since 2013.[113] Additionally, in the 2016 national study, 45 percent of people surveyed expressed their view that it is time to further reform the Family Code.[114]

In April 2011, Morocco withdrew certain reservations to the United Nations Convention on the Elimination of All Forms of Discrimination against Women, namely to articles 9(2) on the transfer of nationality to children, and 16 on equality in marriage and divorce. The official withdrawal of reservations to the CEDAW was long awaited, having been announced by both the minister of justice in March 2006 and in a royal speech in December 2008.

It did not however lift its declarations to article 2, stating that the provision would apply only when it did not conflict with the Islamic *Shari'a*. Morocco also did not lift its declaration to article 15(4) provisions on the right of women to choose their residence and domicile, to the extent that they conflict with "articles 34 and 36 of the Code of Personal Status."[115]

On November 2011, national legislative elections brought to power a governmental coalition led by the Islamist PJD for the first time in Moroccan history. The party was reelected in 2016 elections, winning 125 out of the 395 seats in the first chamber. Only four of the twenty-four member cabinet were women.[116]

The United Nations Working Group on the issue of discrimination against women in law and in practice notes concerns by Moroccan women's groups that the gains of the last decade on women's rights are at risk of being reversed and progress impeded.[117] Indeed, the Working Group was unable to secure a meeting with the then Family Minister during their eight day mission to Morocco, a fact it "regrets" in an official press release.[118] When the previous family minister was a member of Parliament, she declared that "the type of equality (provided for in Article 16 of the CEDAW) is against the Islamic Sharia."[119]

The PJD government had made it clear that it opposed Family Code reforms. This was made particularly evident during the 2017 Universal Periodic Review, when Morocco rejected a record number of 44 out of 244 Human Rights Council recommendations. A good number of these rejected recommendations called for eliminating discriminatory provisions in the Family Code. The government justified its position by referring to constitutional provisions establishing "the special framework of the federative constants of the Moroccan nation, (including) the moderate Muslim identity . . ."[120]

A law creating the Advisory Council on the Family and Children was enacted in May 2016. It must be noted that this was mandated by Article 169 of the 2011 Constitution, a royal initiative.[121]

The 2004 Family Code illustrated the limited capacity of elected political institutions to produce consensus for social reform through a democratic process.[122] The problematic implementation of the Code raises questions about how an independent judiciary could be detrimental for women's rights. The future of the relationship between the Palace and the different branches of government, of the responsiveness of national authorities to international human rights bodies, and of the substance of women's rights in the law, remain to be tighten up space seen.

Notes

1 In his July 2022 Throne Day speech, King Mohammed VI of Morocco called for reforms to the Family Code. The Minister of Justice then held consultations with civil society in November 2022 to solicit input into the reforms.

2 Dahir n° 1-04-22 du 12 hija 1424 (3 février 2004) portant promulgation de la loi n° 70-03 portant Code de la Famille ("Family Code").

3 Dahir n° 1-11-91 du 27 chaabane 1432 (29 juillet 2011) portant promulgation du texte de la constitution, Articles 1, 41, 42, 60–86. The King is also Head of the Judiciary (Article 56).

4 www.youtube.com/watch?v=E81HCCNCv_k.

5 Morocco Constitution Preamble.

6 Constitution, Article 19.

7 Constitution Articles 3, 19, 32.

8 Morocco Family Code Article 400.

9 Dahir n° 1-57-343 du 28 rebia II 1377 (22 novembre 1957) portant application des livres I et II du code de statut personnel et des successions, Dahir n° 1-57-379 du 25 joumada I 1377 (18 décembre 1957) portant application du livre III du code de statut personnel et des successions, and Dahir n° 1-58-019 du 4 rejeb 1377 (25 janvier 1958) portant application du livre IV du code du statut personnel et des successions.

10 Family Code Article 3.

11 Family Code Articles 65-69.

12 Religious notaries acting in their capacity as civil servants, traditionally responsible for drawing up personal status acts.

13 Family Code Articles 19, 20. Article 21 requires the legal guardian's consent.

14 Conseil Economique, Social et Environnemental, "Que faire, face à la persistence du mariage d'enfants au Maroc?" (2019).

15 Committee on the Elimination of Discrimination against women, "Combined Third and Fourth Periodic Report of States Parties: Morocco" (18 September 2006) CEDAW/C/MAR/4.

16 Ligue démocratique de défense des droits des femmes (LDDF), "Droits des femmes et code de la famille après 4 ans d'application" (2007).

17 Conseil Economique, Social et Environnemental (2019).

18 Ministère de la Justice, "Guide Pratique du code de la famille" (2005).

19 Family Code Article 20.

20 Moroccan NGO interviews with authors, May 2012.

21 Dahir n° 1-59-413 du 28 joumada II 1382 (26 novembre 1962) portant approbation du texte du code pénal, as amended, Article 490.

22 Abdallah Ounnir, "Les justiciables dans le circuit judiciaire relatif au contentieux de la famille," in *Le Code de la famille: Perceptions et pratique judiciaire* (Friedrich Ebert Stiftung, 2007), pp. 89–139; LDDF, "Droits des femmes"; Association Démocratique des Femmes du Maroc(ADFM), "Implementation of the CEDAW Convention: Non-Governmental Organisations' Shadow Report to the Third and the Fourth Periodic Report of the Moroccan Government" (November 2007).

23 Morocco Personal Status Code Articles 5, 11, 12.

24 Family Code Articles 24, 25.

25 Ministère de la Justice et des Libertés, "Statistiques des sections de la justice de la famille Année 2011," http://adala.justice.gov.ma/production/statistiques/SJF/FR/30-10-12%20VR%20Finale%20Statistique%20Francais.pdf.

26 Family Code Articles 4, 10(1), 11, 12, 57(3), 63.

27 Family Code Articles 47, 48, 98, 99.

28 "Promoting Women's Human Rights in Morocco, Algeria and Tunisia through Strategic Use of the Marriage Contract: Researching and Documenting the Use of Marriage Contracts among Local Authorities" (Global Rights 2011).

29 Family Code Article 16.

30 Dahir n° 1-10-103 du 3 chaabane 1431 (16 juillet 2010) portant promulgation de la loi n° 08-09 modifiant l'article 16 de la loi n° 70-03 portant Code de la famille.

31 Dahir n° 1-16-2 du 1er rabii II 1437 (12 janvier 2016) portant promulgation de la loi n° 102-15; Bulletin Officiel n° 6436 du 24 rabii II 1437 (4 février 2016), p. 163.

32 Ministère de la Justice et des Libertés, "Statistiques."

33 Présidence du Ministère Public, "Public Prosecution Activity in Family Cases in Courts" (2018), www.pmp.ma/%d8%a5%d8%b5%d8%af%d8%a7%d8%b1%d8%a7%d8%aa/.

34 Family Code Article 40.

35 Global Rights, "Promoting Women's Human Rights in Morocco, Algeria and Tunisia through Strategic Use of the Marriage Contract."

36 Family Code Articles 41, 43, 44, 45, 46.

37 Personal Status Code Article 31.

38 Personal Status Code Article 30.

39 Alami M'chichi, "Changement social et perceptions du nouveau code de la famille."

40 Mohamed Chafi, "Code de statut personnel annoté," Article 29(2) (Marrakech, 1996).

41 Family Code Article 41. Fatna Serehane, "Décryptage du nouveau code de la famille," *Femmes du Maroc* Supplément March 2004.

42 Ministère de la Justice et des Libertés, "Statistiques."

43 Association Démocratique des Femmes du Maroc (ADFM), "Rapport des ONG de défense des droits des femmes au Maroc au titre du 2e Examen Périodique Universel (EPU)" (November 2011).

44 LDDF, "Droits des femmes."

45 Serehane, "Décryptage du nouveau code de la famille."

46 Personal Status Code Article 1.

47 Personal Status Code Article 36(2).

48 Family Code Article 51. Ministère de la Justice, Guide Pratique.

49 Family Code Articles 4, 51.

50 Penal Code Articles 494–496.
51 Family Code Article 53.
52 Présidence du Ministère Public, "Public Prosecution Activity in Family Cases in Courts" (2018).
53 Serehane, "Décryptage du nouveau code de la famille."
54 Ministère de la Justice, Guide Pratique.
55 Haut-Commissariat au Plan, "Mariage et divorce de la femme marocaine : Tendances d'évolution," www.hcp.ma/Mariage-et-divorce-de-la-femme-marocaine-Tendances-d-evolution_a1261.html.
56 Family Code Articles 78–93.
57 Family Code Articles 94–113.
58 Family Code Articles 114–120.
59 Abderrazak Moulay Rachid, *La Condition de la femme au Maroc* (Faculté des sciences, 1985).
60 Family Code Articles 79, 81–87, 123–127.
61 Family Code Article 89.
62 Global Rights, "Conditions, not Conflict" (2008).
63 Global Rights, "Promoting Women's Human Rights in Morocco, Algeria and Tunisia through Strategic Use of the Marriage Contract."
64 Family Code Article 114.
65 Family Code Articles 115–120.
66 LDDF, "Droits des femmes."
67 Family Code Articles 94–97.
68 Rabha Zeidguy, "Analyse de la jurisprudence," *Le Code de la famille: Perceptions et pratique judiciaire* (Friedrich Ebert Stiftung, 2007), pp. 217–271.
69 Family Code Articles 98–112.
70 Ministère de la Justice, Guide Pratique.
71 Family Code Article 113.
72 Stephanie Willman Bordat, "Difficultés pratiques d'accès des femmes à la justice," Colloque "Droits des femmes et révolutions arabes," Le Mans, Université du Maine (June 29, 2012).
73 Family Code Articles 81–82.
74 Ministère de la Justice et des Libertés, "Statistiques."
75 Family Code Articles 122–123.
76 Family Code Article 128.
77 Haut-Commissariat au Plan, Annuaire Statistique du Maroc, 2018.
78 Haut-Commissariat au Plan, Annuaire Statistique du Maroc, 2018. These statistics are the percentages of the 51,913 judicial divorces pronounced, not all divorces.
79 Haut-Commissariat au Plan, Annuaire Statistique du Maroc, 2018.
80 Family Code Articles 13(2), 26–33.
81 Family Code Article 34.
82 Family Code Articles 129–137, 194–196.
83 Family Code Article 84.
84 Family Code Article 97. First Instance Court in Meknes, Family Division, Number 1783, July 9, 2009, Number 1931/8/ 5M.
85 CEDAW/C/MAR/4.
86 Ministère de la Justice et des Libertés, "Statistiques."

87 Committee on the Elimination of Discrimination against Women, "Combined Fifth and Sixth Periodic Reports Submitted by Morocco under Article 18 of the Convention CEDAW/C/MAR/5-6" (January 16, 2020).

88 Global Rights, "Promoting Women's Human Rights in Morocco, Algeria and Tunisia through Strategic Use of the Marriage Contract."

89 Committee on the Elimination of Discrimination against Women, Summary Record of the 825th meeting (February 21, 2008), CEDAW/C/SR.825.

90 10 ans d'Application du Code de la Famille.

91 Houssein Malki, *The Kad o saiya system: examples from Moroccan jurisprudence* (Dar es Salaam, 1999).

92 Family Code Articles 142–162.

93 Family Code Articles 142–162.

94 Family Code Articles 153 and 156.

95 Family Code Article 156.

96 Stephanie Willman Bordat and Saida Kouzzi, "Legal Empowerment of Unwed Mothers: Experiences of Moroccan NGOs," in Stephen Golub (ed.), *Legal Empowerment: Practitioners' Perspectives* (IDLO, 2010).

97 Family Code Articles 231, 236, 238.

98 Family Code Article 179; www.justice.gov.ma/console/Uploads/Doc/Garde%20de%20l'enfant%20Fr.pdf.

99 Family Code Articles 51(3), (4).

100 Family Code Articles 164, 166,171, 174, 175, 178.

101 Family Code Articles 198-199.

102 Family Code Article 168.

103 Family Code Articles 190, 191.

104 Zahia Ammoumou, "Les droits matériels de la femme divorcée," in *Regard sur le droit de la famille dans les pays du Maghreb* (CIDEAL, 2008); A. Ounnir, "Les justiciables dans le circuit judiciaire relatif au contentieux de la famille," *Le Code de la famille: Perceptions et pratique judiciaire* (Friedrich Ebert Stiftung, 2007); LDDF, "Droits des femmes."

105 LDDF, "Droits des femmes."

106 Présidence du Ministère Public, "Public Prosecution Activity in Family Cases in Courts" (2018).

107 Dahir No. 1-10-191 du 7 Moharrem 1432 (13 décembre 2010) portant promulgation de la loi No. 4110 fixant les conditions et procédures pour bénéficier des prestations du Fonds d'entraide familiale, modifiée par le Dahir n° 1-18-20 du 5 joumada II 1439 (22 février 2018) portant promulgation de la loi n° 83-17.

108 Committee on the Elimination of Discrimination against Women, "Combined Fifth and Sixth Periodic Reports Submitted by Morocco under Article 18 of the Convention."

109 For a good description and analysis in this sense, see Žvan Elliott, Katja, *Modernizing Patriarchy: The Politics of Women's Rights in Morocco* (University of Texas Press, 2015).

110 CEDAW/C/MAR/4.

111 ADFM, "Implementation of the CEDAW Convention"; LDDF, "Droits des femmes"; Global Rights, "Promoting Women's Human Rights in Morocco, Algeria and Tunisia through Strategic Use of the Marriage Contract."

112 LDDF, "Rapport de la Fédération de la Ligue Démocratique des Droits des Femmes, Examen Périodique Universel Maroc" (June 2012); ADFM, "Rapport des ONG de défense des droits des femmes"; ADFM, "Implementation of the CEDAW Convention"; LDDF, "Droits des femmes"; Concluding Comments of the Committee on the Elimination of Discrimination against Women, 8 April 2008, CEDAW/C/MAR/CO/4; Report of the Working Group on the issue of discrimination against women in law and in practice, Addendum Mission to Morocco, 19 June 2012, A/HRC/20/28/Add.1; Draft report of the Working Group on the Universal Periodic Review, Morocco, 25 May 2012, A/HRC/WG.6/13/L.1; CCPR/C/MAR/CO/6 Human Rights Committee, Concluding Observations on the sixth periodic report of Morocco, 1 December 2016;

113 www.chambredesrepresentants.ma/fr/action-legislative.

114 10 ans d'Application du Code de la Famillle.

115 http://treaties.un.org/Pages/ViewDetails.aspx?src=TREATY&mtdsg_no=IV-8&chapter=4&lang=en. Morocco acceded to the Convention in 1993, so the declaration was made under the previous law, prior to 2004 reforms. Previous article 36 concerned the wife's duties to her husband, including obedience and management of household affairs, which was eliminated in the 2004 reforms. However, provisions of the previous article 34 on mutual obligations included cohabitation, which remains (article 51).

116 www.cg.gov.ma/fr/composition-du-gouvernement-0.

117 A/HRC/20/28/Add.1.

118 www.ohchr.org/EN/NewsEvents/Pages/DisplayNews.aspx?NewsID=11842&LangID=E.

119 LDDF, "Rapport de la Fédération de la Ligue Démocratique des Droits des Femmes."

120 A/HRC/36/6 Add.1 Human Rights Council Report of the Working Group on the Universal Periodic Review, Morocco, August 2017.

121 Loi n° 78-14 relative au Conseil Consultatif de la Famille et de l'Enfance publiée au B.O n° 6491 du 15 Aout 2016.

122 Jean-Philippe Bras, "La réforme du code de la famille au Maroc et en Algérie: quelles avancées pour la démocratie?"(2007) 37*Critique internationale*, pp. 93–125.

Postponing Equality in the Algerian Family Code

STEPHANIE WILLMAN BORDAT AND SAIDA KOUZZI

4.1 Introduction

Like other family laws in the Maghreb, the Algerian Family Code is prescriptive rather than descriptive or responsive to current social realities. It is situated in an idealized historical past and glorified construction of national identity, based on ideology and a vision of what the family should be rather than what it is. The Code's provisions also reflect tensions and incongruities on issues of equality between women and men.

The process of promulgating the 1984 Family Code and 2005 amendments raises interesting questions about political decision-making. The authoritarian, unilateral manner in which it was enacted highlights challenges to the democratic process. Over the past fifty years, Algeria has confronted many difficult democratic transition issues – civil war, a strong military, and the rise of extremist groups. Within this difficult context, Algerian women's groups continue to lobby and press for reforms.

4.2 Background

The French occupation of Algeria began in 1830 and did not end until 1962, after an eight-year war. Algeria was a French department during colonization, and the French judicial and administrative systems were maintained after independence. Algeria is a People's Democratic Republic with a strong executive branch and an entrenched state bureaucracy. Although multiple parties are represented in Parliament, the military has traditionally had strong influence on defense affairs, foreign policy, and internal politics.

During the 1992 legislative elections in which the Islamist FIS party was poised to win, the military leadership canceled the elections, took control of the country, forced the president to resign, and imposed a state of emergency that lasted until 2011.[1] From 1992 to 2002, Algeria then went through a brutal civil war waged between state security forces and armed Islamic groups, which resulted in approximately 100,000 deaths and thousands of citizens missing and still unaccounted for.[2] Much of the violence was targeted at civilian populations, especially against human rights activists, intellectuals, journalists, and artists. Women were a particular target of politicized, extremist violence, with attacks, murders, rapes, torture, and kidnappings of women by armed insurgent groups.

The previous president, Abdel Aziz Bouteflika, was not officially affiliated with any political party when first elected in 1999. October 2008 constitutional amendments eliminated term limits for the presidency, and in April 2014 Bouteflika was reelected for a fourth term as the National Liberation Front's (FLN) candidate with 81.5 percent of votes.[3] After pressure from the army and popular protests against his intention to seek a fifth term, he was forced to resign in April 2019.[4]

Women activists in Algeria have led a multifaceted struggle against sexist traditions, armed religious extremist groups, and State repression. Women from the Amazigh population in the Kabylie region have also long suffered from ethnic discrimination.

Another challenge to women's rights advocacy work in Algeria has been the major crises and conflicts in the country that have made women's rights seem a "luxury" and not a priority. Women activists have needed to avoid being criticized as ignoring the "important" problems. Recent issues that have taken precedence include not only the violent civil conflict and the rise of religious extremism but the severe natural disasters including major earthquakes and mudslides that destroyed entire towns, killed thousands, and left thousands homeless.

Despite this difficult context, women's NGOs in Algeria have played a key role in legislative reform. Examples from the 1990s include the repeal of discriminatory laws that allowed men to vote for five members of their family by proxy in elections (resulting in men voting on behalf of their female family members), eliminated sports for girls in schools, and established mandatory retirement for female teachers at an earlier age than their male counterparts.[5]

4.3   Constitutional Framework[6]

The constitution establishes Islam as the state religion.[7] The section on Rights and Freedoms provides that "all citizens are equal before the law. No discrimination shall prevail because of birth, race, sex, opinion or any other personal or social condition or circumstance."[8] It further declares that "the aim of the institutions is to ensure equality of rights and duties of all citizens, men and women, by removing the obstacles which hinder the progress of human beings and impede the effective participation of all in the political, economic, social and cultural life."[9] The 2016 Constitutional revisions establish that "the family enjoys the protection of the state."[10]

However, Article 81 opens the possibility for limiting these rights in the interests of obligations to the community, through the qualification that "each person exercises their freedoms in respect of the rights given to others by the Constitution, particularly in respect of the right to honor, privacy and protection of the family, youth and childhood."

Duly ratified and published international human rights conventions take precedence over domestic law[11] and may be invoked by any citizen before the courts.[12] However, the Article 86 provision that the president of the Republic is the ultimate judicial power raises questions about the independence of the judiciary.

4.4   Family Code Promulgation: 1984 Family Code[13]

Prior to the promulgation of the Family Code in 1984, there was no legislation in Algeria covering family issues. The courts applied general provisions of the civil code, while inheritance was covered by religious precepts. The Civil Code promulgated in 1975, and still in force, established in its first article that "in the absence of a legal disposition, the judge decides on the basis of Muslim law, or in its absence, according to custom."[14]

Ever since independence from France, the issue of family law has been the subject of conflict between women's rights groups and other modernists, on the one hand, and more conservative forces, on the other. Several versions of draft family code bills were presented and rejected in less than transparent processes, in 1966, 1973, and 1979 (the latter was submitted to the National Assembly in 1981). One important factor leading to their withdrawal was opposition from women's groups, including the moujahidat (women who fought in the war of independence). In 1984, the political situation, including the repression of the opposition, allowed the then President Benjedid to pass the Family Code through Parliament. The 1984 Family Code reflected a victory for the conservative position. Despite the active participation of women in the war of independence and the country's official revolutionary socialist identity, the 1984 Family Code in Algeria was similar in content and conservatism to the Moroccan Personal Status Code of 1957–1958.

4.4.1   2005 Amendments[15]

Reforms to the 1984 Family Code were first initiated in 1997, when the then solidarity minister organized consultations with women's associations and proposed twenty-two amendments to the Family Code. In 1998, the bill was adopted by the Council of Ministers and transferred to the National Assembly, where it was never debated. The government tried, albeit unsuccessfully, to amend the 1984 Family Code again in 2002. In 2003, a collective of Algerian women's groups at home and abroad launched a campaign under the theme "20 *ans barakat!*" (20 years is enough!). A reform commission organized under the Ministry of Justice prepared a report in the summer of 2004, the text of which was not released publicly.

After the Government Council adopted a family code bill in late summer 2004, active opposition to reforms increased in intensity, particularly among the Islamist political parties MRN (Mouvement du Renouveau national – el Islah) and the MSP (Mouvement de la société pour la paix). The fact that the latter had chosen to support President Bouteflika was one factor that blocked reform. Mobilization included a call for a national referendum against reforms. This reflected the weakness of the presidential majority and placed doubts on the likelihood of the bill being approved by the National Assembly. Religious authorities, although technically under the state's tutelage, also opposed the bill. Islamist opposition claimed that some of the more progressive proposed reforms were against Islam, the State religion, and hence unconstitutional on that basis. Many women's groups, critical of the reforms for not going far enough to establish gender equality, did not actively defend the bill and some called for its replacement with a purely civil code.

Given this deadlock, President Bouteflika withdrew the bill from consideration from the Council of Ministers in September 2004. In February 2005, he invoked the then Article 124 of the Constitution, which allows the president to legislate by ordinance in between sessions and issued amendments to the Family Code. The ordinance was thus ratified as a mere formality at the next parliamentary session in March 2005, with the support of the MSP and abstention of several other parties.

Women's rights proponents argue that the Family Code violates Constitutional provisions of equality. They also assert that then

President Bouteflika caved in on women's rights issues and did not push through real reforms in order to appease the Islamists and obtain their support for his Charter for Peace and National Reconciliation, passed by national referendum in September 2005.[16] On the other hand, Islamist opposition claimed that several of the more progressive reforms were against Islam as the State religion and hence unconstitutional on that basis.

4.5   Family Code Provisions

In substance, the Algerian Family Code reflects the combined heritage of the Malikite school of Islam and French bureaucratic legal procedures. As one analyst describes it, the "ambiguity" toward women's emancipation is reflected in the political discourse since independence, mixing elements of revolution, modernity, equality in the communitarian sense, and religion.[17]

The 2005 reforms resulted in an amended version of same 1984 Code rather than an entirely new law. The Presidential Ordinance amended forty-two articles (eight added, twenty-nine modified, five abrogated). State control over family legal matters was increased, as the public prosecutor is henceforth a party to all cases involving the Family Law.[18] However, Article 222, unmodified by the 2005 reforms, still provides that in the absence of a provision in the law, reference should be made to the dispositions of the "shari'a".

4.5.1   Marriage

Marriage is defined as a "consensual contract concluded between a man and a woman."[19] The minimum age of marriage is nineteen for both spouses; however, the judge may grant a dispensation for reasons of interest or necessity.[20] Under the 1984 version of the Code, the age of marriage was twenty-one for men and eighteen for women. Marriage by proxy was eliminated to prevent forced marriages. Despite this, activists reported over 500 marriages of girls younger than seventeen from 2017–2018.[21]

Fatiha[22] concurrent to the engagement el-khitba does not constitute marriage; however fatiha concurrent to the engagement el-khitba in a contractual meeting does constitute marriage if the two parties consent and the legal conditions for marriage are fulfilled.[23]

Both spouses must present a medical certificate attesting that they do not have any disease or risk factor that would jeopardize the marriage. The law requires the civil status officer to verify that spouses have undergone tests, are aware of illnesses and risk factors, and to note this in the marriage act.[24]

Under Article 8, men may marry more than one wife "within the limits of *Shari'a*, if the motive is justified, and if the conditions and equitable intent are present." Reforms increased judicial control over polygamy. Under the 1984 code, the husband was simply required to notify the current and future wife; under the 2005 amendment, the husband must now petition for judicial authorization. The court authorizes the new marriage only if both women consent and if the husband has proven a justified motive and his aptitude to treat all wives equally.[25] In case of deceit, either wife can file for divorce from the husband.[26] Nothing prevents the husband from simply divorcing the first wife if she does not consent to the new marriage.

One argument in Algeria in support of polygamy is that there are more women than men of marrying age because of the larger number of men who disappeared or were killed during the long civil conflict in the 1990s.[27]

The "marriage contract" is concluded when there are no legal impediments to the marriage, the spouses consent to the marriage, both have the legal capacity to marry, payment of the dower, and the presence of two witnesses and *el wali* (the marital guardian for the bride).[28] Article 13 forbids the *wali* to force a minor girl to get married or to marry her without her consent.

An adult woman concludes her marriage contract "in the presence of her *wali*," who is her father or close relative or any other person of her choice.[29] The text of the final ordinance had a major change from the original bill – it reinstated the mandatory presence of the bride's *wali*. The bill adopted by government in fall 2004 had made the *wali's* presence optional. This modification in the final ordinance is considered a major concession of President Bouteflika to the Islamists, as the Islamist parties and the Imams (even though under the auspices of the Ministry of Religious Affairs) had denounced the abrogation of the *wali* as against *shari'a*. Reforms did eliminate the previous Article 12, which first affirmed that the *wali* could not oppose a marriage if the woman wanted it and it was beneficial to her but then had also provided that a father could oppose the marriage of his virgin daughter if it was in her interests.

The dower must be fixed in the marriage contract, and in its absence, the "parity" or "proper" dower, "*sadaq el mithl*," assessed as a sum usually paid to women on the bride's father's side, is paid the wife.[30] The marriage act is concluded before a private notary or public civil servant legally charged with this task.[31] The two spouses may stipulate in the marriage contract or in a subsequent act any clause they judge useful, such as limiting the number of wives the husband may marry at the same time and allowing the wife to work outside the home without her husband's permission.[32] Marriages not registered at the civil status office must be recognized and validated by a court judgment to be considered legal marriage.[33]

The 1984 Code enumerated respective, distinct obligations of spouses, including the (now eliminated) wife's duty to obey her husband as the head of household and to breastfeed his children. Article 36 as amended established reciprocal obligations between the two spouses. The code makes it the responsibility of both spouses to preserve conjugal ties and maintain a common life, for the spouses to have harmonious cohabitation and mutual respect, and to jointly contribute to the preservation of the family interests. The spouses are to protect their children and ensure their upbringing and mutually consult on management of family affairs and reproductive planning. Each spouse must respect the other's parents and relatives and visit them, preserve kinship ties and good relationships with parents and relatives, and has the right to visit and receive his or her own parents and relatives.

However, husbands are still required to financially support their wives and children. Fathers are obligated to support their boys until the age of majority and girls until they marry.[34] If the father is incapable of supporting his children, the children's financial support falls to their mother if she has the means to provide for them.[35] Article 78 defines financial support as food, clothing, medical care, lodging, and all else necessary according to custom and usage.

Each spouse retains his or her own personal property. However, the two spouses may agree in the marriage contract or in a subsequent notarized contract on joint ownership of property acquired during the marriage and determine the proportion to be attributed to each of them.[36]

4.5.2 Divorce

Article 48 defines divorce as the dissolution of marriage. Divorce may occur unilaterally at the husband's volition (repudiation), by mutual consent of both spouses, or upon the wife's request in the limits established under the law. The judge may not grant the divorce until after several reconciliation attempts have failed.[37] If the judge decides the husband has abused his power of divorce, or in the event of a fault-based divorce upon the demand of the wife, the judge may award her damages for the prejudice she suffered.[38]

The wife may seek divorce for one of ten causes specifically enumerated in the code, including lack of payment of financial support, violation of polygamy provisions, immoral seriously reprehensible fault, persistent disharmony, violation of clauses stipulated in the marriage contract, or any other legally recognized prejudice.[39] Given the difficulties women face to bring proof of such fault, these only comprise 8 percent of divorces.[40]

The wife may also divorce her husband, without his consent, by paying a sum of *khol'à*, and if there is disagreement as to the amount, the judge will fix the amount at no greater than that of the "parity dower" at the time of the divorce.[41] Unlike Moroccan law, here the husband's agreement is not required for a *khol'à* divorce. Nonetheless, *khol'à* only accounts for 11 percent of all divorces, while 49 percent are by repudiation, and 32 percent by mutual consent.[42]

Child custody is awarded to the mother, then the father, then a list of female relatives on both the maternal and paternal side.[43] Custody ceases when the custodian no longer fulfills the conditions enumerated in Article 62; the woman's work is not a motive justifying loss of custody; however, in all cases the interests of the child should be considered.[44]

Custody of boys ends at age ten, although it can be extended to sixteen by a judge if the custodian is the mother and she has not remarried; custody ends for girls at the age of capacity to marry.[45] The custodian who marries someone not related to the child by a prohibited degree of kinship loses custody.[46] If the custodian moves to another country, the judge can decide to maintain custody or withdraw it based on the interests of the child.[47]

In the event of divorce, the father must guarantee the custodian a decent lodging or payment of rent. The wife with custody remains in the conjugal home until the father fulfills the judicial decision on lodging.[48] Previously, rights of the ex-wife were limited, and divorce often rendered women and children homeless.

Fathers are the legal guardians of their children. Guardianship reverts to the mother upon his death. The mother may substitute for the father in urgent matters in case of the father's absence or impediments. In the event of divorce, the judge awards legal guardianship to the parent who has child custody, that is, the mother, if she has custody.[49]

In case of abandonment of the conjugal home by one of the two spouses, the judge awards the divorce and awards damages to the spouse who suffered the prejudice.[50]

4.6   Assessments of Family Code and Calls for Further Reforms

Women's groups expressed their disappointment and anger at the 2005 reforms,[51] described in one newspaper as a mere "makeover" of the 1984 Code.[52] One frequently hears the Family Code referred to as the "Code of Infamy" or the "Family Noose" or "Code of Disgrace." Several of the amendments were not really innovations but basically codified into legislation previous Supreme Court jurisprudence.[53]

Women's groups point out that the law still discriminates against women in numerous ways, including how the mandatory presence of the male marital guardian (*wali*) maintains women in a position of inferiority as legal minors. They also cite the impossibility for women to obtain divorce except for very specific reasons limited by the law, the persistence of polygamy, and unilateral divorce at will by the husband and unequal inheritance rights for men and women. A number of women's groups call for the abolition of the Family Code altogether and its replacement by secular laws.

Divorced women in Algeria also face another grim reality – lack of adequate housing, especially in the capital Algiers and larger cities. The severe housing shortage combined with the lack of alimony and no division of marital property means that women frequently end up homeless with no place to live after a divorce. While the 2005 Family Code reforms guarantee the right of women who have custody of their children to remain in the conjugal home until the father provides adequate alternative housing, the law remains largely unenforced and only applies as long as women have minor children in their custody.

Observers have noted that unemployment means that men have difficulty paying rent, and because of the housing crisis, judges frequently allow men to stay in the conjugal home. This adequate alternative housing provision also encourages men to more vigorously seek custody of their children[54] and makes women vulnerable to violence by their ex-husband to force them to abandon the conjugal home.[55]

Previously unregistered "fatiha" marriages allowed by Article 6 may be proven and formally recorded in the Civil Status Registry by court order, as stipulated by Family Code Article 22. As a result of the combination of these two provisions, a man wishing to take another wife can in reality do so without the consent of the first spouse and without judicial authorization, despite Article 8 limits on the husband's right to practice polygamy.

Observers have also expressed concern that the article requiring spouses to provide medical certificates has led some civil status officers to request virginity certificates from the bride to include in the marriage file.[56] Furthermore, NGO reviews of marriage contracts have found a frequent number that do not mention the dower or its amount, which leads to problems and litigation upon divorce or the husband's death.

During the civil conflict, the majority of the "disappeared" were men, who were believed to be taken into custody by state security forces and whose fate and whereabouts are unknown. Female relatives of the disappeared left behind suffer from numerous legal and administrative difficulties, such as obtaining official documentation of the husband's absence in order to be declared the legal guardian of children. Under the Family Code, men are the legal guardians of their children unless the court rules that they are dead or missing. Women need such a ruling in order to be able to sign legal and administrative documents for their children themselves. Women are left in limbo with no access to bank accounts, property registered in their missing husband's name, or to pensions or other social benefits. Even obtaining a death certificate for men abducted and presumed killed can take years.[57]

Other laws in Algeria were not amended to reflect 2005 Family Code amendments; the resulting inconsistencies and contradictions between the texts prevent women from fully accessing their new rights. This is particularly evident with spouses' rights under Article 19 to stipulate rights-protective clauses into their marriage contract.[58]

Family Code Article 21 provides that the provisions of the 1970 Civil Status Code govern marriage contract registration procedures. Family Code Article 18 refers to either a legally designated civil servant or a notary as the parties competent to conclude marriage contracts. Articles 71 and 72 of the Civil Status Code (as amended in 2014) state that marriage contracts are drawn up either by notaries or by civil status officers. The notary has apparently replaced the judge in the conclusion of marriage contracts, with the judge's role now limited to authorizing the marriage of minors and polygamous marriages.

Article 73 of the Civil Status Code provides that the marriage contract must include the spouses' names, dates and places of birth, their parents' names, the witnesses' names and ages, and any legal authorization or exemption necessary to conclude the marriage. Civil Status Code article 31 prohibits civil status officers from adding anything written or heard into documents other than the required information or from drawing up a legal document on their own initiative. Even though under the 2005 code the marriage contract can include stipulated conditions, the contract template used (based on 1970) practically does not allow for any such amendments. Additionally, nowhere does the law require the civil status officer to inform the two spouses of their legal rights to stipulate additional clauses in their marriage contract or in a subsequent notarized contract.

As a result, Family Code Article 19 has not served its intended purpose, notably the protection of the spouses' rights through the stipulation of conditions into the marriage contracts. The only way to stipulate conditions in the marriage contract in Algeria is by drawing it up in front of a notary. This is not a viable solution because, in addition to their prohibitively high fees, most notaries avoid drawing up such detailed, negotiated marriage contracts. Notaries fear that conflicts might arise later between the spouses over the wording of the contract or the conditions included, in which case the notaries would be drawn into any litigation.

4.7   Conclusion

Algeria ratified the United Nations Convention on the Elimination of All Forms of Discrimination against Women in 1996. The government maintains its official reservations to Article 2, Article 15(4) on the right of women to choose their residence, and Article 16 on equal rights for men and women in marriage and at its dissolution, stating that would only apply these articles to the extent that they do not contradict the provisions of the Family Code.

On July 15, 2009, Algeria withdrew the reservation it had made upon accession to Article 9(2) granting women equal rights with men with respect to the nationality of their children. Reforms made to the Nationality Code in 2005 allow Algerian women married to foreigners to transmit Algerian nationality to their children.

Some additional improvements to women's rights in the family have been made in recent years, notably with the 2015 creation of a Maintenance Fund for payments of alimony and child support post-divorce,[59] as well as a couple of revisions to the Penal Code increasing penalties for violence committed between spouses.[60]

In February 2012 at its 51st session, the Committee on the Elimination of Discrimination against Women expressed its concern at the discrimination against women in the Family Code and made recommendations for additional reforms to bring Algeria into compliance with its international obligations.[61] Those provisions the Committee cited specifically as needing review and amendment include the requirement of the *wali*, polygamy, women's limited access to divorce, inequality of women in custodial and guardianship rights, unequal rights to property acquired during marriage upon divorce, and inequality in inheritance.

Five years later, the United Nations Human Rights Council reiterated these same concerns, with numerous member countries calling on Algeria to modify the aforementioned discriminatory provisions of the Family Code.[62] In its reply, Algeria rejected recommendations pertaining to women's rights in the family, stating that, "personal status questions are inspired by Muslim law." It did, however, assure the Council that a working group had been created to examine possible reforms to the Family Code,[63] repeating a 2015 presidential announcement to this effect.[64] At the time of publication, no such reforms had been made. The future of the Family Code and women's rights in Algeria remains to be seen; activists across the region highlight the challenges to women's rights that have emerged after the so-called Arab Spring. The *Hirak* (popular protest movement) emerged in Algeria in February 2019; for several years regular mass protests have taken place every Friday calling for institutional and democratic reforms. For his part, former President Bouteflika himself had declared on the occasion of International Woman's Day on March 8, 2005, "you wanted Family Code amendments, you got them, but I couldn't do any more .... Be 'fair play' (English in the original) ladies."[65]

Notes

1 See, e.g., David B. Ottaway, "Algeria: Bloody Past and Fractious Factions," *Wilson Center* (August 27, 2015), www.wilsoncenter.org/article/algeria-bloody-past-and-fractious-factions.

2 Ottaway, "Algeria."

3 Patrick Markey and Lamine Chikhi, "Algeria's Bouteflika Wins Re-election with 81.5 Percent: Official Results," *Reuters* (April 18, 2014), www.reuters.com/article/us-algeria-election-idUSBREA3H0D620140418.

4 "Algeria's Abdelaziz Bouteflika Reigns after Mass Protests," *Al Jazeera* (April 3, 2019), www.aljazeera.com/news/2019/4/3/algerias-abdelaziz-bouteflika-resigns-after-mass-protests.

5 Committee on the Elimination of Discrimination against Women, "Combined Third and Fourth Periodic Reports of States Parties," Algeria, March 24, 2010, CEDAW/C/DZA/CO/3–4.

6 Constitution de la République Algérienne Démocratique et Populaire, JORADP N° 76 du 8 décembre 1996 modifiée par: Loi n°02-03 du 10 avril 2002 JORADP N°25 du 14 avril 2002; Loi n°08-19 du 15 novembre 2008 JORADP N°63 du 16 novembre 2008 ; Loi n° 16-01 du 6 mars 2016 – *Journal officiel* n° 14 du 7 mars 2016; JORADP N° 82 du 30 décembre 2020.

7 Algeria Constitution Article 2.

8 Algeria Constitution Article 37.

9 Algeria Constitution Article 35.

10 Algeria Constitution Article 71.

11 Algeria Constitution Article 154.

12 Decision of the Constitutional Court, August 20, 1989, www.conseil-constitutionnel.dz/indexFR.htm.

13 Loi n° 84-11 du 9 juin 1984 portant code de la famille.

14 Ordonnance no. 75-58 du Ramadhan 1395 correspondant au 26 septembre 1975 portant code civil, modifié et complétée.

15 Ordonnance n° 05-02 du 18 moharram 1426 correspondant au 27 février 2005 modifiant et complétant la loi n° 84-11 du 9 juin 1984 portant code de la famille.

16 For an in-depth description of the Algerian Family Code promulgation process, see Jean-Philippe Bras, "La réforme du code de la famille au Maroc et en Algérie: quelles avancées pour la démocratie?" (2007) 37*Critique internationale*, 93–125.

17 Boutheina Cheriet, "Le cas algérien," in *Femmes, droit de la famille et système judiciaire en Algérie, au Maroc et en Tunisie* (UNESCO, 2010).

18 Algeria Family Code Article 3bis.

19 Algeria Family Code Article 4.

20 Algeria Family Code Article 7.

21 Wahiba Soleimani, "Report on the Phenomenon to the Human Rights Office, Nouria Hafsi: 500 Algerian Women Are Victims of Underage Marriage in Less Than Two Years,"
Echorouckonline (June 30, 2018), www.echoroukonline.com/500-%D8%AC%D8%B2%D8%A7%D8%A6%D8%B1%D9%8A%D8%A9-%D8%B6%D8%AD%D9%8A%D8%A9-%D8%B2%D9%88%D8%A7%D8%AC-%D8%A7%D9%84%D9%82%D8%A7%D8%B5%D8%B1%D8%A7%D8%AA-%D9%81%D9%8A-%D8%A3%D9%82%D9%84-%D9%85%D9%86-%D8%B3/.

22 A verbal marriage without a written contract whereby two persons are declared married after the reading of the Koranic verses from the *Surah* of the *fatiha*.

23 Family Code Article 6.

24 Family Code Article 7bis.

25 Family Code Article 8.

26 Family Code Article 8bis.

27 See Nadia Marzouki, "Algeria," in Sanja Kelly and July Breslin (eds.), *Women's Rights in the Middle East and North Africa: Progress Amid Resistance* (Freedom House, 2010).

28 Algeria Family Code Articles 9 and 9bis.

29 Algeria Family Code Article 11.

30 Algeria Family Code Article 15.
31 Algeria Family Code Article 18.
32 Algeria Family Code Article 19.
33 Algeria Family Code Article 22.
34 Algeria Family Code Articles 74 and 75.
35 Algeria Family Code Article 76.
36 Algeria Family Code Article 37.
37 Algeria Family Code Article 49.
38 Algeria Family Code Articles 52 and 53bis.
39 Algeria Family Code Article 53. Other legal reasons include infirmity preventing fulfillment of the purpose of marriage, refusal of the husband to have sexual relations with his wife for more than four months, conviction of the husband for an infraction that dishonors the family and makes conjugal life impossible, and more than a year's absence without valid excuse or financial support.
40 "La répudiation représente 49% des divorces, le khol'â 11%," *El Watan* (February 20, 2018), www.elwatan.com/archives/actualites/la-repudiation-represente-49-des-divorces-le-khola-11-2-20-02-2018.
41 Family Code Article 54.
42 "La répudiation représente 49% des divorces, le khol'â 11%."
43 Family Code Article 64.
44 Family Code Article 67.
45 Family Code Article 65.
46 Family Code Article 66.
47 Family Code Article 69.
48 Family Code Article 72.
49 Family Code Article 87.
50 Family Code Article 55.
51 Communiqué du collectif "20 ans barakat " *Une nouvelle fois les droits des femmes sont bafoués* (8 mars 2005); Florence Beaugé, "En Algérie, le code de la famille récemment reformé maintient la femme sous tutelle," *Le Monde* (February 24, 2005).
52 Samir Rekik, "Le code Algérien de la famille: Pourquoi a-t-il relégué la femme algérienne au statut de 'deuxième sexe?," *El Watan* (March 27, 2007).
53 Nadia Ait-Zai, "Le divorce dans le droit de la famille algérien," www.proyectoadl.com.
54 Marzouki, "Algeria."
55 Mission to Algeria, "Report of the Special Rapporteur on Violence against Women, Its Causes and Consequences," 19 May 2011 A/HRC/17/26/Add.3.
56 Rekik, "Le code Algérien de la famille."
57 Amnesty International, "Algeria: Briefing to the Committee on the Elimination of Discrimination against Women" (December 2004).
58 Information from this section on marriage contracts in Algeria based on Global Rights, "Conditions, not Conflict: Promoting Women's Rights in the Maghreb through Strategic Use of the Marriage Contract" (2008).
59 Loi n° 15-01 du 13 Rabie El Aouel 1436 correspondant au 4 janvier 2015 portant création d'un fonds de la pension alimentaire.
60 Loi n° 15-19 du 18 Rabie El Aouel 1437 correspondant au 30 Décembre 2015 modifiant et complétant l'ordonnance n° 66-156 du 8 juin 1966 portant code pénal.

61 CEDAW/C/DZA/CO/3–4.
62 A/HRC/36/13, July 19, 2017, Human Rights Council Report of the Working Group on the Universal Periodic Review, Algeria.
63 A/HRC/36/13/Add.1 19 septembre 2017 Conseil des droits de l'homme Rapport du Groupe de travail sur l'Examen périodique universel Algérie, Additif Observations sur les conclusions et/ou recommandations, engagements et réponses de l'État examiné.
64 See, e.g., Le Monde avec AFP, "Algérie : Bouteflika annonce une réforme du code de la famille" (March 9, 2015), www.lemonde.fr/afrique/article/2015/03/09/algerie-bou teflika-annonce-une-reforme-du-code-de-la-famille_4590103_3212.html.
65 Rachid Abbar, "Algérie : le code de la famille de la discorde", *Aujourd'hui le Maroc* (March 11–13, 2005), www.aujourdhui.ma/monde/algerie-le-code-de-la-famille-de-la-discorde-28522.

Juristic and Legislative Rulemaking

A History of the Personal Status Code of Iraq, 1959–2022

HAIDER ALA HAMOUDI

5.1 Introduction

Of all the laws that have been enacted throughout Iraq's near century of existence, none has engendered the same sustained level of controversy as Iraq's Personal Status Code, No. 188 of 1959.[1] Much of the attention in the global media has been on the relatively progressive nature of the law, the backlash that the law has generated across generations, and the potential effect that any retrenchment would have on women. Certainly, it would be a mistake to gainsay this dimension of the historic controversy associated with the codification of personal status law in Iraq. However, there is a second, equally important and unappreciated dimension as well. This is the central role that personal status law has played in the Iraqi nationalization project and the backlash against it from particularist groups historically suspicious of Baghdad's intentions, most notably the Shi'a. Hence, from the inception of the Personal Status Code, Shi'i jurists and their political supporters have objected to its universality, demanding in its place the right of the Shi'a to live by the Islamic rules that their own jurists have derived from sacred, revelatory text. That this is more about particularist principle than substantive rule is demonstrated by the fact that, for all of their vociferous objections, the Shi'a Islamist groupings have never actually managed to come together to produce a coherent alternative to the Personal Status Code, nearly two decades after the removal of Saddam Husayn from power. Nationalists, whether Sunni or Shi'i, have fiercely defended the uniform law for the same reasons that the Shi'i Islamist groups have objected to it; namely, that it provides one law for all Iraqis.

Along with the lack of a credible alternative to the Code, recent political unrest has largely ensured its continuation. Across sect and ethnicity, Iraqis are thoroughly disenchanted with their government and the ruling political classes. Demagogic appeals to revamping family law for whatever reason are unlikely to placate or distract those masses. Moreover, existing political divisions *within* each of Iraq's major groups, long underemphasized, have increased in importance, with the most recent political divisions lying across sect and ethnicity rather than on the basis of them. To offer the simplest example, the Shi'i Sadrists have most recently allied with the Kurdish KDP, while the KDP's long time Kurdish rival, the PUK, is closely aligned with the Shi'i militia groups affiliated with Iran, known as "The Coordination Framework." Despite these developments, Iraq's sectarian divisions are unlikely to disappear; and when they rise in importance again, debates over the future of the Personal Status Code will almost surely accompany them.

This chapter will describe the origins and evolution of the Personal Status Code, its substantive provisions as they have been interpreted by Iraqi courts over time, and the long-standing, and continuing, efforts to overturn it as a matter of principle. In so doing, the chapter demonstrates the extent to which the debates over personal status in fact reflect quite closely the serious internal divisions that are the cause of so many of Iraq's difficulties.

5.2   Personal Status before the 1958 Revolution

Personal status law was uncodified and nonuniform from the formation of the British Mandate in Iraq after the First World War until 1959. Throughout this period, two court systems existed to administer personal status, one for the Sunni population, and one for the Shi'a.[2] Each was competent to administer Sunni Hanafi and Shi'i Ja'fari rules, respectively, and each did so by referring primarily to the rules of clerical and juristic authorities in issuing decisions.[3]

The Iraqi government attempted at various times during the monarchy to enact a personal status code to replace this dual system that relied so heavily on premodern juristic rules. The most notable of these efforts culminated in a 1947 proposal that contained some uniform elements, while significant matters were left to determination by sect. However, due to opposition from various elements, very much including the jurists of Najaf, neither that proposal nor any other initiative was successful prior to the overthrow of the monarchy in 1958.[4]

5.3   The Enactment and Evolution of the Personal Status Code until 2003

The impasse as concerned matters of personal status came to a swift end on July 14, 1958, when military strongman Abdul Kareem Qasim seized control of the state in a military coup, ended the monarchy, and declared Iraq to be an independent republic.[5] A committed nationalist, Qasim found neither Iraq's existing personal status regime nor the 1947 proposals particularly appealing. In his view, both deferred to particularist preferences of subnational communities and did little to raise national consciousness. Qasim desired the unification of Iraq's rules of personal status so that all Iraqis would be governed by a single, national code. Less than two years after Qasim took power, Iraq had drafted and enacted into law the Personal Status Code, No. 188 of 1959, which remains in force to this day. Key features of the Code, both as originally drafted and as they have evolved over time, are discussed below.

5.3.1   Entering into Marriage

In keeping with Qasim's leftist tendencies,[6] the Personal Status Code was remarkably progressive for its time. Much of this was achieved through *talfiq*, or the patching together of rules from various schools and sects within Islam to achieve the most progressive result possible. Hence, for example, though beyond the scope of this chapter, the Code's rules on inheritance favor Shi'i rules over Sunni ones.[7] By contrast, its rules on entering into marriage tend to favor the Hanafi Sunni rules to a significant degree. Hence, for example, the Code makes no reference to the Shi'i "temporary" marriage, whereby a marriage is set for a given duration and then automatically terminates.[8] It also permits Muslim men (but not women) to marry adherents of other monotheistic faiths (referred to in *shari'a* discourse as "People of the Book") – another Hanafi principle, but not a Shi'i one.[9] Finally, it requires two witnesses to a marriage, as per Hanafi doctrine, where the Shi'a require none but the couple themselves.[10]

There are two primary progressive innovations that the Code introduces that are worth noting. The first concerns child marriage. While premodern jurists across the schools generally permitted a father or paternal grandfather to bind a child into marriage,[11] the Code from its outset indicated in Article 8 that "the capacity for marriage is completed at eighteen."[12] This type of progressivity, which derogated from classical rules that were uncharacteristically uniform, resulted in resistance not only from jurists and religious institutions across sect and school but from other state actors as well. Thus, in a notable 1963 case, the Court of Cassation, Iraq's highest court of general appeal, interpreted Article 8 very narrowly. According to the Court, Article 8 only meant that a person had the capacity to marry *themselves* at the age of eighteen. However, according to the Court, the Code was silent as to marriages of children undertaken by guardians. Given the legislative silence, the Court indicated, the rules of the *shari'a* prevailed.[13] On that basis, the marriage of an eleven-year-old girl arranged by her father was deemed valid and binding.[14] This problem was not corrected until 1978, when a new Article 9 was added to the Code, which rendered it a criminal act to force a child into marriage without their consent and deemed unconsummated marriages invalid (*bāṭil*) if they were so coerced. The same provision prohibited the forced marriage of any person with capacity to marry.[15]

The effect of this provision is debatable, as the response among many guardians has been to ignore the restriction, contract their children into marriage, and then have the couple wait until eighteen to actually register the marriage.[16] The Personal Status Code had a rather blunt method of dealing with this problem, which was to impose a prison sentence against the husband for contracting an unregistered marriage, should the couple later appear to register the marriage. This has proved remarkably ineffectual, for perhaps obvious reasons.[17] Judges are naturally reticent to impose prison terms on the breadwinners of poor rural families whose crime was to accede to a marriage arranged by their parents when they were teenagers. As a consequence of all of this, child marriage remains disturbingly common in Iraq, with 5 percent of children married by fifteen, and nearly 25 percent married by eighteen, according to estimates provided by UNICEF in 2016.[18]

The second innovation to the rules of entering into marriage lay in the area of polygamy. Traditionally, again uniformly across the schools and sects, classical law imposed upon a husband the obligation to support all of his wives and required him to spend equal time with each of them.[19] Importantly, these were obligations created by the marriages, not conditions to enter into them. A court had no more right under classical law to prevent a polygamous marriage than it could prevent any free person from undertaking an improvident financial obligation. By contrast, the Personal Status Code since its inception required court permission to practice polygamy. Hence, Article 10(5) imposes criminal penalties for entering into an out of court polygamous marriage.

The discretion available to a court to deny permission for a polygamous marriage is broad under Article 3 of the Code.[20] In fact, a court is only supposed to grant permission if the court is convinced that the husband has financial capacity, that the husband will treat his multiple wives equally, and most notably, that there is a "legitimate interest" (*maṣlaḥa mashrū'a*) in the husband having an additional wife.[21] The Code provides no guidance as to what a "legitimate interest" might be. These provisions have remained largely in force, with only modest revisions, the most significant of which was a 1980 amendment removing these conditions when the second wife is a widow.[22]

Generally, and with wide variation, Iraqi courts apply the maddeningly vague criteria of "legitimate interest" set forth in Article 3(4) in a manner that imposes meaningful constraints on husbands seeking additional wives, though not so strictly as to render it extremely burdensome to marry multiple wives. Two cases decided in 2010 are illustrative. In the first, a wife in Samarra' indicated that she had in no way failed in her marital duties and hence there was no "legitimate interest" in her husband taking a second wife. The highest court of general appeal, the Federal Court of Cassation, upheld a lower court ruling permitting the husband to take a second wife because the legal criteria had been met, implying without explanation that a "legitimate interest" in polygamy could indeed arise even if the first wife had not somehow been deemed to have been at fault or derelict in her marital duties.[23] In the second case, arising in Hamdaniya, the same Federal Court of Cassation overruled a lower court ruling granting permission to take a second wife. The reason was that the husband had provided no documentation demonstrating that he had a second home in which to keep his second wife and that he had not even offered a legitimate interest for the court to consider.[24]

It is fair to say that the discretion granted to courts leads to broad uncertainties in result. By way of example, a personal status court in Sadr City in 2009 denied a request for a polygamous marriage to a husband whose salary was a respectable $1,000 monthly, whose first wife, who had born him four children, was agreeable to the marriage, and whose prospective second wife was a divorcee who desired remarriage to avoid social stigma. In so doing, the court rejected a government social worker's conclusion that the additional marriage would not lead to family discord. The court based its denial on the fact that: (i) there was no guarantee that the husband's salary would remain as high as it was, in particular given that most of it was "danger pay" and conditions in Iraq might stabilize; (ii) the husband's desire for more children could be achieved through his first wife, who remained relatively young; and (iii) Iraq is a signatory to the Convention on the Elimination of All Forms of Discrimination Against Women (CEDAW) and therefore any suggestion that divorcees are to be pitied or stigmatized relative to married women is firmly rejected in the state.[25] Leaving aside the irony of both invoking CEDAW and suggesting that a woman who had borne four children could readily bear more without seeming to have taken her view on the matter, it seems clear that this particular court is exceedingly unlikely to ever grant permission for a man to take an additional wife. Other judges across the country seem far less reticent.

In the end, the courts have not settled on a consistent approach in deciding whether to approve polygamous unions, and the matter seems to depend largely on the worldview of the judge hearing the case.

5.3.2 Obligations of Marriage

The Code does not make wholesale changes to the traditional Islamic obligations of marriage. The husband must financially provide for his wife, and the wife must obey her husband.[26] Most court cases in this area involve a dispute between a husband and a wife on whether he is providing a suitable marital home and financial support, whether she is "rebellious" by abandoning the marital home or otherwise refusing him sexual intercourse, or, quite often, cross claims by each of them on these grounds.

Nevertheless, there are areas of development worth remarking upon. One involves the extent of the husband's ability to force his wife to move to a new city, or even a new country, so long as he is able to provide her a suitable marital home after the move. Initially, Iraqi courts seemed to regard it as axiomatic that a woman's obligation of obedience included an obligation to move to a husband's place of work, even where, in one 1969 Court of Cassation case, that place of work was a different country entirely.[27] Interestingly, Iraqi courts have reversed themselves on this question, relying on their own very expansive reading of a 1980 amendment to the Code, which indicates that a wife need not obey her husband if his order to obey is deemed capricious or intended to harm her.[28] On this basis, a husband whose employer relocated him from Basra to Umm Qasr, about thirty-five miles away, can no longer obligate his wife to move with him.[29]

Also interesting is expanded court recognition of a wife's right to work over the objections of her husband. Initially, Iraqi courts routinely granted requests from a husband to declare a wife rebellious for continuing out of home work after her husband asked her to quit. The exceptions were circumstances where the husband's demand appeared to be made in bad faith. Hence, for example, the Court of Cassation ruled in 1963 on a case involving a husband who had no objection to his wife having a career when he married her and who later left her without initiating a divorce, presumably to avoid paying her dower. Upon her suit for financial support, he demanded that she stop working and remain in the marital home. The Court denied his claim. In so doing, it quoted from the Hanafi jurist Ibn ʿAbidin, who indicated that a husband could prevent his wife from working if it interfered with his marital rights. The Court then indicated that it was hard to see how this was the case under the facts presented, given that the husband had abandoned the wife.[30]

Over the course of the 1970s, Iraqi courts began to deny with increasing frequency husbands' demands that their wives stop working, using a variety of disparate grounds. Finally, in 1980, an amendment to the Personal Status Code was enacted that prevents a husband from requiring his wife to occupy the marital home if it is "far from the place of work of the wife, such that she cannot be successful in her home and work responsibilities."[31] Iraqi courts have regularly applied this provision to permit wives to refuse to occupy marital homes if they would need to quit their jobs to do so.

Thus, the general traditional framework of the Islamic marriage, where the husband provides the support for the household and the wife remains in the marital home and submits to his demands, and in particular his sexual demands, remains largely in place in Iraq. At the same time, there is increased recognition of the interests of wives to their lives outside of the home, such that the husband cannot force his wife to move capriciously, nor may he put her in a position where she must abandon her career in order to be with him.

5.3.3 Marital Dissolution

The Code's provisions on the right of a husband to repudiate the marriage through the historic doctrine of *talāq* remain largely determined by sectarian juristic rules, despite any reference in the Code to the sects. Hence, for example, courts require a Shiʿi husband to obtain two witnesses to the divorce to render it effective, and they do not require the

same for a Sunni. Similarly, courts treat a Shiʿi pronouncement of *ṭalāq*
when the wife is menstruating as invalid, where the Sunni pronouncement is sinful but valid.[32]

There are significant progressive provisions respecting the pronouncement of *ṭalāq* that are worth mentioning. The first of these is Article 34 of
the Personal Status Code.[33] It requires that a husband obtain a *ṭalāq* in
court and that the legal effect of the marriage remains in place until the
court orders the divorce complete. Only if it is impracticable to pronounce the *ṭalāq* in court may a husband register it after the fact, and
even then he is required to register it during the period during which the
ṭalāq remains revocable, known as the *ʿidda*.

Iraqi judicial practice has done much to erode these substantive
restrictions. First of all, husbands almost never pronounce *ṭalāq* in court.
The vast majority of husbands register the *ṭalāq* in court after the fact, in
some cases after the passage of years. Courts as a matter of routine deem
such divorces effective despite the obvious violations of Article 34. In
addition, I have not found a case where a wife was successful in pursuing
a case for support after the pronouncement of an out of court *ṭalāq* but
prior to its registration in court. The provision in Article 34 indicating
that the "legal effects" of the marriage remain in force until the *ṭalāq* is
registered in court seems limited, therefore, to questions of proof of the
existence of the *ṭalāq*. Hence, for example, a daughter cannot deny her
mother a share of her decedent husband's inheritance on the basis of a
claim that the decedent father divorced the mother when there is no
court record of a *ṭalāq*, simply because it cannot be proven that the *ṭalāq*
took place.[34]

A second significant innovation in the area of *ṭalāq* is the Code's
adoption of the Shiʿi rule that the notorious "triple *ṭalāq*" is ineffective.
That is, to quote Article 37(2) of the Code, "the *ṭalāq* linked by a multiple
number, pronounced or by signal, only occurs once."[35] Rather incredibly,
the Court of Cassation originally suggested that this wording only meant
that the statement "I divorce you thrice" was deemed a single divorce. By
contrast, the repetition of the words "I divorce you" three successive
times rendered the divorce irrevocable, as per historic Sunni rules.[36] The
courts have since reconsidered the matter. Currently in Iraq, the universal rule is the Shiʿi one – the pronouncement of *ṭalāq* in a single setting is
deemed a single, revocable divorce when pronounced, even when pronounced more than once.

The other major innovations in *ṭalāq* concern a husband's support
obligations after it is pronounced. Specifically, under a 1985 amendment,

the Code adopted a form of Egypt's infamous "Jihan's Law."[37] The amendment authorized a court to order a husband to continue paying maintenance for up to two years following the divorce if it determined that a husband's divorce had been "capricious."[38] Examples of caprice endorsed by the Court of Cassation include divorces undertaken via text message, and divorces pronounced at a wife's place of work. They do not include the refusal of a husband to conduct the *ṭalāq* in court as required by Article 34 of the Code.[39] Though not formally part of the Personal Status Code, there is a separate law that gives a wife the right to remain in the marital home for up to three years following *ṭalāq*, whether or not the *ṭalāq* was pronounced capriciously. This right is available so long as the wife did not consent to the divorce and there is an independent marital home in which she was living at the time that the *ṭalāq* was pronounced.[40]

With regard to marital dissolutions initiated by the wife, the Personal Status Code realizes particular progressive ambitions through a liberal use of *talfīq*, or "patching," of rules from various Islamic sources.[41] For example, adopting a Maliki rule, the Code permits a wife to seek marital dissolution if her husband either refuses to fulfill his maintenance obligations to her for a period greater than sixty days or is unable to do so because he is missing, in hiding, or incarcerated.[42] Courts tend to read these provisions narrowly, requiring sixty days to pass from the time that a husband receives actual or constructive notice from a government agency that his failure to pay maintenance will give his wife the right to dissolve the marriage. A wife is also able to seek dissolution if a husband supports her but has left the marital home for a period of two years or longer or if he is convicted of a crime that carries with it a sentence of three years or greater.[43]

Also seemingly taken from the Maliki school is a provision permitting a party that has suffered harm to make a claim for judicial dissolution where the harm is so severe that it renders that party "unable to continue the marital association."[44] Most of the cases respecting severe harm involve a court trying to distinguish between the "moderate" physical discipline that a husband is permitted under classical law to impose upon a recalcitrant wife and what the court would regard as more significant domestic abuse. Generally, courts require some sort of record of severe violence, usually in the form of a hospital visit or the initiation of a criminal case.[45] In particularly egregious cases, such as a husband attempting to drown his wife in a bathtub in front of several witnesses, medical evidence need not be presented.[46]

Finally, a wife may seek to dissolve her marriage to her husband if he marries an additional wife out of court. By initiating the dissolution, she waives her right to press criminal charges for the out of court polygamous union.[47]

No fault dissolution appears to exist in Iraq in Article 41.[48] That provision permits either party to seek a dissolution if "discord" (*shiqāq*) arises between them. The dissolution process involves first extensive mediation among representatives of each of the families of the husband and the wife. In the end, if the court is satisfied that the differences are indeed irreconcilable, it apportions the delayed dower owed to the wife on the basis of the fault of the respective parties for the discord. Both husbands and wives attempt to make use of Article 41 with some frequency. Wives invoke it when no other basis to dissolve the marriage affords itself. Husbands invoke it because the pronouncement of *ṭalāq* requires payment of the entire deferred dower, where the Article 41 dissolution does not, to the extent that the court finds that the wife bore some responsibility for the discord.

Iraqi courts are remarkably hostile to granting dissolutions under Article 41 under almost any circumstance, instead dismissing such claims on the grounds that the discord alleged is not deep-rooted enough to merit dissolution.[49] In fact, I have yet to see a court authorize a marital dissolution under Article 41 that it could not have dissolved on some other ground, such as harm or failure to maintain. This judicial hostility does not seem to have resulted in any drop in Article 41 cases filed, based on a cursory review of the number of published Court of Cassation cases on the subject through the end of 2022.

5.3.4   Child Custody

One final area within personal status that has seen significant change over the years concerns child custody. In keeping with Islamic law, the original code distinguished between the right to "raise" (*ḥaḍāna*) the child and a right to "guardianship" (*wilāya*) over the child. A mother had the right to raise a child until the age of seven, but the father, or the legal guardian in the father's absence, had the right to look into the conditions of education and upbringing.[50] The mother's right to raise the child was extinguished if she married another person unrelated to the child.[51]

As amended in 1978, the distinction between guardianship and raising continues to be in force, but it has lost much of its meaning as concerns custody matters because the father no longer has the right to interfere in education and upbringing while the mother is raising the child. Moreover, the amendments extend the mother's right to raise the child to the age of ten, and the court can extend it to fifteen if an investigating committee finds it in the child's interest to do so.[52] Upon reaching the age of fifteen, the child is left to decide where to reside.[53] A 1987 amendment also removed the automatic denial of the right of the mother to custody upon remarriage, instead empowering the court in such instances to decide where custody is best, based on the best interests of the child.[54] It should be noted that this is one of the few circumstances where the best interests of the child are specifically given precedence, in stark contrast to prevailing practice in most of the developed world.

5.4   Controversies over the Personal Status Code (1959–2003)

Some of the criticism concerning the Personal Status Code was directed at its more progressive elements. For example, Sheikh Ahmed Al-Kubaisi, a Sunni whose work on the Code remains highly influential within Iraqi courts to this day, objected at length to the provisions of the Personal Status Code requiring judicial approval of a second marriage.[55] Other elements of the Code, including the prohibition against child marriage, the possibility of no fault divorce, and the right of a woman to refuse to accompany her husband if he relocates to another city, have likewise engendered resistance from Sunni and Shi'i religious authorities from time to time.

However, the objections among the Shi'i religious elite and their political allies ran much deeper than individual progressive provisions and to the very *principle* of a uniform personal status code enacted by a state legislature. Hence, the prominent jurist Muhammad Bahr al-Ulum published a lengthy and detailed objection to the Personal Status Code when it was first enacted, rejecting outright the idea that there could be a single set of rules that could unite all Iraqis on the matter of personal status, given their sectarian differences.[56] Bahr al-Ulum instead demanded space and accommodation for rulemaking on the part of both Najaf's jurists and their Sunni counterparts. These objections were initially short lived. The rise of the Ba'ath party in 1968, and its prolonged period of severe repression of the Najaf seminaries, stifled the Shi'i opposition for a period of time, but circumstances changed radically after 2003, when the Ba'ath regime was forcibly displaced by the United States.

5.5   The Personal Status Code since 2003

That decades of repression had done nothing to soften Shi'i Islamist objections to the Personal Status Code in principle became obvious in late 2003 in a rather stunning fashion, through a move undertaken by purported allies of the United States. Prior to the restoration of Iraqi sovereignty, the occupying forces recognized by the UN Security Council, known as the Coalition Provisional Authority (CPA), handpicked a group of prominent former Iraqi opposition figures to advise them during the post conflict transition. This Iraqi advisory group, given the Orwellian name of the Iraq Governing Council (IGC), enacted a resolution in December of 2003 respecting personal status.[57] Proposed by the Shi'i Islamist representatives of the IGC and enacted during the period that a prominent Shi'i Islamist, Abdul Aziz al-Hakim, served as its President, the resolution called for the repeal of the Personal Status Code and its replacement with uncodified *shari'a* based on the school of thought of the affected parties in any given matter.[58]

Legally, the resolution had no effect. The IGC could only advise the CPA, not make its own law. The US-dominated CPA made its staunch opposition to the law abundantly clear, and the IGC ultimately repealed the law in a contentious session that ended in a Shi'i Islamist walkout.[59] Yet the move still reverberated throughout much of Iraq's legal community. After all, Shi'i Islamist groups had just made their preferences respecting personal status rather clear, they were likely to remain a potent political force for some period of time, and the United States would not forever be around to restrain them.

The culmination of the Shi'i Islamist efforts to repeal the Personal Status Code was the inclusion of Article 41 into Iraq's current constitution. That Article reads in full as follows:

> Iraqis are free in their personal status obligations, based on their religions, sects, beliefs and choices, and this shall be regulated by law.[60]

The provision was the subject of much negotiation between secularists and nationalists, on the one hand, who preferred to keep matters of personal status as they were, and Shi'i Islamists, on the other hand, who sought the formal constitutional repeal of the Personal Status Code.[61] As a result, the article is, to say the least, inelegantly drafted. When faced with the nearly impossible task of interpreting Article 41, in order to determine the limits of the individual "freedom" to live by a family law of one's own choosing, the Federal Supreme Court in 2011 used the reference in Article 41 to the enactment of a regulating law to turn the matter back to the legislature for resolution. The Court held that it could not simply set aside provisions of the Personal Status Code to which any given litigant objected on the grounds that such a provision violated that litigant's individualized belief, even if that belief was based on the juristic consensus of an established Islamic school. Rather, what was required was "specialized study in the opinions of all of the Islamic schools" such that there is a text for Iraqis "in light of their differences, so that the removal of a requested provision does not exceed or contradict what the various opinions on the matter have agreed upon, or whatever is reconciled between them."[62] This, the Court determined, required the intervention of the legislative branch.

Draft legislation for the Shi'i population arrived three years later, in the spring of 2014, when the minister of justice deposited a draft in the sacred tomb of the Prophet Muhammad's son in law Ali ibn Abi Talib, the first Imam of the Shi'a. The gesture was pure demagoguery, and the draft was amateurish and clumsy, little more than a hasty effort to codify the rules of marriage and divorce laid out by the Najaf's current senior cleric, Grand Ayatollah Ali al-Sistani, just in advance of upcoming national elections. That Sistani was providing rules by which the faithful would be able to live a virtuous life, and not the laws that a state could be expected to rationally enforce and adjudicate, did not seem to trouble the drafters. Hence, they included provisions that could only be described as bizarre. These included, for example, determining capacity to marry on the part of boys to be based on whether their bodies showed sufficient signs of puberty as determined by jurists. The problem is that jurists identify primarily two signs of male puberty – the onset of wet dreams and the appearance of pubic hair. It is hard to imagine any modern judge using criteria of this sort in order to rule on the capacity of a party to marry.[63]

Internal contradictions and ambiguous terminology also abounded in the draft.[64] Thus, one is left completely unclear as to whether a central feature of Shi'i marriage law – the temporary marriage – is part of the Code or not. On the one hand, no reference is made to its rules, including the requirement of a dower in advance paid to the woman, the specification of a period of time for the marriage, and the absence of a right of the husband to pronounce *ṭalāq*. On the other hand, the Code recites the familiar Shi'i rule that a man may not enter into a "permanent marriage" with anyone but a Muslim woman, thereby implying strongly that there are marriages other than permanent ones permitted by the Code.[65]

Critics pointed out other problematic provisions, in particular those permitting a father to marry off his children at any age and those declaring a female as capable of entering into a marriage contract at the age of nine.[66]

The draft never became law, partly because Najaf's jurists were concerned enough about the atrocious state of the draft to oppose it and partly because, shortly after its introduction, the so-called Islamic State overran the city of Mosul, thereby refocusing national priorities.[67] After the state managed to free Mosul and other Iraqi territories from ISIS, other sporadic efforts were made to amend the Personal Status Code for a period of years, though none advanced as far as the 2014 draft. The repeated cycle of poorly considered draft legislation, almost designed to fail, suggests that the Shi'i Islamists do not have an actual, credible alternative to the existing Personal Status Code. Their continued objections in this sense could be thought of more as a matter of principle to the very idea of uniformity, and subjecting family law to state rather than juristic governance, than any actual attempt to change rules to reflect Shi'i traditional teachings more closely.

Since the end of 2019, around the tenth anniversary of the Arab Spring, the repeal efforts have further abated due to broader popular unrest and dissatisfaction with the current political classes as a whole. The original Arab Spring had failed to ignite the same level of political upheaval in Iraq as it had elsewhere, at least among the Shi'a. With memories still fresh of Ba'ath totalitarianism and the unspeakable repression of Shi'is and Shi'ism, the Shi'i population seemed at that time to be in no mood to threaten a new political order that had established their domination. Ten years later, in a state characterized by rampant corruption, appalling governance, and little by way of legislative accomplishment, Shi'is across Iraq's south clearly felt differently and initiated demonstrations against the ruling elites. Their demands were not merely similar to those of demonstrators in Egypt, Tunisia, Yemen, and elsewhere a decade earlier – they were virtually identical. Al-sha'ab yurīd isqāṭ al-niẓām – the people want the fall of the regime – was the rallying cry, just as it had been in Tahrir Square in Cairo. The intensity and popularity of the demonstrations did not ultimately lead to the type of deep-rooted political change that those leading them had sought, and indeed for the most part the state was able to repress the demonstrators rather than engage them. Nevertheless, the protests were successful enough to lead to the resignation of the prime minister at the time and the promulgation of a new Elections Law designed to blunt the power of the existing political parties whom many Iraqis blame for the current, deplorable state of affairs.[68] Indeed, the 2021 elections resulted in a broad repudiation of the parties most closely associated with the repression of the demonstrators, and the rise of the Sadrist movement. While the Sadrists did not actually take control of the government, due to political machinations that lie beyond the scope of this article to describe, it is fair to note that the broader lesson has been learned. Iraq's legislators have fairly been criticized for seeming out of touch with the demonstrators, and unwilling to truly respond to their concerns. However, none are so out of touch as to think the matter could be addressed, or even ameliorated, by another demagogic deposit of a new draft Personal Status Code inside the tomb of a revered Shi'i holy figure.

Moreover, it bears noting that further evidence that sectarian tensions have eased in deference to broader ones concerning governance lies in Iraq's significant political realignment. Gone, at least for now, are the days when each of the major political groupings were dominated by a single sect or ethnicity. Currently, each of the Shi'i dominated "Coordination Framework" and Sadrist Movement have major, credible Sunni and Kurdish allies, which form core parts of their respective coalitions. There is nothing to be gained by either of them in making the restructuring of personal status law in Iraq a major political priority. This would only work to splinter each coalition along sectarian lines.

As a result, to date, the Personal Status Code remains the law of the land in Iraq, unamended since the fall of the Ba'ath regime in 2003. Indeed, the Code is probably in its least precarious state since 2003.

As a final note, there is an interesting exception to this state of affairs respecting the evolution of the Personal Status Code, applicable only to the Kurdistan Region of Iraq. The constitution's adoption of a federal system of governance resulted in the immediate creation of the autonomous region of Iraqi Kurdistan, entitled to make its own law and indeed to amend or nullify Iraqi law as applied in the region, so long as the law does not impinge on particular, narrow prerogatives of the national sovereign in Baghdad.[69] The Kurdistan Regional Government has used this power broadly in any number of contexts, including the enactment of a far-reaching amendment to the Personal Status Code applicable in the Kurdish region that is, on balance, remarkably progressive.[70] The Kurdistan Code thus comes close to abolishing polygamy entirely, removing the "legitimate interest" language of the Code and replacing it with a series of conditions that include, most significantly, permission of the first wife and the existence of a serious medical condition as determined by a panel of doctors.[71] In similarly unprecedented fashion, the Kurdistan Code permits a mother to act as guardian to her child in permitting the child to marry at an age under eighteen.[72]

With regard to the traditional obligation of the husband to maintain his wife and his wife to obey, the Kurdistan Code attempts modest revisions. For example, it permits the obligation of maintenance to be shared between the parties if the wife agrees and it does not create a burden for her.[73] The Kurdistan Code also generally makes the condition of rebelliousness or disobedience one that could be attributed to a wife or a husband, though significantly, a rebellious husband is one who "flees" the marital home while a rebellious wife is one who "leaves" it.[74]

The Kurdistan Code adopts the familiar Shi'i rule that two witnesses must be present for an out of court divorce to be pronounced by a man, even though Iraq's Kurdish population is overwhelmingly Sunni.[75] A wife divorced by her husband through *ṭalāq* is not obligated to return to her husband during the three month period of the *'idda* unless she so desires, a quite significant change from traditional understandings of the *shari'a* across the major Sunni and Shi'a schools.[76] Finally, a related innovation makes clear that a wife may seek dissolution of the marriage through the process of *khul'* without permission of her husband if a judge is convinced following a mediation process that the wife can no longer live with the husband.[77] This is a significant departure from traditionalist understandings, and it has caused controversy in countries such as Egypt, which has adopted a similar rule.[78] However, this change in the actual text of the Personal Status Code is rather minor. As demonstrated above, a wife may already theoretically seek a judicial dissolution of her marriage if there is "discord" between them, and courts in Iraq's south have made such a dissolution all but impossible to attain. The extent to which the Kurdish courts will actually prove more receptive than the Arab courts to no fault marital dissolutions remains unclear.

5.6   Conclusion

Controversial from its inception, the Personal Status Code is the subject of serious contention along two axes. The first, paralleling the Kurdish-Arab divide, concerns the degree to which the Code should adhere to traditional understandings of the *shari'a*, as opposed to innovating in favor of modern conceptions of women's rights in particular. Quite clearly, the Kurds have moved the Personal Status Code as it applies in their region very much in the direction of innovation and change. Though generally reasonably progressive by regional standards, the Code as applied in Arab-dominated Iraq is considerably more conservative. In theory, and seemingly in principle, it is subject to more pressure from conservative forces than from liberal ones. That said, it is quite helpful to the cause of liberals that Iraqis of various levels of religiosity are currently focused on other things; specifically, a complete overhaul of the state and the near total replacement of its ruling factions who have served Iraq so poorly over the previous two decades. It is also helpful that conservative forces have yet to present a credible alternative to the Code, thereby suggesting that their actual objections to the progressive innovations of the Code are more theoretical than they are real.

The second axis, which reflects the Shi'a-Sunni divide, concerns whether there should be a personal status code at all, with Shi'i Islamist political forces seemingly hostile to the very existence of a uniform code, preferring devolution of the authority to make rules of the family to jurists and clerics. Currently, the political circumstances plainly favor the proponents of the Code, Article 41 of the Constitution notwithstanding. The judiciary has made clear it will not enforce Article 41 absent the enactment of an implementing law, and efforts to achieve wholesale abolition of the Code have to date failed. Moreover, they are unlikely to succeed any time soon, in light of the fact that sectarian tensions have eased, and most focus at this point is on the appalling governance problems that exist in Iraq. In the longer term, it is hard to believe that the divisions that have long defined Iraq will not result in further episodes of significant instability. It seems inevitable that debates over the substantive provisions of the Personal Status Code, or indeed whether there should be one at all, will at some point in the future reemerge.

Notes

1 The Personal Status Code of Iraq, No. 188 of 1959, enacted December 30, 1959.

2 Law of the *Shari'a* Courts (not numbered), issued by King Feysal I, June 30, 1923.

3 Law of the *Shari'a* Courts, Arts. 6–7 (requiring formal reference to established scholars when the judge hearing the case is not of the sect of the litigating parties).

4 K. Stilt, "Islamic Law and the Making and Remaking of the Iraqi Legal System" (2004) 36 *George Washington International Law Review*, 748–749.

5 M. Farouk-Sluglett and P. Sluglett, *Iraq Since 1958: From Revolution to Dictatorship* (Palgrave Macmillan Press, 2003), pp. 49–50.

6 Qasim was sympathetic to the Iraq Communist Party and certainly regarded the Communists as allies in his earliest years. Y. Nakash, *The Shi'is of Iraq*, 2nd ed. (Princeton University Press, 2003), p. 135.

7 For example, Article 91(2) of the Code permits a daughter in the absence of sons to inherit the residue of an estate, precisely as the son would, rather than take one-half of the estate and have the balance devolve to the nearest male agnate, usually the brother of the decedent. This resembles more closely the Shi'i rule than the Sunni.

8 Respecting the temporary marriage, see H. A. Hamoudi, "Sex and the Shari'a: Defining Gender Norms and Sexual Deviancy in Shi'i Islam" (2015) 39 *Fordham International Law Journal*, 41–45.

9 Personal Status Code, Art. 17; cf. Minhal al-Saliheen, 3:¶205 (indicating that as a matter of obligatory precaution, a Muslim man may not permanently marry anyone but a Muslim woman).

10 Personal Status Code, Art. 6(1)(d).

11 "Sex and the Shari'a," pp. 91–92 (respecting Shi'i rules); K. Ali, *Marriage and Slavery in Early Islam* (Harvard University Press, 2014), p. 31 (respecting Sunni rules).

12 Personal Status Code, Art. 8 (original text). In addition, as per original Article 9, minors as young as fifteen marry with the permission of both the court and their father.

13 Article 1(2) of the Personal Status Code indicates that "where there is no legislative provision which may be implemented, the principles of the *shari'a* most in accordance with the provisions of this law shall be applied."

14 Iraq Court of Cassation, *Shari'a* Panel, Case 520/1963, decided December 26, 1963.

15 Personal Status Code, Art. 9 (as amended).

16 H. Hamoudi, "Decolonizing the Legal Centralist Mind: Legal Pluralism and the Rule of Law," in *The International Rule of Law Movement: A Crisis of Legitimacy and the Way Forward* (Harvard University Press, 2014) pp. 149–150.

17 Personal Status Code, Art. 10(5) (as amended).

18 UNICEF, The State of the World's Children 2016, www.unicef.org/publications/files/UNICEF_SOWC_2016.pdf, p. 151.

19 J. Tucker, *Women, Family and Gender in Islamic Law* (Cambridge University Press, 2008), pp. 56–57.

20 Personal Status Code, Art. 3.

21 Personal Status Code, Art. 4.

22 Personal Status Code, Art. 3(7), added to the Personal Status Code as Law 189 of 1980, the Sixth Amendment to the Personal Status Code.

23 Federal Court of Cassation, First Personal Status Panel, Case 2076/2010, decided April 22, 2010.

24 Federal Court of Cassation, First Personal Status Panel, Case 2289/2010, decided March 4, 2010.

25 Personal Status Court of Hay Al-Sha'ab, decided August 5, 2009.

26 Personal Status Code, Arts. 24–25 (original text).

27 Iraq Court of Cassation, *Shari'a* Panel, Case 527/1969, decided June 29, 1969.

28 Fourth Amendment to the Personal Status Code, No. 57 of 1980, Art. 1.

29 Federal Court of Cassation, First Personal Status Panel, Case 2964/2010, decided November 7, 2010.

30 Iraq Court of Cassation, *Shari'a* Panel, Case 539/1968, decided October 3, 1968.

31 Personal Status Code, Art. 25(2)(b) (as amended).
32 See, e.g., Iraq Court of Cassation, *Shari'a* Panel, Case 708/1968, decided November 24, 1968 (applying Shi'i rule to Shi'i husband seeking a divorce without witnesses); Personal Status Court of Hayy al-Sha'ab, decided September 14, 2009 (applying Shi'i rule to Shi'i husband seeking to divorce just after his wife's giving birth); Personal Status Court of Baya' (Sitting in Cassation), Case 5145/186, decided January 14, 2009 (applying Sunni rule to Sunni husband seeking a divorce without witnesses).
33 Personal Status Code, Art. 34.
34 Federal Court of Cassation, Personal Status Panel I, Case 3888/2010, decided November 2, 2010.
35 Personal Status Code, Art. 37(2).
36 Iraq Court of Cassation, *Shari'a* Panel, Case 385/1968, decided August 22, 1968.
37 C. Lombardi, *State Law as Islamic Law in Modern Egypt: The Incorporation of the Shari'a into Egyptian Constitutional Law* (Brill, 2006), p. 170.
38 Personal Status Code, Art. 39(3) (as amended by Article 1 of Law 51 of 1985).
39 Iraq Court of Cassation, Personal Status I Panel, Case 899/2011.
40 Law of the Right of the Divorced Wife to Housing, No. 77 of 1983.
41 This is a common practice in modern Islamic states. See, e.g., Lombardi, *State Law as Islamic Law*, pp. 81–82 (describing process in Egypt).
42 Personal Status Code, Art. 43(1)(7)–(9).
43 Personal Status Code, Art. 43(1)–(2)(as amended).
44 Personal Status Code, Art. 40 (original text).
45 Federal Court of Cassation, Personal Status I Panel, Case 4765/2011, decided September 25, 2011.
46 Personal Status Court of Kadhmiyya, Case 2601/2001, decided September 5, 2001.
47 Personal Status Code, Art. 40(5) (as amended).
48 Personal Status Code, Art. 41.
49 Federal Court of Cassation, Personal Status Court I, Case 3356/2011.
50 Personal Status Code, Art. 57(1), (4) (original text).
51 Personal Status Code, Art. 57(2) (original text).
52 Personal Status Code, Art. 57(4) (as amended by Law No. 21 of 1978).
53 Personal Status Code, Art. 57(5) (as amended by Law No. 21 of 1978).
54 Personal Status Code, Art. 57(2) (as amended by Law No. 106 of 1987).
55 A. Kubaisi, *Personal Status in the Fiqh, the Courts and the Law*, vol. 1, rev. ed. (Legal Bookstore, 2007), pp. 110–115.
56 M. Bahr Al-Ulum, *Shedding Light on the Iraqi Personal Status Code* (Nu'man, 1963).
57 Stilt, "Making and Remaking," 700–701.
58 Stilt, "Making and Remaking," 710.
59 L. Diamond, *Squandered Victory: The American Occupation and the Bungled Effort to Bring Democracy to Iraq* (Owl Books, 2005), p. 172.
60 Constitution, Art. 41.
61 A. S. Deeks and M. D. Burton, "Iraq's Constitution: A Drafting History" (2007) 40 *Cornell International Law Journal*, 21–23.
62 Federal Supreme Court of Iraq, Decision 59 of 2011.
63 Draft Ja'fari Personal Status Code of 2014, Art. 16(1).

64 H. A. Hamoudi, "The Political Codification of Islamic Law" (2016) 33 *Arizona Journal of International & Comparative Law*, 340–341.

65 Draft Ja'fari Personal Status Code, Art. 63.

66 Draft Ja'fari Personal Status Code, Arts. 16, 50–51.

67 Hamoudi, "The Political Codification of Islamic Law," pp. 342–343.

68 F. Hassan and A. Rubin, "Iraq's New Election Law Draws Much Criticism and Few Cheers," *New York Times* (December 24, 2019).

69 H. A. Hamoudi, "Notes in Defense of the Iraq Constitution" (2012) 33 *University of Pennsylvania Journal of International Law*, 1126–1129.

70 Law No. 15 of 2008 (Kurdistan), The Amendment of the Implementation of the Personal Status Code, No. 188 of 1959 in the Region of Kurdistan (hereinafter "Kurdistan Personal Status Code Amendment.")

71 Personal Status Code, Art. 3(2), as amended by Article 1 of the Kurdistan Personal Status Code Amendment.

72 Personal Status Code, Art. 7, as amended by Article 4 of the Kurdistan Personal Status Code Amendment.

73 Personal Status Code, Art. 23, as amended by Article 8 of the Kurdistan Personal Status Code Amendment.

74 Personal Status Code, Art. 25(1), as amended by Article 10(1) of the Kurdistan Personal Status Code Amendment.

75 Personal Status Code, Art. 34, as amended by Article 13 of the Kurdistan Personal Status Code Amendment.

76 Personal Status Code, Art. 38, as amended by Article 16 of the Kurdistan Personal Status Code Amendment.

77 Personal Status Code, Art. 46, as amended by Article 21 of the Kurdistan Personal Status Code Amendment.

78 Y. Sezgin, "Women's Rights in the Triangle of State, Law and Religion: A Comparison of Egypt and India" (2011) 25 *Emory International Law Review* 1020–1022.

The Status of Muslim Women in the Mosaic of Islamic Family Law in Lebanon

NADA AMMAR

6.1 Introduction: Brief Overview of the Lebanese Legal System

Lebanon is a republic, a parliamentary democracy, and a multi-confessional country that hides behind the image of a unique modern state and is based on a precarious sectarian foundation. Praised by some as a "political remedy" and deplored by others as a "social malady" as Max Weiss rightfully terms,[1] it is uncontestable that sectarianism defined both Lebanon's political life and social identity. To understand the nature of family law in Lebanon and its impact on the status of women, it is necessary to draw the political culture in which it has emerged.

After ending an era of "relative autonomy"[2] under Ottoman rule, Lebanon became a French Mandate from 1920 to 1943. Apart from the adoption of its first Constitution in 1926, the most significant event that followed was Lebanon's independence in 1943.[3] Lebanon's political life was marked by a "special nature"[4] stemming from the diversity of its confessional groups and leading to a structure of power sharing between the major religious communities.

The institutionalization of religious groups as political entities expanded to other areas like the family law system. Personal status matters remain under the domain of religious laws and are regulated by different codes. By the same logic, there exists no common jurisdiction ruling on family law matters, which are adjudicated by each sect's own religious courts.

6.2 The Genesis of Islamic Family Law

6.2.1 Sources of Law

Certain authors consider that the administration of personal status law in Lebanon derives from the millet system that prevailed under Ottoman rule,[5] while others deny direct causality.[6] The legal pluralism in family law finds its roots in the Lebanese Constitution.[7] It is through legislative Decree N 60 L/R (March 13, 1936) that the mandatory authorities began organizing the personal status law system. The Decree conferred to the recognized religious denominations in Lebanon the right to administer their own affairs and the exclusive prerogative to act as legislators and pass judgments in respect of issues of personal status.[8] The Decree officially recognized seventeen religious communities: eleven Christian denominations, five Muslims denominations, and one Jewish denomination.

In Lebanon, the main Islamic sects are the Sunnis and Shi'as, with Druzes, Alawite, and Ismailis as minorities. Although Lebanon is not a Muslim state, *Shari'a* as a source of law is manifested in family law for Muslim communities.

Adherents of the Sunni and Shi'a denominations are subject to the 1962 Judiciary Act regulating the Sunni and Jaafaree judiciaries and the 1917 Ottoman Family Rights Law (Ottoman PSC), which is still in force for the Sunnis, and in certain instances for the Shi'as as long as it does not contradict with the Jaafaree school. For matters not provided for in these two laws, the provisions of the Hanafee School for Sunnis and the Jaafaree School for Shi'as apply.[9] The *Shari'a* courts decide questions of marriage, divorce, custody, and inheritance.

The Druze community has a distinct personal status code promulgated on February 24, 1948 (Druze PSC). Article 171 of the said law stipulates: "for all matters falling under the jurisdiction of the *madhab* judge and not explicitly provided for in this law, the judge shall refer to *Shari'a* Law according to the Hanafee School." The law of March 5, 1960, regulates the Druze judiciary, which is composed of courts of first instance and a higher court of appeal.

6.2.2   Gender and the Law

In the midst of this highly pluralized system, the status of women in Lebanon, albeit advanced when compared to other Arab countries, still suffers from an important setback. The lack of a unified secular personal status code violates the principle of equality before the law.[10] Concomitantly, the religious courts are generally headed by men, which can hinder a woman's ability to assert equal marriage rights and break patriarchal norms. Although under the French Mandate, the legal status of women was upgraded when equal civil and political rights were granted for all Lebanese citizens in the 1926 Constitution,[11] gender equality was and is far from being realized. While it could be asserted that deeply rooted patriarchal stereotypes and customs rather than Islamic principles affect the status of women, one cannot negate that gendered interpretations still transpire on different levels. Even if the Ottoman Family Rights Law altered certain aspects of the *Shari'a*, this law has codified selected rules from the dominant Sunni legal schools.[12] Thus, the protection and rights conferred by *Shari'a* teachings, although greater than customary laws from a historic standpoint, are not likely to be equal to those conferred by a secular civil law.[13]

The difference between equality and sameness of rights for men and women in Islam, while crucial to understanding the status of women is beyond the scope of our discussion. We will be focusing below on the salient issues where the codes play in disfavor of women across the different Muslim sects: (1) marriageable age, (2) matrimonial guardianship, (3) obedience, (4) divorce, and (5) custody.

6.2.3 Age of Marriage and Matrimonial Guardianship

With regard to legal capacity for marriage, different provisions exist for the Sunnis, Shi'as and Druzes.[14] While the scope of judicial discretion on the basis of puberty and the *wali'* (guardian) permission varies among the sects,[15] they all converge in that marriageable age for women remains younger than that of men. The following table[16] illustrates the marriageable age across the different Muslim sects.

Religious community	Required age of marriage		Alternative age of marriage		Permission given by	Articles of law
	Female	Male	Female	Male		
Sunni	17	18	9 (provided she reaches puberty)	17	Religious judge	4, 5, 6
Shia	Puberty		9	15	Religious judge	Jaafaree school
Druze	17	18	15	16	Religious judge	1, 2, 3

Article 35 of the Ottoman PSC and Article 14 of the Druze PSC provide that consent by both parties is sufficient to validate a marriage contract. For the consent to be valid, the person must have the capacity to consent and the consent must be unconditional.

The right of a woman to contract her own marriage is mostly affected by the issue of matrimonial guardianship. In Lebanon, a Muslim woman needs a *wali* to contract the marriage on her behalf. He is typically the woman's father or, if deceased, paternal grandfather or uncle. Islamic Sunni sects differentiate between a minor female and male. According to the Sunni Sect, a minor male does not need his guardian's consent but must obtain a judge's permission to marry. The judge is more likely to give his permission if the minor male reached puberty and can afford to marry.[17] Pursuant to Article 7 of the Ottoman PSC, under no circumstances may a minor male under seventeen years of age and a girl under the age of nine be married.[18]

For the Druze, according to Article 5 of the 1948 PSC, "it shall not be permitted in principle for any person to give in marriage a minor boy who has not reached sixteen years or a minor girl who has not reached fifteen years of age."[19] Further, for the Sunni sect, the minor girl may marry between the ages of nine and seventeen by court permission and the consent of her *wali*, so long as she has reached puberty and is physically able to perform the obligations of marriage.[20] It should be noted that despite this provision, it is no longer customary to marry a girl at nine years old.

The code allows a pubescent woman who is over seventeen years old to make a marriage request, upon which the judge informs the *wali*, and if the latter does not object or where the objection is frivolous and unfounded, the judge could act as her guardian and is allowed to approve the marriage on her behalf.[21]

In the case of marriage concluded by a legally capable woman on her own accord without the consent of her guardian, the marriage is valid. The *wali*, however, has the right to demand judicial annulment provided that the pubescent women is not pregnant and married a person considered not of equal socioeconomic status.[22] This right granted to the *wali* to demand judicial annulment raises the question of why women are subject to a *wali* requirement, while men are not.[23] Not only does the *wali* requirement jeopardize the right of a woman to contract their own marriage, but a misuse of such powers could also block a marriage forever.[24]

The Jaafaree sect makes no distinction between female or male minors, who both need the consent of their guardian and judicial approval to enter into a marriage contract. In the instance where the guardian refuses to grant the consent for whatever reason, the judge is not entitled to proceed with the marriage on his or her behalf regardless of the grounds of refusal.[25]

Guardianship with the right of compulsion (*Ijbar*) was a common practice among the Sunni sect, which used to follow the precepts of the Hanafee doctrine. Nonetheless, such practice came to an end with the promulgation of the Family Rights Law of 1917,[26] which limited the right of compulsion to the marriage of "insane" male or female in case of extreme necessity and upon the judge's approval.[27] According to the Jaafaree view, the guardian could force the minor to marry regardless of their consent. Upon reaching majority, however, the minor may either affirm the marriage or disaffirm it and seek dissolution.[28] Compulsory marriages are no longer customary. For the Druze sect, a guardian's approval and consent of a religious judge are also required until the age of twenty-one.[29]

The case of coercion merits mention. If coercion is exercised in a manner that vitiates a person's will, the consent will be invalidated. Marriage contracted under coercion, is automatically void.[30] Seduction does not automatically nullify the marriage but grants the wife or her *wali* the opportunity to seek an annulment.

The Islamic precepts governing the Sunni sect provide that where the parity in the husband's social condition was explicitly provided for in the marriage contract or where the husband misrepresented himself as having a certain social rank, and evidence was later found showing the falsity of such representation, the wife or her *wali* may request annulment.[31] The same rules apply to the Jaafaree and Druze sect.[32] Such practice has become uncommon.

6.2.4   Marital Authority: Duty of Obedience (Ta'ah)

Maintenance and obedience are regulated by customary law. Pursuant to Islamic *Shari'a*, the husband is regarded as the head of the family. However, today's economic realities depart from this traditional patriarchal stereotype. Article 73 of the Ottoman PSC provides that a wife must obey her husband in all lawful matters, and a husband must treat his wife with respect.[33] Article 70 states that the husband shall provide his wife with housing of his choice, as well as with all the necessities.[34] This means that a married woman is considered legally residing in the husband's place of residence. Thus, the husband is responsible for financially maintaining his wife.

If the wife is disobedient, her maintenance shall be forfeited.[35] The Jaafaree view provides that a "wife shall be proven to be recalcitrant, if she refuses to obey her husband and leaves his house without his permission. Her recalcitrance established, the obligation to support her financially becomes null and void."[36] However, the prevailing stance of *the Shari'a* court is that a wife's refusal to obey her husband does not mean that she is disobedient and thus forfeits her rights to financial support.[37] In contrast and still according to the Jaafaree view, if "a husband … does not give his wife adequate maintenance … and if her remaining in his house is a cause of anguish and distress, she has the right to leave his house and return to the house of her family or others."[38]

Article 28 of the Druze PSC reads that "maintenance shall include food, clothing, housing; medical treatment and domestic services for the wife based on her social status, infirmity or sickness. This obligation is due by virtue of the mutual consent or agreement of the parties or by a court decision."[39] A disobedient wife also forfeits her right to maintenance.[40]

6.2.5 Polygamy

Polygamy in Lebanon is not outlawed. A man can marry up to four wives at the same time with the classical condition to treat the wives equally.[41] While the background and historic context in which the verse allowing polygamy was revealed is beyond the scope of this study, it is irrefutable that this practice is discriminatory against women and reveals that equality between women and men has not yet been actualized. Article 74 of the Ottoman PSC reiterates this tenet.[42] Article 38 of the Ottoman PSC merits special attention. This article expressly recognizes the validity of a condition in the contract restricting the husband's right to marry polygynously.[43] This departs from the traditional Hanafee view that considers the condition prohibiting the husband from taking another wife null and void because it infringes upon a legitimate right of the husband.[44] In fact, if the condition is not honored, either the wife or the new co-wife is considered divorced.[45]

With regard to the Jaafaree sect, two sets of conditions exist. Legal conditions which do not contradict with *Shari'a* can be stipulated in a marriage contract and are binding upon each spouse. Prohibited conditions contradicting with the *Shari'a* will be declared void by the competent judge, and the contract will survive the condition and remain fully valid.[46] Among those conditions, one that retains our attention is the one where the wife conditionally agrees to marry based on her husband's agreement not to marry a second wife. While the principle of contractual freedom is manifested by allowing marriage contract stipulations, limitation to such freedom seems to be detrimental to women. It is important to note that the Druze Personal Status Law Article 10 prohibits polygamy.[47]

6.2.6   Divorce

While Muslim women do not have an unfettered right of divorce equal to that of men, they can still have access to divorce either by stipulating such right as a condition in the marriage contract or by seeking judicial dissolution based on certain grounds. There are two categories of divorce under the *Shari'a* – revocable and irrevocable divorce. Men may divorce either verbally or by usages denoting unequivocal intention to end the marital relationship.[48] Repudiation becomes absolutely irrevocable after reiterating it three times.[49]

Two major differences exist between Shia's and Sunnis. While Sunnis recognize contingent repudiation subject to a condition or relegated to some event in the future,[50] the Shi'a sect requires that repudiation be unconditional.[51] Further, the Shi'a requires two male witnesses to be present for the repudiation to be valid. Conversely, Sunni doctrine does not require such evidence.[52] Another discriminatory aspect derives from the fact that when the husband decides to revoke his repudiation, he retains the right to take back his wife without her consent within the waiting period.[53]

While a husband can divorce at will, the wife needs to have grounds for divorce. A wife may seek judicial divorce in the following situations: the "husband's failure to consummate the marriage; the husband's affliction making cohabitation without harm impossible; husband's insanity; husband's failure to maintain and concealment of his whereabouts, or his absence, disappearance, or intermittent cohabitation with his wife."[54] In the Sunni denomination, a woman can request dissolution of the marriage by decree of a judge as a result of damage resulting from discord or ill-treatment such as cruelty, insult, or coercion to commit religiously prohibited acts, and after failure of the reconciliation efforts.[55]

The 1962 Judiciary Act introduced the concept of marriage concili-
ation as a method of family conflict resolution.[56] Shi'as do not recognize
the woman's right to request divorce by court, but the *Shari'a* courts
accept marriage contracts in which the woman has reserved her right to
divorce.[57] For the Druze sect, divorce can only be effected by the court[58]
and should be pronounced by the *madhab* judge. Thus, repudiation is
not possible. Further, in the absence of legal justification for divorce, the
judge could award the wife damages taking into consideration any moral
and physical harm she may have suffered.[59] Financial compensation for
harm inflicted is not available for Sunni and Shi'a women. A wife may
request separation in certain cases, and dissolution of marriage by mutual
consent is allowed provided it is declared in the presence of two witnesses
before a judge.[60]

6.2.7   Custody and Guardianship

In the case of divorce, women's custody rights over her children vary
among the different sects. For the Druze sect, her custody rights end at
the age of seven for boys and nine for girls. The Sunni sect amended the
age of custody to twelve for both genders.[61] For the Shi'as, the custody
period lasts until the age of two for boys and seven for girls, unless the
mother remarries subject to the child's best interest.

The Druze community has introduced a bill in which the custody of
the mother is renewed every two years, and until the age of eighteen.[62]
The Sunni sect had submitted a bill establishing the age of custody to the
mother at fifteen for girls and thirteen for boys.[63] No such steps have
been taken by the Shi'a sect. Even where the mother has custody, the
father retains guardianship over the minor and his assets. Obligations of
maintenance are undertaken exclusively by the father or, by default, the
next person given the legal status of guardian in the agnatic line. Thus,
the mother has no parental authority over the child. Guardianship can be
transferred to a woman only in the Druze sect.[64]

Although things seem to evolve gradually on a case-by-case basis, the
religious authorities appear to be slowly moving forward. Precedents
have emerged ruling on issues of compensation in case of divorce and
the need of reevaluation of the dower, *mahr mua'khar* in Sunni and
Druze communities.[65] Two bills have also been introduced on the question of the age of the children in the custody of their mothers and the
amount and the evaluation criteria in case of compensation due to the
dissolution.[66]

6.3   Secular vs. Religious

6.3.1   Dual Legal System

In certain instances, the civil and religious systems intertwine, leading some authors to talk about a "dual legal system."[67] The duality is mostly witnessed in marriage formalities, the judicial oversight exercised over religious courts, and in the case of civil marriage contracted abroad. Marriage registration is a requirement regulated by both the Family Rights Law and the 1962 Judiciary Act. The *Shari'a* Court, having jurisdiction over the domicile of either spouse, has sole and exclusive competence to solemnize marriage contracts for Muslims.[68] As for the Druze sect, according to Article 16 of the Druze Personal Status Law, in order for a marriage contract to be valid it must be solemnized by the Druze religious chief Cheikh Aql or a judge or their duly delegated deputies.[69]

Another law of December 7, 1951,[70] governs registration of civil status acts such as marriage before the civil registry. All Lebanese regardless of their religious sects are subject to this law. Under Article 22, a person must submit a marriage certificate signed by the religious court, a local government executive (*mokhtar*), and by two witnesses to the Personal Status Affairs office in the area of his residence within a month from the date of his marriage.[71] Further, the *Shari'a* courts are subject to judicial oversight from the Court of Cassation.[72] However, this oversight is limited to the issue of jurisdictional conflict between the courts or violation of public order without monitoring the legality of their decisions.[73]

Interestingly, Lebanese law[74] recognizes civil marriages contracted abroad. The Lebanese civil judiciary has authority to decide disputes arising from such marriages according to the foreign law under which the marriage was contracted.

6.3.2   Attempted Reforms

As Chibli Mallat has noted, Lebanon has been living in a "legislative lull" as matters of family law and personal status have remained unmodified for several decades.[75] As things stand, marriage in Lebanon still must be contracted by a religious official or via a religious contract. Several attempts to reform personal status laws and enact a unified civil personal status code have been made over the span of the years to no avail. Under the French Mandate, a decree on April 28, 1936, aiming at limiting the judicial competence of religious courts to marriage proceedings was repealed due to fierce objections.[76] Debates on the need for reforms arose again in the 1950s, 1960s, and 1970s, all of which were unsuccessful.[77]

In 1998, President Elias Hrawi proposed an optional civil marriage bill in order to remedy complications arising out of interfaith marriages and the multiplicity of laws. The draft bill was endorsed in the cabinet but was not delivered to parliament for ratification. Albeit voluntary, the shelved bill would have reinstated gender equalities when it comes to marriage and its effects.[78] Nadia El Cheikh explained that the reasons behind such vocal objection can be traced to a few provisions contradicting the precepts of *Shari'a*. The draft bill implicitly permitted Muslim women to marry a non-Muslim.[79] Article 9 of the bill outlawed polygamy by stating that it is prohibited to contract a marriage between two parties, if one of them is already bound by a marriage.[80] Furthermore, Article 25 establishes gender equality in divorce by conferring equal rights to women and men in initiating divorce.[81] It also disregards certain impediments to marriage by allowing marriage between two persons connected through the relationship of suckling (*rida'ah*).[82]

Opposition was also raised with regard to Article 34, which provides that a woman could remarry only 300 days after the nullification of the previous marriage, contravening the three-month waiting period (*iddah*) as defined by *Shari'a*.[83] Another article recognizes the principle of adoption which contravenes the *Shari'a*.[84] An interesting feature is that although the marriageable age was modified, it was still set as different ages by gender – eighteen for males and sixteen for females.

Again, in 2007 and 2009,[85] the debate over an optional civil personal status code was revived. Other draft civil personal status code proposals in 2009 and 2011[86] with minor changes were considered but were not adopted by the parliament.

In February 2013, a Justice Ministry committee ruled that a civil marriage contracted in Lebanon was legal[87] after a couple disregarded religious marriage formalities. The couple crossed off their religious affiliation from their identification and used a loophole in the 1936 Legislative Decree that makes reference to civil unions. The Decree required that another law be made for those opting to remain outside religious institutions' authority as long as it does not conflict with laws of public order.[88] In such instance, Articles 10[89] and 17 of the said law stipulate that those not affiliated with a sect shall be subject to civil law.[90] Accordingly, those articles that put citizens not belonging to any sect under civil law, should be activated.

In 2014, the Ministry of Justice drafted a bill to regulate optional civil marriage. It would have required amending several articles. No law was promulgated.[91] The attempts to reform family law have continued to be obstructed, because in Lebanon the structure and regulation of family matters has always been identified as the aegis of Islamic law.[92] Stripping religious authorities from their control over matters of personal status and putting an end to the sectarian culture, albeit challenged, is not likely to be successful in the near future. The debate over civil marriage in Lebanon was brought up again in 2022, but to date no legislative changes have been formally introduced.

6.4   Conclusion

In conclusion, the adoption of a secular civil family law is not likely to be actualized, although it would be ideal. Thus, another avenue would be for Lebanese Muslim feminists to call for the reading and rethinking of Islamic Family law from an egalitarian viewpoint reflecting the true essence of Islamic principles. Calling for new exegesis and "engaging in creative *ijtihad* [reasoning] could very well reform and renew the position of Islam on the issue of the status of women."[93] As Moroccan feminist Fatema Mernissi writes: "if the women's rights are often a problem for some modern Muslim men, it is neither because of the Qur'an ... nor Islamic tradition but simply because those rights conflict with the interests of a male elite ... not only to have the sacred texts always been manipulated, but the manipulation of them is a structural characteristic of the practice of power."[94]

Notes

1 Max Weiss, *In the Shadow of Sectarianism: Law, Shi'ism and the Making of Modern of Lebanon* (Harvard University Press, 2010), p. 2.
2 Abdullahi A. An Na'im, *Islamic Family Law in a Changing World: A Global Resource Book*, 4 vols. (Zed Books, 2002), vol. II, p. 126.
3 Farid El Khazen, "The Communal Pact of National Identities: The Making and Politics of the 1943 National Pact," Centre for Lebanese Studies (Oxford, October 1991), p. 3.
4 Maurus Reinkowski, *Ottoman "Multiculturalism"? The Example of the Confessional System in Lebanon* (Orient Institute of the Deutsche Morgenlandische Gesellschaft, 1997), p. 5 https://freidok.uni-freiburg.de/fedora/objects/freidok:4403/datastreams/FILE1/content.
5 Weiss, *In the Shadow of Sectarianism*, p. 98.
6 See Reinkowski, *Ottoman "Multiculturalism"?*

7 Lebanese Constitution Article 9.

8 "Third Periodic Report of State Parties: Lebanon" (New York, UN Committee on the Elimination of Discrimination Against Women, July 7, 2006),

9 1962 Judiciary Act Article 242.

10 S. Kelly and J. Breslin (eds.), *Woman's Rights in the Middle East and North Africa: Progress amid Tesistance* (Freedom House, 2010), p. 249.

11 Constitution Article 7.

12 S. Jeppie, E. Moosa, and Richard L. Roberts, *Muslim Family Law in Sub Saharan Africa and Post-colonial challenges* (Amsterdam University Press, 2010).

13 Adrien K. Wing, "Custom, Religion and Rights: The Future Legal Status of Palestinian Woman" (1994) 35 *Harvard International Law Journal*, 149.

14 Jamal J. Nasir, *The Islamic Law of Personal Status*, Arab and Islamic Laws Series, 3rd ed. (Kluwer Law International, 2001), vol. 23, p. 50.

15 Abdullahi A An-Nai'im, *Islamic Family Law in a Changing World: A Global Resource Book* (Zed Books, 2002), vol. 2, p. 127.

16 Antoine Elias El Gemayel, "The Lebanese Legal System" (International Law Institute in cooperation with Georgetown University, 1985), vol. I.

17 Nasir, *The Islamic Law of Personal Status*, p. 54.

18 The texts of the articles can be found at Maher Mahmassani and Ibtissam Messara, *Statut personnel: textes en vigueur au Liban*, Documents Huvelin, FDSP (Beyrouth-Liban, 1971) (in French).

19 D. El Alami and D. Hinchcliffe, *Islamic Marriage and Divorce Laws of the Arab World* (Kluwer Law International, 1996), p. 172.

20 Ottoman PSC Article 6.

21 Ottoman PSC Article 8.

22 Ottoman PSC Article 47 and Article 50. Ottoman PSC Article 45 defines the characteristics for finding a husband eligible (fit) such as equal social status in terms of financial means, and occupation.

23 Aziza Alhibri, "Islam, Law and Custom: Redefining Muslim Women's Rights" (1997) 12 *American University Journal of International Law and Policy*, 1.

24 Alhibri, "Islam, Law and Custom."

25 Nasir, *The Islamic Law of Personal Status*, p. 55.

26 El Gemayel, "The Lebanese Legal System" (International Law Institute in cooperation with Georgetown University, 1985), vol. I, p. 279.

27 Ottoman PSC Article 9.

28 El Gemayel, *The Lebanese Legal System*, p. 279.

29 Druze PSC Article 6; El Gemayel, *The Lebanese Legal System*, p. 280.

30 Ottoman PSC Article 57. The text of Article 57 does not explicitly exclude the guardian's right of compulsion, but such meaning can be inferred.

31 Ottoman PSC Article 48; El Gemayel, *Lebanese Legal System*, p. 276.

32 El Gemayel, *Lebanese Legal System*, p. 276.

33 Ottoman PSC Article 73.

34 Ottoman PSC Article 70.

35 Ottoman PSC Article 101.

36 "Third Periodic State Report," p. 85 referring to Jaafaree Legal Manual Article 310 (1994).

37 "Third Periodic State Report," p. 90; Decisions of Tyre *Shari'a* Court, judgement 259, record 11 (February 9, 2000) and of the Supreme Ja'fari *Shari'a* Court, judgement 59/466, record 116 (June 18, 2002).

38 "Third Periodic State Report," p. 90; Jaafaree Legal Manual Article 313.

39 See Article 28 in Mahmassani and Messara, *Statut personnel: textes en vigueur au Liban*, p. 94.

40 Druze PSC Article 36.

41 An Naim, *Islamic Family Law in a Changing World*, p. 128.

42 Ottoman PSC Article 74.

43 An Naim, *Islamic Family Law in a Changing World*, p. 128; Ottoman PSC Article 38.

44 Alhibri, *Islam, Law and Custom*, p. 23.

45 Ottoman PSC Article 38.

46 El Gemayel, *Lebanese Legal System*, p. 277.

47 Druze PSC Article 10.

48 Ottoman PSC Article 109.

49 Ottoman PSC Article 115.

50 Ottoman PSC Articles 106 and 107.

51 Nasir, *The Islamic Law of Personal Status*, p. 109.

52 Nasir, *The Islamic Law of Personal Status*, p. 109.

53 Ottoman PSC Article 113.

54 An-Naim, *Islamic Family Law*, p. 128; Ottoman PSC Articles 119–129.

55 1962 Judiciary Act Articles 337–345 cover the rules related to the reconciliation process in divorce proceedings. Ottoman PSC Articles 130–132 are the equivalent.

56 1962 Judiciary Act.

57 Nasir, *The Islamic Law of Personal Status*, p. 119.

58 Druze PSC Article 37.

59 Druze PSC Article 49.

60 Druze PSC Article 42.

61 Article 15 of Decision no. 46, issued by the Higher Islamic Shariah Council on October 1, 2011, pursuant to Law no. 177 (August 29, 2011); See UN Committee on the Elimination of Discrimination Against Women (CEDAW), "Consideration of Reports Submitted by States Parties under Article 18 of the Convention, Fourth and Fifth Periodic Reports of States Parties Due in 2014," p. 115, Lebanon, May 15, 2014, CEDAW/C/LBN/4-5, www.refworld.org/docid/564edad14.html.

62 Alexa Hechaime, "Actualites du Statut personnel des communautes Musulmanes au Liban, Droit et Cultures," http://droitcultures.revues.org/1992.

63 Hechaime, "Actualites du Statut personnel des communautes Musulmanes au Liban."

64 Druze PSC Articles 67 and 70.

65 For details, see Nasir, *The Islamic Law of Personal Status*.

66 Nasir, *The Islamic Law of Personal Status*.

67 Weiss, *In the Shadow of Sectarianism*, p. 159.

68 Ottoman PSC Article 37.

69 Nasir, *The Islamic law of Personal Status*, p. 71.

70 The law was modified in 1954 and 1956. It governs registration of civil status acts such as birth certificates and death certificates.

71 George Dib, *Law and Population in Lebanon* (Law and Population Programme, 1975).

72 The Cassation Court is the highest civil court in the judicial system that reviews civil and criminal cases.

73 UNDP, "Lebanon National Development Report: Towards a Citizen State," Lebanon 2008–2009.

74 Lebanon Code of Civil Procedure Article 79.

75 Jane O. Connors and Chibli Mallat, *Islamic Family Law*, Arab and Islamic Laws Series, Centre of Islamic & Middle East Law (CIMEL) (School of Oriental and African Studies, 1990), p. 1.

76 Nadia M. El Cheikh, "The 1998 Proposed Civil Marriage Law in Lebanon: The Reaction of Muslim Communities" (1998–1999) 5 *Yearbook of Islamic Studies & Middle East Law*, 148.

77 Sherifa Zuhur, "Empowering Women or Dislodging Sectarianism: Civil Marriage in Lebanon" (2002) 14 *Yale Journal of Law & Feminism* 177, 185.

78 Zuhur, "Empowering Women or Dislodging Sectarianism."

79 El Cheikh, "The 1998 Proposed Civil Marriage Law in Lebanon."

80 Civil Marriage Proposal Draft bill Article 9. The text of the 1998 draft bill can be found at www.civilmarriagelebanon.com/CivilMarriage98Proposal.pdf.

81 Draft bill Article 25.

82 Draft bill Article 10.

83 Draft bill Article 10.

84 Draft bill Article 10.

85 Sanja Kelly and Juslin Breslin (eds.), *Woman's Rights in the Middle East and North Africa* (Freedom House, 2010).

86 Texts of the draft optional civil laws can be found in Arabic at www.civil-marriage-lebanon.com.

87 Retrieved from www.dailystar.com.lb/News/Politics/2013/Feb-15/206602-charbel-urged-to-approve-lebanon-civil-marriage.ashx#ixzz2P5Ay8nEJ.

88 1936 Decree Articles 14 and 15.

89 Nizar Saghieh, *Beyond Civil Marriage: Freedom Is the Principle* (Legal Agenda, 2013).

90 UNDP, "National Human Development Report 2008–2009," p. 76.

91 See UN Committee on the Elimination of Discrimination Against Women (CEDAW), "Consideration of Reports Submitted by States Parties under Article 18 of the Convention, Fourth and Fifth Periodic Reports of States Parties Due in 2014," p 115, Lebanon, May 15, 2014, CEDAW/C/LBN/4–5, www.refworld.org/docid/564edad14.html.

92 Kail. C Ellis, *Lebanon Second Republic, Prospects for the Twentieth Century* (Florida University Press, 2009), p. 10.

93 Asma Barlas, *Believing Women in Islam, Unreading Patriarchal Interpretations of the Qu'ran* (University of Texas Press, 2002), p. 3.

94 Gunawan Adnan, *Women and the Glorious Qu'ran: An Analytical Study of Women Related Verses of Sura An-Nisa'* (University of Gottingen, 2004), p. 171.

In Circles We Go

A Historical Overview of the Jordanian Personal Status Law

SARA ABABNEH *

7.1 Introduction

This chapter outlines some of the changes that the Jordanian Personal Status Law (JPSL)[1] has undergone since its inception as the Ottoman Family Rights Law (OFRL) written in 1917[2] to the newest amendments, which were made in 2019.[3] A historical perspective allows us to see that changes in the law are not progressive. Instead they were often circular with laws being changed, changed back again, and then altered once more. Examining the historical development of the code enables the reader to appreciate that rather than being based on *divine shari'a* law, as many Jordanians believe, the law is an outcome of human decision, politics, and choices. Finally, a comparative approach highlights that codification resulted in limiting women's ability to negotiate matters related to marriage, divorce, and child custody.

While most of the literature focuses on the discriminating nature[4] of the JPSL in terms of gender, with the exception of a few texts on classical jurisprudence, there has been no discussion of discrimination based on social class.[5] I show that through the concept of *kafa'a* (financial compatibility), the law enshrines class hierarchies by attempting to restrict the marriage of women from affluent families to economically marginalized men (men who are considered of a lesser economic standing). In addition, the law does not grant all women the same rights in terms of the amount of maintenance and dowry.

Methodologically, the chapter draws on primary legal texts, including the Arabic translation of the OFRL, interviews conducted by the author with women's rights activists and legal practitioners, participant observation, meeting minutes obtained from participating in lower and upper house legal committees and sessions, newspaper articles, and academic scholarship.

In Section 7.2, I define the main concepts used in this chapter such as *shari'a* and *fiqh* and discuss the supposed divinity of the code. Section 7.3 focuses on the historical development of some of the clauses in the JPSL concerning marital rights, obligations of husbands and wives, in addition to divorce, guardianship, and child custody. In the conclusion (Section 7.7), I argue that refraining from revising the idea of men as breadwinners and women as receivers of maintenance is the reason gender and class discrimination continues to be enshrined in the JPSL.

7.2   *Shari'a* or *Fiqh*? The "Divinity" of the Personal Status Law

Jordan has a dual legal system. The law is based on two conceptually different legal traditions. This legal duality results in two separate court systems and two separate legal bodies of the law: one for criminal and civil codes mostly – but not exclusively – based on a Western legal tradition, and one for personal status law based mostly – but also not exclusively – on *fiqh*, that is Islamic jurisprudence.[6]

Religious Courts are divided into *Shari'a* Courts, which have jurisdiction over Muslim personal status, and religious tribunals (church courts) that apply the canon law of Christian denominations.[7] Concerning inheritance, which will not be discussed in this chapter, the Muslim PSL is applied to all Jordanian citizens regardless of their religion. Matters of personal status regarding foreign nationals come under the jurisprudence of regular courts.[8]

This duality of the law is a legacy of the Ottoman era. For the most part, Ottoman criminal and civil laws were both modelled in form and content on nineteenth-century Napoleonic code.[9] The OFRL, on the other hand, was mostly derived from the Sunni schools of *fiqh*. This led to the popular perception that while civil and criminal codes were secular, personal status law was *Islamic* in nature, or based on *shari'a*.

In reality, Ottoman family law was a mixture of different Islamic schools of *fiqh*, in addition to local customs of the time and Western laws.[10] Since many Muslims believe that the *shari'a* is literally the will of God as derived from the *Qur'an* and the *Sunnah* of Prophet Mohammad, *shari'a* has gained an almost sacred status beyond human critique.[11]

Historical investigation of the writing process of the OFRL highlights the amount of human deliberation that went into drafting the law. Firstly, following the jurists of *fiqh*, the authors of the OFRL and their successors took certain parts of the Qur'an and set aside others. An example of this is the idea of *qiwamah*. As Ziba Mir-Hosseini argues, all marital relations in the JPSL are based on the idea that a husband has *qiwamah* – is financially responsible for his wife – and that his wife therefore has to obey him.

> Yet [there] is only [one] appearance in the Qur'an of the word *qawwamun* .... In relation to marriage and relations between spouses, two other terms appear over twenty times: *ma'ruf* (good way, decent) and *rahmah wa muwadah*, (compassion and love). Why did the jurists choose not to translate these two terms into legal rulings?[12]

Secondly, modern ideas were enshrined in the law. An example of this is the idea of the nuclear family. The nuclear family as conceptualized by the law and as we understand it today is foreign to Islamic jurisprudence.[13] Not only does the state establish the family as a basic social unit, it also empowers men to rule these families. As a result, the state transfers some of its sovereign rights to its male citizens. The law restricts female citizens' direct access to the state by placing male relatives in intermediary roles, as I will discuss later.[14]

Finally, the main sources that the authors of the OFRL go back to are not the *Qur'an* and the *Sunnah* but *fiqh*. While, drawing on the Qur'an at times, using a method called *takhayyur* (selection), most of the OFRL is based on Hanafi law and other Sunni schools of jurisprudence.[15] As a result, the JPSL enacts a type of patriarchy that has very little to do with the Islamic *shari'a*[16] or even *fiqh*, on which it claims to be based.

The JPSL makes no claims to establish equality between the sexes. Rather women and men are given different rights, duties, and obligations depending on their position in the family. Men are obliged to financially provide for their families, demand obedience from their wives, and can divorce at will. Women have the right to be financially provided for. Their access to divorce is limited unless they stipulate that right in their marriage contract or, since 2001, give up some of their rights and parts of their back-end dowry through using *khulu'*.

The following two sections outline how these regulations developed in the various Jordanian personal status laws. First, I highlight some main differences between the Ottoman law and later Jordanian laws. Then, I examine the historical development of the JPSL.

7.3   Differences between the Ottoman and Later More Modern Jordanian Family Laws

A quick note is necessary to elaborate on the key differences between the OFRL and the JPSLs that followed. This discussion highlights that many of the present-day problems stemming from the JPSL do not go back to the Ottoman era but are more modern in nature.

The OFRL defines many of the legal concepts, which makes it a much more accessible document than subsequent versions of the law. The authors of the OFRL also provide a detailed explanation of the rationale behind choosing certain rulings over others. In what is perhaps the most interesting part for the purposes of our chapter, the authors of the code explain why they decided to make certain rulings and refrain from making others. The authors are unapologetic about using the rulings of different schools of *fiqh* and sometimes not using any of the schools at all but modern needs. The OFRL authors assert this in their explanatory introduction:

> It has been found that the *ijtihad* and *fatwas* of some of the jurists from different schools [not that of Abu Hanifa] are for some matters more appropriate for people's interactions and the demands of this time than the great Hanafi jurists who are fathers of this school.[17]

This flexibility and openness to debate the underlying assumptions and rulings would be unthinkable today. The authors' discussion of polygyny illustrates this point. Polygyny is discussed at length in the introduction to the law. The authors reason that polygyny is *mubah* (allowed) and not *wajeb* (required), which means that they are free to decide whether to include it in the law or not.[18] Today, many lay Muslim men regard it as their personal divinely enshrined right to marry more than one wife.[19] The authors of the OFRL, by contrast, tell the reader that they seriously considered banning polygyny or at least conditioning it upon the approval of the first wife. They maintain that the *shari'a*'s legalization of polygyny is based on whether society needs such provisions. In this matter, rather than returning to *fiqh*, the authors refer to verses two and three of *Surat al Niss'a* (chapter 4:2,3): Yusuf Ali's translation of the verses reads as follows: "To orphans restore their property (When they reach their age), nor substitute (your) worthless things for (their) good ones; and devour not their substance (by mixing it up) with your own. For this is indeed a great sin. If ye fear that ye shall not be able to deal justly with the orphans, Marry women of your choice, Two or three or four; but if ye fear that ye shall not be able to deal justly (with them), then only one, or [marry] (a captive) that your right hands possess, that will be more suitable, to prevent you from doing injustice."[20] The Qur'an suggests polygyny as a solution to a particular problem faced by society at that time, in this case the great number of orphans in the aftermath of a battle, referred to in Qur'an 4:3. The authors reason that the need of "current time" – the context of the authors' being World War I – is as high as it was in the early days of Islam when women far outnumbered men. It is important to underline that the authors do not assume that it is the divine right of a Muslim man to marry up to four wives. Instead, drawing on the Qur'an, they argue that in times of crises, polygyny might be used as a remedy to solve the social problem of orphans. In other words, polygyny is a suggested solution to a social problem, not an eternal divinely granted right of men.

This rationale places the authors in a dilemma regarding whether the approval of the first wife for a second marriage should be required or not. In theory, the authors seem to regard this as the first wife's right. But they recognize "that no woman will allow her husband to marry another wife."[21] They conclude that making the legality of a second marriage dependent on the first wife's approval would be equivalent to banning it. They solve the matter by arguing that each woman has the right to make stipulations in her marriage contract preventing her husband from taking another wife.

Article 38 of the OFRL states a woman can stipulate that her husband not marry another wife. Unlike later Jordanian laws, a wife can also make the decision of whether taking another wife will result in her divorce from her husband or the immediate divorce of a second wife, in other words, the annulment of any future marriage.

> If the fiancée sets the condition that her husband cannot marry another woman, then if he gets married either she or the second wife is divorced, if she stipulates this in the contract.[22]

The above discussion shows Ottoman authors used flexibility in discussing polygyny that would be unthinkable to most Muslims today. Section 7.4 discusses the historical development of the JPSL.

7.4 The Jordanian Personal Status Law's Historical Journey

The first codified Family law, which was used in the area that is now Jordan, was the OFRL, which was adopted officially in Transjordan in 1933. A year after its independence in 1946, the temporary law of Family Rights was released.[23] In 1951, Jordan became the first independent Arab country[24] to establish a code of family law (JLFR).[25]

The early seventies were characterized by numerous efforts by the Jordanian state to establish greater gender equality. Internationally, this was triggered by the 1972 United Nations General Assembly resolution 3010 in which the year 1975 was declared Women's International Year.[26] The JPSL of 1976[27] was written in this context.[28]

The temporary law of 2001 emerged in the midst of a huge controversy.[29] The law had been drafted by a Royal Commission for Human Rights (RCHR), chaired by Queen Rania while the parliament was not in session.[30] The commission recommended amendments to the personal status law.[31] Upon the election of a new parliament in June 2003, the three amendments to the personal status law were debated almost immediately. The most controversial aspect of this law was a clause allowing women to get a divorce through *khulu'*.

Despite numerous efforts by women's rights organizations, the law was voted down a second time by parliament on June 27, 2004, with forty-four out of eighty-three Members of Parliament (MPs) voting against the amendments.[32] It has to be noted that in spite of the notorious reputation that the law got for breaking with tradition, the 2001 law[33] is, in fact, almost identical to the 1976 law.

The temporary law 36 (2010)[34] was celebrated by many in the media as having emerged from national consensus.[35] Chief Justice Ahmad Hlayel argued that the law recognizes the importance of protecting the family and society in general and women's and children's rights in particular.[36] Women's rights organizations saw things differently. The Jordanian Women's Union pointed out that despite being asked to give feedback and discuss the draft, their recommendations were not included in the new law.[37] Furthermore, none of the people who participated in drafting the law were women.[38] Centrally, *Dairat Qadi al Quda'* the Supreme Justice Department (SJD) came to dominate the reform process.[39] The SJD was able to maintain its role as key player and expert in the debate over the amendments in 2018–2019.

In late 2018, the executive branch of government proposed thirty amendments to the 2010 PSL. These amendments were discussed by the lower and upper houses of parliament. Women's rights activists under the leadership of the Jordanian National Commission for Women hereinafter JNCW met with both lower and upper house legal committees and provided them with a document of proposed changes for nineteen out of the thirty articles up for discussion. With the exception of one (article 172 b,[40] which was revoked),[41] all of the suggestions made by women's rights activists were rejected by lower house legal committee.[42] In the end, the discussion boiled down to two articles, namely, article 10, which stipulates the minimum age of marriage in exceptional cases,[43] and article 279 which concerns "obligatory bequest" (*al-wasiya al-wajiba*).

Women's rights activists argued that there should be no exceptional cases in terms of marriage and that eighteen should be the minimum age for all cases. When the lower house committee rejected this suggestion, the JNCW and other women's rights activists conceded that the exceptional age should at least be sixteen and not fifteen as it was before. When the amendments were discussed in the Upper House, the Senate voted in favor of the amendments to increasing the age of marriage for women in exceptional cases to sixteen. The Senate also supported giving inheritance rights to grandchildren born to female children equally with male children.[44]

Eventually, what determined the outcome of the parliamentary vote was a politically insensitive statement by the Human Rights Watch (HRW) deputy Middle East director. Even though inheritance was not among the amendments to the law up for discussion, HRW director Michael Page urged Jordanians to seize this opportunity to finally have women and men be equal in inheritance, divorce, and marriage.[45] The statements by Page led to a backlash from many MPs and *Shari'a* judges seeing HRW as interfering in internal Jordanian matters, making suggestions in terms of inheritance that MPs saw as a direct violation of the word of God. One MP refused the Senate's suggestions saying that they were the outcome of "civil society organizations pressure funded by embassy money."[46] Another MP argued that the amendments that the Senate suggested would be "stopping the work of the book [the Qur'an] and law of God".[47]

Centrally, MPs critiqued what they called a foreign-funded civil society. To appreciate the incident, a note of clarification is in order. Women's rights initiatives are often popularly understood as extensions of imperialist policies. Given a history of colonial[48] and contemporary policies (US invasions of Iraq and Afghanistan to "liberate women" come to mind here) that have used women's rights to further control the population, this is not a totally unfounded fear. The claim of wanting to save Arab women by states whose track record has not been much better than the states they are attempting to save[49] has been detrimental for women's rights activists on the ground.[50] The statements made by HRW were understood in the same context. In a heated debate, women's rights activists and by extension all the reforms they suggested were portrayed as extensions of foreign intervention and imperial politics.

The reforms were portrayed as anti-Islamic. At the end of the parliamentary session, Supreme Justice Abd al Karim Khasawneh ended by saying
that anyone voting for allowing the obligatory bequest for children of
predeceased daughters would be "sinning (athmeen) in the eyes of
God".[51] Many MPs saw the Supreme Judge as speaking for Islam and
the amendments as anti-Islamic imperialist schemes to destroy Jordanian
culture.[52] The session ended with the parliament voting against increasing the exceptional age of marriage. The majority of those present also
voted against extending the obligatory bequest to orphaned grandchildren through predeceased daughters.[53]

After having examined the history of the PSL, let me now turn to some
of the main reforms that the law has undergone. I particularly discuss
marriage, the concept of kafa'a, forms of divorce, the marriage contract,
and custody and guardianship.

7.5   Marriage, Divorce, and Custody in the Jordanian Personal Status Law

7.5.1   Marriage: Between Paying Maintenance and Obedience

In the Qur'an "marriage is presented as a major source of comfort and
joy for both spouses."[54] Jurists, however, discussed marriage mostly in
terms of the sexual rights of husbands and wives to each other's bodies.
In the JPSL, the discussion on marriage is limited to issues of maintenance, obedience, and since 1976, procreation.

The 1976 JPSL is the first law to define marriage. Article 2 reads:
"marriage is a contract between a man and a woman whom he can marry
according to the shari'a in order to form a family and start a lineage
(nasel)."[55] Despite the fact that the word nasel and the logic of marriage
as a means of procreation are absent from the Qur'an, this definition of
marriage is still used in the JPSL.[56]

The logic for requiring a wife's obedience is derived from the argument
that husbands need to financially provide for their wives. Current circumstances in which more and more women work and contribute to
paying family maintenance have not been taken into account in any
recent debate concerning legal reform.[57] Women's rights activists have
not challenged the Islamic nature of the law or demanded alternative
Islamic interpretations to be used like in Tunisia or Morocco.[58]

Maintenance (nafaqa) is stipulated as a wife's right. It is determined
between husband and wife, or by judicial estimate, and can be increased

or decreased depending on general price increases or changes in the husband's financial condition.[59] Over the years, the law increasingly added examples of what falls under maintenance, effectively expanding it. The current law lists "food, *kuswa* (clothing), living, health care, and providing servants for the wife whose likes have servants,"[60] as an example of what maintenance entails.

Although the JPSL enshrines maintenance as a wife's right, the state has faced numerous problems trying to guarantee this right to women. With each redrafting of the law, additional clauses were included to ensure that husbands pay their wives the *nafaqa* (Arabic for maintenance). The OFRL tried to ensure that wives actually got their maintenance by allowing wives to take the money their husbands owed them from those who are otherwise responsible for their alimony. The money paid was later seen as a debt by the husband, which he had to repay.[61]

More recently, the temporary law of 2010, Article 321 has been regarded as a major advancement by women's rights groups. This article sets up provisions for a *nafaqa* fund, which lends money to the wives of husbands who are unable, unwilling, or absent. It is then the obligation of the husbands to repay this debt to the fund. The *nafaqa* fund was finally activated in late 2017. Since then, beneficiaries have been provided with electronic cards through which they can withdraw their maintenance directly. During the Corona lock down (March–May 2020), the Supreme Justice Department (SJD) made payment of *nafaqa* one of its primary priorities. For those beneficiaries who had no cards, the SJD sent out their due maintenance by post.[62]

In return for being provided for by her husband, the JPSL obliges a wife to obey her husband. What obedience entails exactly remains rather vague. In none of the family laws used in Jordan is obedience defined clearly. Disobedience (*nushuz*) is discussed in a bit more detail but also lacks a clear definition.[63] Once the husband pays the dower, his wife is required to obey him. A disobedient wife (*nashez*), who leaves her house without a *musawegh shar'i* (religiously legal reason), forfeits her right to maintenance.[64] In 1976, a working wife[65] was entitled to maintenance if (1) her work is legitimate and (2) her husband has given his permission for her to work.[66] A husband cannot withdraw his permission unless there is a legitimate reason to do so and without inflicting any harm on his wife.

This is an example of how the state places men as intermediaries between female citizens and itself.[67] Women's rights activists pointed out that when there is rule of law, illegal work should be prevented by the state and not by individuals.[68] The JNCW argued that article 61b should be revoked as only the state, not its citizens, is responsible for law enforcement.

7.6 Kafa'a

The rationale of *kafa'a* (literally "compatibility," but in this context, financial compatibility) is one that is taken from the *fiqh* literature and goes through the OFRL and continues in the JPSL until today. Article 45 of the OFRL stipulates that a husband has to be a woman's *kafu'* in money and profession. Monetary *kafa'a* is defined as the husband's ability to pay a woman's dower and her maintenance in a manner that she is accustomed to in her paternal home. It is one of the conditions for a marriage to be valid that a man is a women's financial *kafu*.[69] Professional *kafa'a* is that "the business of the husband or the profession that he has chosen [has to be] similar in honor to that of the guardians of the wife."[70] In other words, *kafa'a* attempts to ensure that a woman does not get married to someone who is considered to be of a lower socio-economic background to her father's.[71]

In the 1951 JLFR, compatibility in profession between the husband and father in law was dropped as a condition to marriage.[72] In 2010, the concept of *kafa'a* was expanded to include religiosity.[73] The current law defines *kafa'a* to be in "religiosity and money."[74] Monetary *kafa'a* is defined as "that the husband is able to pay the dowry and the wife's maintenance."[75]

It is important to note that the concept of *kafa'a* is not only absent in the Qur'an but directly contradicts *Surat Al Baqara*, verse 221. It also contradicts the Sunna. I have argued elsewhere that Prophet Mohammad's inability to pay his first wife Khadijah's dowry,[76] would not have passed the *kafa'a* conditions of the JPSL.[77] Through using the logic of men as maintainers, apart from not treating men and women equally, the JPSL also treats people of different classes differently and effectually establishes barriers between women from more affluent families and less affluent men. Even though the provision that a groom is to be equal to the bride's father in professional status has been dropped, a woman's guardian can still dissolve a marriage conducted without his approval if the husband is not of the financial status of the bride's family.[78] The concept of *kafa'a* thus enshrines socioeconomic hierarchies in the law.

7.6.1 Marriage Contracts

"A prenuptial condition in a marriage contract is undoubtedly one of the most important instruments that women in Islamic societies ... used to ensure control over marriage".[79] Despite being one of the few countries whose law allows the inclusion of prenuptial agreements in the marriage contract, making stipulations has been increasingly restricted. Judith Tucker shows that at various times during Islamic history the use of marriage contracts was fairly widespread. Rather than doctrinal differences, Tucker argues, local customs were the reason that women used marriage contracts to insert stipulations.[80]

In what is now Jordan, the power of stipulations women can make in a marriage contract decreased with time. As shown earlier in the chapter, article 38 of the OFRL allowed a woman living in the Ottoman Empire to stipulate that her husband not marry another wife. Unlike later Jordanian laws, a wife could also decide whether her husband could marry another wife.

Article 21 of the 1951 JLFR gives a few examples of what a woman can include in her marriage contract. The clauses that are mentioned include giving the wife the right of divorce, that a husband does not force his wife to live in a country other than the one they agreed to live in together, and that he does not take another wife. In case a husband violates the clauses stipulated by the wife, she can ask to have her contract voided, in other words, demand to be divorced. Unlike the OFRL, the 1951 JLFR and all the laws that followed did not give wives the ability to prevent husbands from taking multiple wives. Instead, if a husband violates any of the stipulations made by his wife in her marriage contract, then she can get a divorce while maintaining all her marital rights (payment of dowry).[81]

While the power of stipulations has decreased, marriage contracts still function as a way in which women can attain more rights in their marriage than the JPSL otherwise gives them. Legal illiteracy and social stigma associated with making demands other than the dowry, however, prevent most women from making use of their right to make stipulations, which could provide them with more legal equality.[82] Even when couples choose some of the stipulations explicitly mentioned in the JPSL, such as a wife's ability to get a divorce, shari'a judges often push back making it very hard for couples to actually include such stipulations in the contract.

The Economic and Social Council recommended establishing marriage contract checklists. Checklists could be part of the paperwork that young couples have to fill out to get married. This way, couples could simply check articles that they would like to include without any family interference.[83] From 2020–22 the Information and Research Center, King Hussein Foundation has worked on compiling a checklist to be used by prospective couples.[84]

7.6.2   Divorce

There are five types of divorce in *fiqh*, four of which are used in the JPSL, namely *talaq*, *tafreeq*, *khulu'*, and *li'an*. In this section, I will discuss the first three, given that li'an[85] is hardly used.

Talaq (divorce) is the prerogative of the husband alone. A man can divorce his wife at any time, place, and for any reason he likes. A wife can only divorce – herself (from herself), not her husband – if she makes this stipulation in her marriage contract or if the husband authorizes her to do so.[86]

Tafreeq (separation or repudiation) is often referred to as women's divorce. Unlike men, women cannot get a divorce unless stipulated in the marriage contract. In the OFRL, there are seven instances in which a woman can be separated from her husband, ranging from separation because of a defect in the husband, to insanity. In each case, a wife has to go to court and ask the judge to grant her separation.[87]

Khulu'/*mukhala'* was added as a way in which women can attain a divorce after 1976. *Mukhala'* is not defined in the law of 1976. Most jurists have agreed that *khulu'* happens when a wife compensates her husband in case she desires divorce.[88] In Jordan, the main disagreement was on whether a husband has to agree to grant his wife the divorce or whether she can get *khulu'* in spite of her husband.

Despite the notorious reputation that the 2001 temporary law got for breaking with tradition and allowing *khulu'*, the 2001 law is in fact almost identical to the law of 1976 concerning *khulu'*. The only substantive difference is article 126(c), which allows a woman to get a divorce in court without the permission of her husband, a clause that was later referred to as the *khulu'* clause. The other articles dealing with *khulu'* (articles 102–112) are the same articles present in the 1976 JPSL.[89]

In the temporary law of 2010, women's rights activists' main opposition concerned the change in the *khulu'* article. Firstly, instead of *khulu'*, the law uses the term *consensual khulu'*. The article dealing with *khulu'* reads "consensual *khulu'* is when a husband divorces his wife in return to a compensation when he utters the words of *khulu'*, divorce."[90] The law makes the husband's approval a precondition for his wife's ability to attain *khulu'*. In article 114b, under the heading of separation, the law enables a woman to pay in return for the court to annul the marriage contract if she compensates her husband and after the court has tried to mediate between the spouses. Even though the word *khulu'* is not used in association with article 114b, the wording and conditions are identical to the article under the heading of *khulu'* in the 2001 JPSL. The final definition of consensual *khulu'* used in the 2019 JPSL is "that the husband divorces his wife in return for a compensation they have agreed upon."[91]

The discussion around *khulu'* is another example of how *fiqh* and the current JPSL depart from primary Islamic sources, in this case rulings of the Qur'an itself. Many interpreters have regarded Surah 2, Verse 229[92] as divine authorization of an "unconditional right on the part of the wife to obtain a divorce from her husband."[93] The hadith literature supports this in the narration of the story of Jamilah, the wife of Thabit ibn Qays.[94]

The present interpretation of *khulu'* is also a departure from local traditions. Ethnographic studies of the Southern Jordanian city of Tafieleh, for example, show that in the 1920s and 1930s *khulu'* was a widely used form of divorce.[95] In regards to *khulu'* the current law is not just a departure of certain Islamic interpretations of the Qur'an and the Sunna, it is also more rigid than historic local practices.

7.6.3   Hadana *and* Wilaya

While *wilaya* (guardianship) is an exclusively male prerogative in the JSPL, *hadana* (custody for minors) can be performed by both women and men. *Wilaya* is a father's guardianship over his children. Without the approval of the *wali* of the bride, a marriage contract cannot be completed.[96] Men do not require the approval of the *wali*, which de facto means that once a boy turns eighteen he is a full citizen without the need for a guardian. Regardless of how old she is, a woman's guardian's approval is a condition for her first marriage.[97] The *wali* of a child[98] is the father, then the representative of the father, the paternal grandfather, and then the paternal grandfather's representative.[99] The issue of guardianship is another matter in which the Jordanian state has adopted laws, which differ from previous Islamic customs.

> The mother as guardian, ubiquitous in the Ottoman era, illustrates the extent to which a woman could play a male role in certain situations, primarily those in which her fitness for the care and nurturing of her children extended to the safekeeping and management of their properties.[100]

Reading the law from a historical perspective, we note that the JPSL has restricted the ability of women to act as their children's guardian. As a result of these guardianship laws, mothers could not legally hospitalize their children, to name only one example. This provision was changed after a boy died when his father refused to allow him to undergo surgery to spite his wife.[101] The death of the boy led to reform article 62 of the penal code. In the amended article, both parents of a child are now able to approve surgery, not only the guardian as it was before.[102] This reform did not, however, change the concept of guardianship.[103]

Hadana is custody over the children in case of the parent's divorce or a husband's death. Over the years, the period in which a custodian can keep her wards has been extended from seven and nine years for boys and girls consecutively in 1951[104] to fifteen in 2010 on the condition that she does not remarry a man who is not the children's *mahram*.[105] The 1976 JPSL[106] is the first law that asserts that custody is the right of the mother. In 2010, fathers' rights to custody were expanded. Before 2010, custody would first go to the mother, then the mother's mother, never reaching the father.[107] In 2010, the law was changed to read that after the mother custody would go to "the mother's mother, then to the father's mother, then to the father."[108] In 2019, the article was amended to include "the interest of the ward"[109] as a criterion for determining custody. This provision allowed fathers to also gain custody. Women's rights activists have suggested allowing mothers to be guardians as well as custodians, or establishing joint guardianship,[110] a practice that is not foreign to Muslim communities.

7.7   Conclusion

What is most striking about the journey of the development of the JPSL is how little the law has changed in the last 106 years. Where alterations have been made, they have not touched the overall rationale of the law. There were no efforts to revisit the sources of the law, to rethink certain assumptions which were based on seventh-century Arabian society but are now no longer relevant, or stem from conservative colonial European laws, or to think of alternative "Islamic versions." Instead, the changes have focused on adjusting particular rulings by giving women or men more choices in a certain matter.

Certainly, important advances have been made. Mothers have been allowed to have custody over their children for longer periods of time.

However, legal reforms have not altered the institution of guardianship as an exclusively male privilege.

In other instances, the current law is more restrictive than earlier laws or social practices. The ability for women to divorce through *khulu'* is an example of this. Another example is that during the Ottoman period, women could stipulate that their husbands could not marry another woman. This legally prevented husbands from entering another marriage.

Unlike their Ottoman predecessors, Jordanian legislators have stayed clear from rethinking the JPSL in terms of current times and requirements. In the 2019 discussions of the PSL, any critique of the law was seen as a critique to the *shari'a*, and Islam itself.

In the JPSL, rights are not universal, but are based on gender and class. While maintenance is a woman's right, the amount of maintenance or the dowry a woman is entitled to is determined by her social class. If there is a disagreement about the dowry, a woman is entitled to *mahr al mithel*, which is the dowry that women of her family and social standing usually receive.[111] In addition, a woman is entitled to servants as part of her maintenance if she had servants in her father's home. It is therefore a rich woman's right to have servants, while it is not the right of a poor woman.[112] Affluent women are entitled to higher maintenance and a more comfortable home than economically marginalized women. While the law does not place affluent women over poor men, it puts certain restrictions in place complicating the process of their marriage to each other. The JPSL is not only a law, which privileges men over women, but also the rich over the poor, in particular: affluent men over poor men and affluent women over poor women.

At the core of the unequal relations between the sexes and the classes is the notion that men are providers and women are entitled to maintenance. Despite the fact that women now often work and provide for themselves, this basic equation has not been rethought. The logic of obedience in return for maintenance continues to act as the main justification for legislation that is discriminatory in terms of sex and class.

Notes

* I want to thank my interns Duha al Shafi', Bayan al Arouri, Bara'a al Hiyyasat, and Lovis Maj Bartholain for all their help with the research process.

1 The JPSLs include the 1976 JPSL, 2001 JPSL, 2010 JPSL, and 2019 JPSL. The original texts of the various family laws and JPSLs used in this chapter were in Arabic. The quotes are my own translations of these Arabic texts.

2 Ottoman Family Rights Law (OFRL) (1917), translated into Arabic by Muhammad Shaker Bin Ragheb Al Hanbali Al Dimashqi, Gazette of Legal Verdicts; Ahmad Jawdat Pasha, Fiqh of Mu'amalat *in the Hanafi School and Family Rights in Civil Marriage and Divorce* (Dar Ibn Hazem, Al Jaffan & Al Jabi, 2004).

3 2019 Jordanian Personal Status Law, Law 15/2019, Official Gazette no. 5578 published June 2, 2019.

4 Mohammad Al Hawamda, *The Historical Development of Personal Status Law in Jordan* (original in Arabic: *Al tatawour al tareekhi liqanoon al ahwal al shakhsiya fil urdun*), Markaz al Rayi Lil Dirasat (Al Rayi Center for Research, 2003, www .alraicenter.com); Abla Amawi, "Gender and Citizenship in Jordan," in Suad Joseph (ed.), *Gender and Citizenship in the Middle East* (Syracuse University Press, 2000), pp. 158–184; Asma Khader, "Jordanian Legal System, 2012," www .asmakhader.com; Valentine M. Moghadam and Farzaneh Roudi-Fahimi, *Reforming Family Laws to Promote Progress in the Middle East and North Africa* (Population Reference Bureau, 2005), www.ptb.org; Annelies Moors, "Debating Islamic Family Law: Legal Texts and Social Practices," in Margaret Meriwether and Judith Tucker (eds.), *Social History of Women and Gender in the Modern Middle East* (Westview Press, 1999), pp. 141–175; Jamal Nasir, *The Status of Women under Islamic Law and Modern Islamic Legislation*, ed. Danvers (MA) (Koninklijke Brill NV, 2009); Amira Azhary Sonbol, *Women of Jordan: Islam, Labour and the Law* (Syracuse University Press, 2003); Gihane Tabet, "Women in Personal Status Laws: Iraq, Jordan" (Gender Equality and Development Section, UNESCO, 2005); Catherine Warrick, *Law in the Service of Legitimacy: Gender and Politics in Jordan* (Ashgate, 2009); Doerthe Engelcke, "Jordan," in Nadjma Yassari, Lena Maria Moeller, Imen Gallala-Arndt (eds.), *Parental Care and the Best Interests of the Child in Muslim Countries* (Asser Press Den Haag, 2017), pp. 121–143; Doerthe Engelcke, "Law-Making in Jordan: Family Law Reform and the Supreme Justice Department," *Islamic Law and Society* (2018) 25(3), 274–309; Doerthe Engelcke, *Reforming Family Law: Social and Politics Change in Jordan and Morocco* (Cambridge University Press, 2019); Doerthe Engelcke and Nadjma Yassari, "Child Law in Muslim Jurisdictions: The Role of the State in establishing Filiation (Nasab) and protecting parentless Children – Symposium Introduction" (2019) 34(3) *Journal of Law and Religion* (Center for Law and Religion at Emory University), pp. 332–335; Doerthe Engelcke, "Establishing Filiation (Nasab) and the Placement of Destitute Children into New Families: What Role Does the State Play?" (2019) 34(3) *Journal of Law and Religion* (Center for Law and Religion at Emory University), pp. 408–432; Doerthe Engelcke, "The Organization of the Greek Orthodox Courts in Jordan and the Application of Byzantine Family Law: Tensions between the 'National' and the 'Transnational,'" in Marie-Claire Foblets, Hatem Elliesie, and Irene Schneider (eds.), *Law, Islam and Anthropology* (Routledge, 2020); Lynn Welchman, "The Development of Islamic Family Law in the Legal System of Jordan" (1988) 37(4) *The International and Comparative Law Quarterly*, 868–886; Paul Scott Prettitore, "Family Law Reform, Gender Equality, and Underage Marriage: A View from Morocco and Jordan" (2015) 13(3) *The Review of Faith & International Affairs*, 32–40.

5 Homa Hoodfar, *Shifting Boundaries in Marriage and Divorce in Muslim Communities* (Women Living Under Muslim Laws, 1996); Judith Tucker,

"Revisiting Reform: Women and the Ottoman Law of Family Rights, 1917" (1996) 4(2) *The Arab Studies Journal*, 4–17; Judith Tucker, *Women, Family, and Gender in Islamic Law* (Cambridge University Press, 2008).

6 Warrick, *Law in the Service of Legitimacy*, p. 39.
7 Engelcke, "Greek Orthodox courts in Jordan," p. 2.
8 Khader, *Jordanian Legal System*; Welchman "Development of Islamic Family Law"; Géraldine Chatelard, "The Constitution of Christian Communal Boundaries and Spheres in Jordan" (2010) 52(3) *Journal of Church and State*, 476–502.
9 Amawi, "Gender and Citizenship in Jordan," p. 175; Warrick, *Law in the Service of Legitimacy*, p. 45.
10 Sonbol, *Women of Jordan*, p. 8.
11 John L. Esposito and Natana J. DeLong-Bas, *Women in Muslim Family Law*, 2nd ed. (Syracuse University Press, 2001); Ziba Mir-Hosseini, "Decoding the "DNA of Patriarchy" in Muslim Family Laws," Open Democracy, May 21, 2012, www.opendemocracy.net/print/65974.
12 Mir-Hosseini, *Decoding the "DNA of Patriarchy."*
13 Sonbol, *Women of Jordan*, pp. 38–39.
14 Amawi, "Gender and Citizenship in Jordan," p. 171.
15 Tucker, *Women, Family, and Gender*, p. 20.
16 *Shari'a* is the word used to commonly refer to the basis of the law. In reality, what jurists, politicians and lay people are refering to is Islamic jurisprudence: *fiqh*. Scholars like Amina Wadud and Ziba Mir Hosseini have cautioned against the conflation of the idea of *Shari'a*, which signifies the path of God, in other words, divine law, with *fiqh*, which is the human endeavor to establish a law. Mir-Hosseini, *Decoding the "DNA of Patriarchy"*; Amina Wadud, *Inside the Gender Jihad: Women's Reform in Islam* (Oneworld, 2006).
17 The original texts of the various family laws and PSLs used in this chapter were in Arabic. The quotes are my own translations of these Arabic texts. OFLR, p. 510.
18 OFRL, p. 511.
19 More than half the female and male respondents of the Jordan Gender Barometer (2020) regarded it as a man's right to marry more than one wife. Sara Ababneh, "Jordan Gender Barometer, Survey Report," Center for Strategic Studies, HIVOS, 2020, p. 18; for infographics, see https://hivos.org/resource/hivos-jordan-gender-barometer/.
20 *The Holy Qur'an*, translated by Abdullah Yusuf Ali (Wordsworth Classics, 2000), p. 60.
21 OFRL, p. 511.
22 OFRL, p. 511.
23 1947 Temporary Law of Family Rights, Law 26/1947, Official Gazette no.915 published on August 2, 1947, www.lob.gov/ui/laws.
24 Welchman, "Development of Islamic Family Law," p. 871.
25 1951 Law of Family Rights, Law 92/1951, Official Gazette no. 1081, published on August 1, 1951 (JLFR), www.lob.gov/ui/laws.
26 Laurie Brand, *Women, the State and Political Liberalization: Middle Eastern and North African Experiences* (Columbia University Press, 1998), pp. 124–125; Sara Ababneh, "The Time to Question, Rethink and Popularize the Notion of 'Women's Issues': Lessons from Jordan's Popular and Labor Movements from

2006 to Now" (2020) 21(1) *Journal of International Women's Studies*, 271–288, https://vc.bridgew.edu/jiws/vol21/iss1/21.

27 1976 Jordanian Personal Status Law, Law 61/1976, Official Gazette no. 2668 published on December 1, 1976, Jordanian Legislative and Opinion Court, www.lob .gov/ui/laws.

28 Welchman, "Development of Islamic Family Law," p. 871.

29 Janine Clark and Amy Young, "Islamism and Family Law Reform in Morocco and Jordan" (2008) 13(3) *Mediterranean Politics*, 333–352.

30 The parliament was suspended for two years from June 2001 until June 2003.

31 King Abdallah II dissolved parliament between 2000 and 2003. During this period, the Ali Abu al Ragheb government passed over 200 laws. The only laws that the parliament did not pass upon its reinstatement were those to do with women (the nationality law and the PSL). Amal Sabbagh, "A Critical Assessment of NWMs: The Case of Jordan" (2006), p. 20; Sara Ababneh, "Islamic Political Parties as a Means to Women's Empowerment? The Case of Hamas and the Islamic Action Front," DPhil Thesis, 2010, Department of Politics and International Relations at the University of Oxford.

32 Clark and Young, "Islamism and Family Law," p. 338.

33 2001 Temporary Personal Status Law, Law 82/2001, Official Gazette no. 4524 published on December 21, 2001, http://samilawfirm.com.

34 2010 Temporary Personal Status Law, Law 36/2010, Official Gazette no. 5061 published on October 17, 2010, www.lob.gov/ui/laws.

35 Rania Sarayrah, "Chief Islamic Justice Department Hands over Personal Status Law to Cabinet Today" (Original in Arabic: *Da'irat Qadi Al Quda tarfa' al yaoum ta'leemat khasa bi qanoon al ahwal al shakhsiah limajles al wisara' li'iqrariha*), *Al Ghad Newspaper*, November 21, 2010, www.alghad.jo; Manal Shamleh, "Important Changes in the New Jordanian JPSL: The Need to Inform the First Wife When Her Husband Marries Another after the Marriage Contract Is Conducted and Prohibiting Beating Using the Excuse of Nushooz" (Original in Arabic), April 20, 2010, www.sahafi.jo/files/51f89b17d8f0daddce0720efe087acd5a3c1b057.html.

36 Ahmad Hlayel, "An Introduction of the Jordanian Personal Status Law" (2011), http://aliftaa.jo/index.php/ar/articels/show/id/109.

37 Amneh Zubi, Personal Interview with Amneh Al Zubi, conducted by the author on May 30, 2012.

38 Nadia Shamroukh, Personal Interview with Nadia Shamroukh, conducted by the author on May 30, 2012.

39 Engelcke, "Law-Making in Jordan," p. 306.

40 This article stated that that non-Muslim mothers lose custody of their children when they turned seventeen. Article, 172 b, 2010 JPSL.

41 Jordanian National Commission for Women (JNCW), "The Comments of the JNCW on the Decisions of the Legal Committee of the House of Representatives on the Temporary Personal Status number 36 for the year 2010" [Mulahadat al Lajneh al Wataniyya li Shu'oon al Mar'a a'la qararat a'la Qararat al-Lajneh al Qanooniyya fi Majles al Nuwwab h'awl Qanoon al Ahwal al Shakhsieyya al Mu'aqat Raqam 36 lisanat 2010]. Presented to the committee on December 4, 2018, p. 7.

42 Lower House Legal Committee discussion of PSL 2010 amendments, Personal Attendance, December 4, 2018.

43 Ana V. Ibáñez Prieto, "JNCW Urges Amendments to Women's Rights Legislation," *Jordan Times*, February 26, 2018, www.jordantimes.com/news/local/jncw-urges-amendments-women's-rights-legislation.

44 Rana Husseini, "Female MPs to Lobby Colleagues for Personal Status Law Amendments," *Jordan Times*, December 26, 2018, www.jordantimes.com/news/local/female-mps-lobby-colleagues-personal-status-law-amendments.

45 Human Rights Watch, "Jordan: End Child Marriage in Status Talks," *Human Rights Watch*, April 3, 2019, www.hrw.org/news/2019/04/03/jordan-end-child-marriage-status-talks.

46 Jo24. 2019, "Parliament`s Session Settling the Controversy Over Inheritance and Marriage" [Original in Arabic] (2019), www.jo24.net/post.php?id=315190.

47 Jo24. 2019, "Parliament`s Session Settling the Controversy Over Inheritance and Marriage"

48 There are many examples in recent colonial history in which the colonizers claimed to be in the country to liberate Arab women. Perhaps the most infamous example is that of Lord Cromer, who was the High Commissioner of Egypt at the time. Cromer claimed that Britain was in Egypt to liberate Egyptian women. The same Lord Cromer was one of the most vocal opponents of the British suffragettes in the House of Lords. The French campaign to unveil Algerian women is another example of colonial claims that they are saving colonized women from colonized men. Mona L. Russell, "Competing, Overlapping, and Contradictory Agendas: Egyptian Education Under British Occupation, 1882–1922" (2001) 21(1–2) *Comparative Studies of South Asia, Africa and the Middle East*, 54; Elizabeth Perego, "The Veil or a Brother's Life: French Manipulations of Muslim Women's Images during the Algerian War 1954–62" (2015) 20(3) *Journal of North African Studies*, 349–373.

49 One example of this is US work around the world to counter early marriage when it is legal for fifteen and even thirteen-year-old girls to get married in some US states. Leti, Volpp, "Blaming Culture for Bad Behavior" (2000) 12(1) *Yale Journal of Law & the Humanities*, 113, 116.

50 MP Dr. Dima Tahboub eluded to that in some US states there is no minimum age to the exceptions for the age of marriage. Dima Tahboub, Joint Session to discuss Amendments to PSL 2010, April 8, 2019, personal Attendance.

51 Abd al Karim Khasawneh, Joint Session to discuss Amendments to PSL 2010, April 8, 2019, personal Attendance.

52 Saleh al Armuti, Yehiya al Saud, Fawaz al Zubi, Joint Session to discuss Amendments to PSL 2010, April 8, 2019, personal Attendance.

53 Sawsan Tabazah, "Jordan's Civil Society Fights for More Rights in Personal Status Law," Al-MONITOR, December 26, 2018, www.al-monitor.com/pulse/originals/2018/12/jordan-civil-status-code-women-marriage-divorce-children.html.

54 Tucker, *Women, Family, and Gender*, p. 38.

55 1976 Jordanian Personal Status Law, Law 61/1976, Official Gazette no. 2668, www.lob.gov/ui/laws.

56 2019 JSPL, Number 15, Article 5.

57 More of a quarter of a million out of two million households are headed by women in Jordan. Tarek Dilwani, "Corona Virus Raises Unemployment Numbers among Women in Jordan," *Independent*, December 9, 2020, www.independent.co.uk/news/world/middle-east/jordan-covid-unemployment-women-b1768479.html.

58 Ziba Mir-Hosseini, Mulki Al-Sharmani, and Jana Rumminger (eds.), *Men in Charge? Rethinking Authority in the Muslim Legal Tradition* (One World, 2014).

59 OFRL.

60 2019 JPSL, Number 15, Article 59b.

61 OFRL Articles 94, 95, 96, and 97.

62 Fatima Dabaas, "The Impact of the Corona Pandemic on Issues of Personal Status" [Ta'theer Jaihat al Corona ala qadaya al-Ahwal al-Shakhsiyya], Solidarity is Global Institute (SIGI), Zoom Round Table, May 19, 2020.

63 According to the OFRL, a woman who is *nashez* is defined as one who leaves her husband's home or prevents the husband from entering the marital home. OFRL Article 101. Later laws expand upon but still fail to clarify what "leaving the home" means.

64 1976 JPSL; 2001 JPSL Article 69; 2010 JPSL Article 62; 2019 JPSL Article 61.

65 Sonbol in *Women of Jordan*, (p. 55), shows that prior to the modern era, work and a woman's ability to engage in business ventures was not regarded to contradict her duties toward her husband. It was also not seen as related to obedience. Obedience mostly concerned a wife's exclusive sexual availability to her husband and was not connected to staying at home.

66 2019 JPSL Article 61. Women's rights activists have pointed out that it is in fact unconstitutional for a husband – or anyone else for that matter – to prevent a woman from working, since article 23 of the constitution asserts that work is the right of every Jordanian.

67 Amawi, "Gender and Citizenship in Jordan."

68 Jordanian National Commission for Women, Comments of the 2010 JPSL.

69 2001 JPSL Article 20.

70 OFRL Article 47.

71 In later laws, age compatibility is added (1951 JLFR Article 6).

72 1951 JLFR Article 23.

73 2010 JPSL Article 21a

74 2019 JPSL Article 21a.

75 2019 JPSL Article 21a.

76 Barbara F. Stowasser, *Women in the Qur'an, Traditions, and Interpretation* (Oxford University Press, 1994), p. 179 n. 38.

77 Shadaab Rahemtulla and Sara Ababneh (2021), "Reclaiming Khadija's and Muhammad's Marriage as an Islamic Paradigm: Towards a New History of the Muslim Present," *Journal of Feminist Studies in Religion*, www.jstor.org/stable/10 .2979/jfemistudreli.37.2.06

78 2019 JPSL Article 22b.

79 Sonbol, *Women of Jordan*, p. 155.

80 Tucker, *Women, Family, and Gender.*

81 1976 JPSL Article 19.

82 Amawi, "Gender and Citizenship in Jordan."

83 Economic and Social Council (2012), Position paper on the Draft Personal Status Law (2010) http://esc.jo/sites/default/files/Draft_Personal_Status_Law_2010_-_ Policy_Position_Paper.pdf.

84 Information and Research Center (2023), Stipulations in the Marriage Contract, "Knowledge, Perceptions, and Practices Related to Stipulations in the Marriage Contract/Jordan".

85 *Li'an* is when a husband accuses his wife of adultery and that a child is not his own. 2019 PSL Articles 164–165.

86 One aspect of the law that has not been taken advantage of by women's rights activists is the provision that allows men to delegate their right to divorce to their wives. 2001 JPSL Article 87; 2010 JPSL Article 85. Provided a man agrees to delegating his wife to divorce herself at any time and place and for any reason she desires, then this wife has the right to divorce. In fact, the 2019 JPSL even states that including the condition that the wife can divorce herself in the marriage contract is equivalent to the husband delegating this right to the wife. 2019 JPSL Article 38b.

87 OFRL Article 125.

88 Tucker, *Women, Family, and Gender*, p. 95.

89 One price a woman can and might have to pay from leaving a marriage is giving up her right to child custody. 2001 JPSL Article 111.

90 2010 JPSL Article 102.

91 2019 JPSL Article 102.

92 "There shall be no sin upon either of them for what the wife may give up [to her husband] in order to free herself." *The Message of the Qur'an*, translated by Muhammad Asad (The Book Foundation England, 2003), p. 61.

93 Asad, *The Message of the Quran*, p. 61.

94 Jamila is said to have come to the Prophet demanding to get a divorce from her husband. She admitted that she could find no fault with his character or behavior but that she simply "disliked him." Thereupon, the Prophet asked her to return her dowry (a garden she had received) to Thabit and decreed that the marriage be dissolved. Asad, *Message of the Qur'an*, p. 62.

95 Ishaq Ahmad Salem Eyal Salman, History of Tafileh from the end of the Ottoman Empire to the Independence of the Hashemite Kingdom of Jordan (1892–1946) [Tarikh al-Tafileh min awakher al-Dawlah al-Uthmaniyya h'ta Istiqlal al-Malaka al-Urduniyya al-Hashimiyya 1892/1309H- 1946/1365H], Ministry of Culture, 2009.

96 2019 JPSL Articles 14, 19.

97 2019 JPSL Article 19.

98 A guardian is responsible to provide for a male ward until he starts working in a way similar to others in his social class and for a female ward until she gets married. While males become responsible for providing for themselves after that, women always have the right to be provided for in the Jordanian JPSL. 2019 JPSL Article 195.

99 2019 JPSL Article 223.

100 Tucker, *Women, Family, and Gender*, p. 222.

101 Jordan Times, "Family Council Seeks Mother's Right to Approve Medical Intervention for Children," *Jordan Times*, May 16, 2015. Al Ra'i, "'Solidarity' Welcomes Parliaments Approval to Change Articles (62) and (98) of the Penal Code' [Tadamun turaheb bimuwafaqat al Nuwwab a'la ta'dil al-Madatayin 62 wa 98 Auqubat], *Al Ra'i*, July 30, 2017.

102 2011 Penal Code No. 18/2011, Published in Official Gazette No. 5090 on May 2, 2011.

103 Hadeel Abd al Aziz, phone interview with the author, May 21, 2020.

104 1951 JLFR, Article 123.

105 A *Mahram* is a family member to whom one is not allowed to get married Islamically. In other words, it is *haram* (forbidden) to get married to this person.
106 1976 JPSL Article 156.
107 1976 JPSL Article 154.
108 2010 JPSL Article 170.
109 2019 JPSL Article 170.
110 Zaina Steityeh, "The Personal Status Quo," *Jordan Business* (December 2010), (77–80), p. 78.
111 2019 JPSL Article 20.
112 2001 JPSL Article 66a.

The Palestinian Minority in Israel

MICHAEL MOUSA KARAYANNI

8.1 Introduction

Two formal sets of norms govern family law and gender among the Palestinian minority in Israel. The first is the respective religious law of the parties. Until today, in Israel, certain matters of personal status are under the adjudicative and prescriptive jurisdiction of the relevant religious community, which in some cases is exclusive in nature. The second is a constitutional quest that seeks to install certain liberal norms of a secular nature in the sphere of family law. The Knesset (the Israeli parliament) has singled out a number of family law issues and subjected them to secular-territorial norms applicable to all Israelis alike, irrespective of their religious affiliation. In some cases, Israeli law went one step further and levied criminal and civil sanctions with respect to certain practices in the domain of family law that happen to be sanctioned by religious law but found inappropriate in terms of gender and public policy considerations in Israel. As I will also try to show, a third set of norms has also come into play within the domain of family law and gender relations, albeit less direct and formal in nature. This third source is Israel's constitutional identity as a Jewish nation-state, which entails certain legal paradigms when dealing with the family law issues of the considerable Palestinian minority that exists in the country.

As one can imagine, covering all these issues would require a much more elaborate discussion than the one dictated by the limitations of space in this chapter. I have nonetheless assembled here an analysis that gives a general impression of how all of these sets of laws worked together in generating the major norms concerning family law and gender issues.

8.2 Demography

The Palestinian minority in Israel constitutes about 20 percent of the total population. At the end of 2017, the total population of Israel stood at 8,797,900,[1] of which 1,838,200 were Palestinian (officially termed "Arabs").[2] In terms of religion, the Palestinian minority in Israel is divided into three main groups: Muslims, numbering 1,561,700 (about 17.7 percent of the total population); Druze, numbering 141,200 (1.6 percent); and Christians, numbering 171,900 (slightly below 2 percent).[3] The Palestinian Christian community is divided into ten recognized religious communities: (1) Eastern (Orthodox), (2) Latin (Catholic), (3) Gregorian Armenian, (4) Armenian (Catholic), (5) Syrian (Catholic), (6) Chaldean (Uniate), (7) Greek (Catholic) Melkite, (8) Maronite, (9) Syrian (Orthodox), and (10) Evangelical Episcopal.[4] This chapter, however, will focus on the Muslim community only and more specifically on the interrelation between state law and Islamic *Shari'a*.

8.3   Adjudicative and Prescriptive Jurisdiction of Palestinian Religious Communities

The basic enactment regulating the jurisdictional authority of *Shari'a* courts in Israel is a British Mandate legal instrument called the Palestine Order-in-Council, 1922 (POC).[5] This enactment, which in effect operated as the semi-constitution of Mandatory Palestine, incorporated, with some major modifications, the Ottoman *millet* system by which parties were relegated to their religious community courts and norms in matters of family law.[6] The relevant provision regulating the jurisdictional capacity of *Shari'a* courts is Article 52 of the POC.[7] In its original form, this provision granted the local *Shari'a* courts exclusive jurisdiction in a wide variety of personal status matters of Muslims, both local citizens and foreigners, who under the law of their nationality (*lex patriae*) were subject in matters of personal status to the jurisdiction of *Shari'a* courts. POC Article 52 did not explicitly list the personal status matters over which *Shari'a* courts were granted exclusive jurisdiction but referred to an Ottoman law called "Law of Procedure of Muslim Religious Courts," enacted in 1917, which (in Section 7) listed the following matters: issues pertaining to endowments, orphans, guardianship, wills and succession, incompetency, absentee, marriage, divorce, *mohar* (*bride price*), and child support.[8]

The jurisdictional capacity accorded to the *Shari'a* courts was much wider than that accorded to the Christian and Druze courts and even that of the rabbinical courts (which was almost the same as that of the Druze courts). This also happens to be a legacy of the Ottoman legal system where the *Shari'a* courts operated for a long period of time as the official state courts of the Empire and were thus granted far-reaching jurisdictional authority.[9] Interestingly, some of this preferred status managed to survive the British Mandate of Palestine as well as the State of Israel (at least in the first decades).[10]

The jurisdiction of the *Shari'a* courts underwent one major transformation in 2001 when their exclusive jurisdictional capacity was restricted to matters of marriage and divorce only. In those other matters over which these courts had exclusive jurisdiction before, they now have concurrent jurisdiction that materializes if they are seized first by one of the parties. The initiative that culminated in these reforms was motivated by the desire to promote gender equality in the realm of family law.[11] The working assumption has long been that the more jurisdictional authority is taken away from the religious courts in favor of the civil courts, the better the chances are that women will receive equal treatment.[12] This is the case for two main reasons. First, religious law on issues of family law tends to be patriarchal in nature, making exclusive jurisdiction of religious courts detrimental to gender equality.[13] Second, the mere fact that women can now opt out of the exclusive jurisdiction of religious courts also works to empower their "voice" from within – the greater the availability of exit the better the chances that the community will take the voices of its members into account and work to accommodate them.

All in all, under present day law in Israel, the *Shari'a* courts of the Palestinian minority have exclusive jurisdiction in matters of marriage and divorce of their members, which to a great extent is also the case with respect to the rabbinical courts. It is true that when defining the jurisdictional capacity of the various religious communities, the law defines the adjudicative jurisdictional capacity of these courts. There is no express provision instructing these courts which law they must apply when adjudicating marriage and divorce claims of their members. Yet it is widely acknowledged that when a religious court operates within the exclusive adjudicative jurisdictional authority, it is free to apply the law of that community in these matters. In fact, in light of the initial interest in guaranteeing the application of religious norms to matters of marriage and divorce, the religious courts were afforded exclusive jurisdiction in these matters.

It is also important to note that issues of marriage and divorce can come up in an ancillary manner before the civil courts. Take, for example, an alimony claim filed by a wife against her husband before the civil court and the husband argues to his defense that the parties are not considered to be married at all, making the claim baseless. It has long been customary in Israel that the law governing marriage and divorce is the personal law of the parties, which in the case of local Israeli citizens, is considered to be their religious law.[14]

Religious courts in Israel can also be competent to deal with certain family law matters under their concurrent jurisdictional capacity. In accordance with a number of enactments, a religious court can adjudicate family law matters if and when a certain precondition is met, otherwise the jurisdiction lies in the civil court – the Court of Family Affairs. For example, an inheritance proceeding can be brought by a party before the relevant religious courts if all of the concerned parties agree to such a jurisdictional capacity.

If the religious court is granted jurisdiction in accordance with its concurrent jurisdictional capacity, it is presumed here as well that the court will apply its religious law. However, at times the religious courts are instructed by a special enactment to abide by a secular norm against their own religious norm, specifically because the latter is discriminatory against women. For example, Israel's Succession Law, 1965, instructs the religious courts dealing with a matter of intestate succession that female minors should get the same share as male heirs, even if the relevant religious norm might instruct otherwise.[15]

8.4   From the Personal-Religious to the Territorial-Secular

8.4.1   Major Enactments

Following establishment of the State of Israel, one can discern a clear trend in the regulation of family law. The *millet* concept of having religious jurisdiction and personal religious law govern matters of family law was gradually pushed out and territorial-secular norms were ushered in.[16] This transformation was not accomplished within one general reform initiative but through piecemeal legislation that began in the 1950s and 1960s.[17] Nor was this transformation complete; it did not cover all family law matters – marriage and divorce are still within the exclusive jurisdiction of religious courts and norms, and religious courts can be empowered to deal with other matters according to their concurrent jurisdiction.

The major enactments that are identified with the shift toward a territorial-secular model are the Adoption of Children Law, 1960 (eventually replaced by Adoption of Children Law, 1981); Legal Capacity and Guardianship Law, 1962;[18] and the Succession Law, 1965. However, each of these laws provided that under certain conditions, primarily the agreement of all concerned parties, the relevant religious courts of the parties can still be competent to deal with issues regulated therein. Yet even then, the religious courts were at times ordered to abide by the secular norms – otherwise their judgment would be considered null and void for lack of subject matter jurisdiction.[19] One example is with respect to minor female heirs, as mentioned earlier. Another important provision was enacted in the Women's Equal Rights Law, 1951 (WERL),[20] which provides that both the father and mother are the guardians of their children.

The most interesting part of this trend was when territorial-secular legislation criminalized some acts in the domain of marriage and divorce, even though these acts were sanctioned by the religious norm of the parties. Criminalization was explicitly carried out in the name of gender equality.[21] The first enactment was the Age of Marriage Law, 1950.[22] This law set the minimum age for marriage at seventeen years (now eighteen). Accordingly, a person who marries an underage spouse solemnizes such a marriage and the parents/guardians of an underage spouse who permitted the marriage to take place can all be fined and sentenced up to two years in prison.[23] Another important feature of this enactment is the provision that recognizes the circumstance of one of the spouses being underage as cause for the dissolution of the marriage. Yet the law does not regard an underage marriage as void; if it is recognized by the relevant religious community of the parties, it is deemed valid under Israeli law.

The second enactment was WERL. In this law, the Knesset abolished the existing defense previously granted to Muslims if they undertake a polygamous marriage, thereby making polygamy a crime for all. Second, unilateral divorce was also made a crime. Yet WERL, as in the case of underage marriage, does not intervene in the religious norms that govern marriage and divorce – so that if these regard a polygamous marriage or a unilateral divorce as valid, Israeli law will do the same, notwithstanding the fact that such acts constitute a crime.[24]

8.4.2   Israeli Supreme Court Activism

Another important source, working to strengthen gender equality and other related interests in the sphere of family law, was the Israeli Supreme Court. Throughout the years this judicial institution, the highest in the country, worked to strike a balance between the governing religious norms in matters of family law, on the one hand, and liberal interests based on individual autonomy, especially one's right to be free from the imposition of religious norms, on the other. In a laborious journey fraught with criticism for its activist role, the Supreme Court did much to entrench norms of a liberal nature, including gender equality, at the expense of religious norms. This process was especially forceful with respect to the Jewish community and eventually it spilled over into the family law matters of the Palestinian minority. The following are three illustrative cases.

8.4.3   Sultan v. Sultan (1984)[25]

A Muslim wife was unilaterally divorced by her Muslim husband without the husband first seeking the approval for such a *tallaq* from the *Shari'a* court. As we have seen before, this constitutes a crime under Israeli law. The record of the case does not indicate whether the husband was actually prosecuted or not. In any event, the wife chose to initiate a civil proceeding claiming that since the husband's action constituted a crime, she is entitled to a civil remedy (compensation) under the Civil Wrongs Ordinance [New Version], 1968,[26] which turns a breach of a statutory duty into a tort. Both the Magistrate Court and the District Court (on appeal) dismissed the claim. The Supreme Court reversed. The Court reasoned that defining the husband's action as a crime was designed to promote gender equality. The plaintiff belonged to the group of individuals the definition under WERL sought to protect, all notwithstanding the fact that the unilateral divorce would still be recognized as binding under *Shari'a* and thus under Israeli law in general. This is indeed an innovative approach whereby a civil cause of action is created in order to further restrict the practice of unilateral divorce and promote gender equality within family law, without meddling in the religious norm on divorce.[27]

8.4.4   Plonit [Jane Doe] v. Ploni [John Doe] (1995)[28]

This case dealt with a paternity claim filed by a Muslim mother and her minor daughter against a man who was alleged to be the girl's father. The defendant, who was already married and the father of eight children, was also asked to provide child support if found to be the biological father. At all relevant times, the mother claimant was single and agreed to have a relationship with the defendant on the basis of his promise to marry her, but no marriage materialized between the two. When seized with this action, the *Shari'a* court summarily dismissed it. The court reasoned that since the mother was not legally married to the defendant, she could not claim that the defendant was the father of her child. The mother-claimant did not give up and filed the same action before the District Court on the basis of its general residual jurisdiction. This court also dismissed the claim on the pretext that it lacked subject matter jurisdiction. According to the jurisdictional principles in effect at the time, paternity (*nassab*, literally family lineage) was deemed to be within the exclusive jurisdiction of the *Shari'a* courts. The mother and daughter were thus faced with a legal deadlock: neither the *Shari'a* court nor the civil court was prepared to adjudicate their claim on the merits. On appeal taken from the judgment of the District Court, the Supreme Court intervened and reversed. In its opinion, the Court stressed the child's basic right to know the identity of her father. The prime purpose of the civil courts, the Court went on to proclaim, is the welfare and happiness of the individual. In the final analysis, this overall objective brought the Court to conclude that irrespective of what an actual paternity proceeding means under the rubric of *nassab*, a *Shari'a* court cannot be regarded as having subject matter jurisdiction over a proceeding when it will summarily dismiss the claim up front as incognizable. Therefore, in such an instance, subject matter jurisdiction lies in civil courts.

8.4.5   Plonit [Jane Doe] v. Shari'a Court of Appeals (2013)[29]

According to an enactment from the time when the Ottomans ruled the country prior to 1917, and that is still binding on *Shari'a* courts to this day, a panel of arbitrators is appointed to settle divorce proceedings between the spouses. Each spouse appoints an arbitrator on his/her behalf. In this case, the wife insisted on choosing a female arbitrator. Both the *Shari'a* court of first instance and the *Shari'a* Court of Appeals denied her request, holding that only male arbitrators are allowed to fill this post. In a special administrative review procedure, the wife then petitioned the Israeli Supreme Court in its capacity as the High Court of Justice arguing that what the *Shari'a* courts did was to disregard the basic norm of the equality between the sexes as determined in WERL. The Court granted the petition and invalidated the judgment of the *Shari'a* courts.

From these decisions, one can clearly discern the Israeli Supreme Court's attitude toward limiting the jurisdictional powers of the

Palestinian religious community in the name of gender equality. But as I will argue in the upcoming discussion, this judicial activism on the part of the Court was of limited influence given the contextual constitutional environment of Israel as a whole.

8.5   The Palestinian Minority's Family Law,
Gender Issues and Israel's Constitutional Definition as a Jewish Nation-State

Generally, there is a close connection between the existing social and political order and the realm of family law.[30] Family law is regarded as a storyteller: it "tells stories about the culture . . . stories about who we are, where we came from, and where we are going."[31] In essence, family law is a mirror of society's basic norms and reflects its hegemonic structure.[32] Israel is no exception. The question of whether it is proper to keep matters of marriage and divorce under the exclusive jurisdiction of the religious courts came to be closely tied with Israel's constitutional iden- tity as a non-assimilative Jewish nation-state that has been in a state of conflict with its Palestinian minority since its establishment.[33] The existing state of jurisdiction helped to preserve endogamy and as a result, guarantee the strengthening of Jewish identity, thereby maintaining Israel's national identity as a Jewish state[34] and its overall social order as a non-assimilative state.[35] It also served to keep the Palestinian community religiously divided, thereby making it more susceptible to the government's policies of control,[36] while at the same time helping dominant patriarchal forces within the Palestinian community maintain their power structure given the basic fact that religious family law is very much patriarchal in nature.[37]

One other major implication Israel's constitutional identity had on the jurisdiction accorded to the Palestinian minority religious communities was the relegation of this jurisdictional authority into Israel's private sphere, while Judaism and the jurisdictional authority accorded to Jewish religious institutions were maintained as part of Israel's public sphere given the fact that Judaism is the state's official religion.[38] As part of this private nature of the jurisdiction accorded to the Palestinian religious communities, it became commonplace to regard it as a form of multicultural accommodation or a liberal-tolerant concession on the part of the Jewish state toward its non-Jewish religious communities.[39] These characteristics had some important implications for issues of family law and gender. Given the private–multicultural–autonomous nature of the jurisdiction accorded to the Palestinian religious communities in Israel, there was more reluctance on the part of the Israeli establishment (the Knesset, ministries, and courts) to intervene in the internal dealings and norms of these communities than in the internal dealings and norms of Jewish religious institutions.[40] In turn, patriarchal norms based on religious community norms had a stronger grip on the Palestinian minority.[41]

This should not be taken to mean that the Israeli establishment did not intervene at all in the internal norms of Palestinian religious communities. As we have already seen, a number of religiously permitted practices in the sphere of marriage and divorce were criminalized in Israel (underage marriage, polygamy, and unilateral divorce); and on a number of occasions, the Israeli Supreme Court did restrict the jurisdiction of Palestinian religious courts in order to protect gender-based interests. However, if we were to zoom out and look at the evolution of these interventions as well as the actual enforcement of criminal and civil restrictions, we will be better able to observe the reluctance of the Israeli establishment as identified earlier. Let us consider the following examples.

8.5.1 Alimony Claims

As far back as 1953, a Jewish wife seeking alimony from her husband was granted the opportunity to file her claim before civil court, with the enactment of Rabbinical Courts Jurisdiction (Marriage and Divorce) Law, 1953 (Sec. 4).[42] However, a Muslim wife seeking to file an alimony claim was granted the opportunity to file her claim before a civil court only in 2001. Until then, Muslim wives had to file their alimony claims before the Shari'a courts since they had exclusive jurisdiction over alimony proceedings. This exclusive jurisdictional authority that the Muslim wives had to endure for forty-eight years more than did Jewish wives can be explained by the reluctance of the Israeli establishment observed earlier. As I argued above, this reluctance had a detrimental impact with respect to gender. It is common knowledge that the religious courts were not particularly generous when fixing alimony payments. If we add to this the fact that their jurisdictional authority was of an exclusive nature, Muslim wives could not opt out. With no other competing jurisdiction, these religious courts had no particular interest in entertaining the "voice" and hence the interests of these wives.

8.5.2   Enforcement in Matters of Underage Marriage and Polygamy

The criminalization of polygamy, unilateral divorce, and underage marriage was no doubt a rather bold act with the aim of abolishing certain practices sanctioned by the religion of the parties. But there seems to be a disparity between the norm on the books and the norm in action. Prosecution for these crimes seems to be minimal,[43] and some very creative ways were found for circumventing these restrictions.[44] This overall tendency is also driven by the basic notion that such practices are those of a religious minority in which the State of Israel is more reluctant to intervene. Particularly telling in this respect is the account of Robert H. Eisenman, author of *Islamic Law in Palestine and Israel* – the most thorough study on *Shari'a*'s institutions in the country. Regarding regulation of underage marriage, Eisenman notes: "Israelis were not anxious to upset local, non-Jewish sensibilities through prosecution and were really more concerned about Oriental Jews newly arriving in the State with similar cultural mores."[45] If this is true with reference to underage marriage, then it is equally true in other spheres, as indeed noted by others.[46] And when there was decline in certain practices, for example, polygamy, the main reasons were "economic, cultural and social factors," rather than the criminal sanction.[47]

8.6   The Arab World and Local Reforms

The recent upheavals in the Middle East, namely the events in different Arab countries in the wake of what came to be known as the "Arab Spring" had many implications, some of which are still unraveling before our eyes. Many of us watching these historic events were baffled at times. The quest for democracy and order left some countries in anarchy or a regime change that differed little from the one that existed before. Was it all in vain? I guess much will still be said and written about this in the future to come. But a vibration of a sort to look around and seek reforms did leave its imprints in many places, including among the Palestinian minority in Israel. I must say that these reforms did not materialize to their full extent, at least in the domain of family law, in light of the crippling effect of the long-standing conflict between the Palestinian minority and the Israeli establishment. Working to reform Palestinian personal law will certainly create cracks from within that will weaken this minority in its major political battles with the Israeli state institutions.

Additionally, the Israeli establishment has traditionally benefited from the existing structure of traditional religious law governing in matters of personal status as it suited its control policy of "divide," or rather "define and rule" (to use Mahmood Mamdani's term).[48] Some reforms did make it through, among which were reforms that took place in other Arab countries. For example, the practice of appointing informants (*mukhbirin*) by a *Shari'a* court to assess alimony payments for Muslim women was abolished while citing its abolishment in other Arab countries. The appointment of a woman to the position of a *Shari'a* court *qaddi* was also facilitated by the fact that such an appointment already took place in other Arab countries.[49] This is a mode of reform that I have called "organic transplantation," and it is hoped that local *Shari'a* reforms will continue to draw on reforms taking place in other Arab countries.

8.7 Conclusion

The Muslim minority's family law and gender issues in Israel are a peculiar entanglement between the personal-religious and the secular-territorial. In addition, the case of the Muslim minority is special given the national tension between it as part of a national minority and the State of Israel – a conflict that adds a dimension of its own. As I have expanded on the topic in my other writings,[50] it does make a difference that Israel is explicitly identified with the Jewish majority and is not a Western democracy, if and when it seeks to intervene in issues pertaining to Muslim personal status. In many respects, it is intervening in the private affairs of "others" and not in the affairs of its "own." This legitimacy deficit is also relevant for Palestinian political minority leaders and reformers from among the Muslim community. Turning to Israeli state institutions in order to amend *Shari'a* and *Shari'a* jurisdiction is compared with seeking the help of a "foreign" entity. Add to this such factors as "define and rule," preserving endogamy as a measure of preserving the Jewish state structure, and internal Palestinian concerns about galvanizing the national political discourse while downplaying minority secular ideals – then one can come to see the rather complicated web of consideration that sustains *Shari'a* jurisdiction among the Palestinians in Israel. In this chapter, I tried to give a general survey of governing norms as well as the general policies that dictate their application.

Notes

1 "CBS Statistical Abstract of Israel 2018," www.cbs.gov.il/reader/shnatonenew_site .htm, table 2.1.

2 "CBS Statistical Abstract of Israel 2018." Of the total population in Israel there are 371,000 citizens identified as neither Jews nor Arabs. This group is composed of immigrants who acquired Israeli citizenship under a special provision in the Law of Return, 1950, that grants the right of immigration to those with a certain family relative who was a Jew ("CBS Statistical Abstract of Israel 2018," table 2.1). Another group is that of foreign workers, estimated at 190,000, who do not appear in the official census ("CBS Statistical Abstract," p. 30).

3 "CBS Statistical Abstract of Israel 2018," table 2.2.

4 See R. Gottschalk, "Personal Status and Religious Law in Israel" (1951) 4 *International Law Quarterly*, 454, 455. The Evangelical Episcopal Church was recognized in 1970; see Order of Recognition of a Religious Community (Evangelical Episcopal Church in Israel), 1970, K.T. 2557, p. 1564. In addition, there is the Bahai Community – a religious group recognized since 1971; see Order of Religious Community (The Bahai Faith), 1971, K.T. 2673, p. 628.

5 Palestine Order-in-Council, 1922 (POC).

6 See Edoardo Vitta, "Codification of Private International Law in Israel?" (1977) 12 *Israel Law Review*, 129; Frederic M. Goadby, *International and Inter-Religious Private Law in Palestine* (Hamadpis Press, 1926), pp. 115–120.

7 POC Article 52.

8 Moussa Abou Ramadan, "Judicial Activism of the Shari'a Appeals Court in Israel (1994–2001): Rise and Crises" (2003) 27 *Fordham International Law Journal*, 254, 264 n. 50.

9 Edoardo Vitta, *The Conflict of Laws in Matters of Personal Status in Palestine* (Bursi, 1947), pp. 103–104. The *Shari'a* court's jurisdiction was severely restricted in the vast legal reforms of the 19th century, widely known as the Tanzimat. In the end, *Shari'a* courts had jurisdiction in matters of family law only.

10 See Edoardo Vitta, "The Conflict of Personal Laws" (1970) 5 *Israel Law Review*, 170, 172–178. One major modification made by the British Mandate was to restrict the jurisdiction of the *Shari'a* courts to Muslims only. During the Ottoman Empire, including in the post-Tanzimat period (and certainly before), the *Shari'a* courts had jurisdictional capacity over non-Muslims as well. See Zeina Ghandour, "Religious Law in a Secular State: The Jurisdiction of the Shari'a Courts of Palestine and Israel" (1990) 5 *Arab Law Quarterly*, 25, 28. At times, this preferred status of the *Shari'a* courts was used by the Israeli establishment in order to highlight Israel's religious tolerance toward its non-Jewish minorities. See Michael M. Karayanni, "Two Concepts of Group Rights for the Palestinian-Arab Minority under Israel's Constitutional Definition as a 'Jewish and Democratic' State" (2012) 10 *I•CON. – International Journal Constitutional Law*, 304–339.

11 Gila Stopler, "Countenancing the Oppression of Women: How Liberals Tolerate Religious and Cultural Practices That Discriminate Against Women" (2003) 12 *Columbia Journal Gender & Law*, 154, 201.

12 See Gila Stopler, "The Free Exercise of Discrimination: Religious Liberty, Civic Community and Women's Equality" (2004) 10 *William & Mary Journal Women & Law*, 459, 485.

13 See Gila Stopler, "'A Rank Usurpation of Power' – The Role of Patriarchal Religion and Culture in the Subordination of Women" (2008) 15 *Duke Journal Gender Law & Policy*, 365.

14 See Menashe Shava, "Civil Marriage Celebrated Abroad: Validity in Israel" (1989) 9 *Tel Aviv University Studies Law*, 311, 320–322.

15 Israel Succession Act (1965).

16 See Menashe Shava, "The Nature and Scope of Jewish Law in Israel as Applied in the Civil Courts as Compared with Its Application in the Rabbinical Courts" (1985) *Jewish Law Annual*, 3, 4.

17 See Robert H. Eisenman, *Islamic Law in Palestine and Israel: A History of the Survival of Tanzimat and Shari'a in the British Mandate and the Jewish State* (E. J. Brill, 1978), pp. 196–223.

18 Adoption of Children Law (1960) (eventually replaced by Adoption of Children Law, 1981); Legal Capacity and Guardianship Law (1962).

19 See Menashe Shava, *Ha-Din ha-Ishi be-Yisra'el* [*The Personal Law in Israel*], 3rd enlarged ed., 2 vols (Masada, 1991), vol. I, p. 223 (in Hebrew); HCJ 187/54 *Biriah v. Qadi of Muslim Shari'a Court*, 9 P.D. 1193 (1955).

20 Women's Equal Rights Law, 1951 (WERL).

21 Eisenman, *Islamic Law*, pp. 168–169.

22 Age of Marriage Law (1950).

23 Exceptions do apply, when, for example, the wife is pregnant or has recently given birth to a child, or if she is sixteen-years-old with other special circumstances.

24 Eisenman, *Islamic Law*, p. 187.

25 CA 245/81, 38(3) P.D. 169 (1984).

26 Civil Wrongs Ordinance [New Version] (1968).

27 Unilateral divorce is also recognized by Druze law on divorce. In HCJ 2820/03 *Plonit v. Druze Appellate Court in Acre* (2006), a Druze wife who was unilaterally divorced from her husband just before he died challenged the proceedings in which the Druze religious courts was asked to recognize this divorce. At the end of the day, she prevailed because of an improper procedural position taken by the Druze religious court. However, one of the justices, Salim Jubran, reasoned that in his opinion the act of a unilateral divorce is void given the fact that it was declared a crime, even when considered by the Druze religious court. This opinion, which remained Justice Jubran's alone, with the other two justices explicitly refraining from taking such a position, is far reaching. For until now, the two realms, the personal-religious and the territorial-secular, went their own ways in matters of marriage and divorce.

28 CA 3077/90, 49(2) PD 578 (1995).

29 HCJ 3856/11 (27.6.2013)

30 See Mary Ann Glendon, *State, Law and Family: Family Law in Transition in the United States and Western Europe* (North Holland, 1977), p. 18; O. Kahn-Freund, "On Uses and Misuses of Comparative Law" (1974) 37 *Modern Law Review*, 1, 13.

31 Mary Ann Glendon, *Abortion and Divorce in Western Law* (Harvard University Press, 1987), p. 8.

32 Michael M. Karayanni, "In the Best Interests of the Group: Religious Matching Under Israeli Adoption Law" (2010) 3 *Berkeley Journal Middle East & Islamic Law*, 1.

33 See Nadim N. Rouhana, *Palestinian Citizens in an Ethnic Jewish State: Identities in Conflict* (Yale University Press, 1997).

34 See Karayanni, "Two Concepts of Group Rights"; Yüksel Sezgin, "The Israeli Millet System: Examining Legal Pluralism through the Lens of Nation Building and Human Rights" (2010) 43 *Israel Law Review*, 631, 632–633, 636–641.

35 Karayanni, "In the Best Interests of the Group," pp. 44–45.

36 Ian Lustick, *Arabs in the Jewish State: Israel's Control of a National Minority* (University of Texas Press, 1980). See also Gad Barzilai, "Fantasies of Liberalism and Liberal Jurisprudence: State Law, Politics and the Israeli Arab-Palestinian Community" (2000) 34 *Israel Law Review*, 425, 436.

37 Michael M Karayanni, "The Separate Nature of the Religious Accommodations for the Palestinian-Arab Minority in Israel" (2006) 5 *Northwestern University Journal International Human Rights*, 41, 64.

38 See Michael M. Karayanni, "Living in a Group of One's Own: Normative Implications Related to the Private Nature of the Religious Accommodations for the Palestinian-Arab Minority in Israel" (2007) 6 *UCLA Journal Islamic & Near Eastern Law*, 1, 2–3.

39 Karayanni, "The Separate Nature of the Religious Accommodations," pp. 45–46. This should not be taken to mean, however, that these accommodations do in fact qualify as such. See Michael M. Karayanni, "Multiculture Me No More! On Multicultural Qualifications and the Palestinian-Arab Minority of Israel" (2007) 54 *Diogenes*, 39.

40 See, e.g., Ori Stendel, *The Minorities in Israel: Trends in the Development of the Arab and Druze Communities 1948-1973* (The Israel Economist, 1973), p. 8 ("from the establishment of the State, the government's policy has been not to interfere in the religious affairs of the various communities," and all communities "maintain a considerable measure of internal autonomy"); Martin Edelman, *Courts, Politics, and Culture in Israel* (University of Virginia Press, 1994), pp. 88, 98–99 (arguing that reforming the personal law of the non-Jewish population in Israel has not been a government priority and that the government refrained from intervening in such issues so as not to aggravate minority religions by insisting that they conform to the majority's norms); Gad Barzilai, *Communities and the Law*, Politics and Cultures of Legal Identities 107 (University of Michigan Press, 2003) ("non-Jewish courts, inter alia, the Shari'a courts, Christian courts, and Druze courts, have received state recognition as having exclusive religious jurisdiction over their respective groups in personal status affairs under the possible review of the Supreme Court. The Supreme Court has rarely intervened in their jurisdiction, and often it has empowered their jurisdiction").

41 It is important to also note that when the Israeli Supreme did intervene in what seemed an internal matter of the *Shari'a* courts, it went out of its way to underscore the fact that Islamic law can also be supportive of the move. This was very much the case, for example, in *Plonit v. Shari'a Court of Appeals*. On the interplay between religious jurisdiction-authority and gender issues, see Monique Deveaux, *Gender and Justice in Multicultural Liberal States* (Oxford University Press, 2006); Ayelet Shachar, *Multicultural Jurisdictions: Cultural Differences and Women's Rights* (Cambridge University Press, 2001); Susan Moller Okin, "Is Multiculturalism Bad for Women?," in Joshua Cohen et al. (eds.), *Is Multiculturalism Bad for Women?* (Princeton University Press, 1999), p 7.

42 Rabbinical Courts Jurisdiction (Marriage and Divorce) Law (1953) (Sec. 4).

43 See Eisenman, *Islamic Law*, p. 179.

44 See Aharon Layish, *Women and Islamic Law in a Non-Muslim State: A Study Based on the Shari'a Courts in Israel* (Wiley; Israel Universities Press, 1975), pp. 16–17; Eisenman, *Islamic Law*, pp. 174–175, 182.

45 Eisenman, *Islamic Law*, p. 172.

46 See Edelman, *Courts, Politics, and Culture*, p. 87; Anat Lapidot-Firilla and Ronny Elhadad, *Forbidden Yet Practiced: Polygamy and the Cyclical Making of Israeli Policy* (The Center for Strategic and Policy Studies, 2006); Andrew Treitel, "Conflicting Traditions: Muslim Shari'a Courts and Marriage Age Regulation in Israel" (1995) 26 *Columbia Human Rights Law Review*, 403–438.

47 Layish, *Women and Islamic Law*, pp. 78–79.

48 See Mahmood Mamdani, *Define and Rule, Native as Political Identity* (Harvard University Press, 2012). On this issue and the whole religion and state configuration in Israel, see Michael Karayanni, *A Multicultural Entrapment, Religion & State among the Palestinian-Arabs in Israel* (Cambridge University Press, 2020).

49 See Karayanni, *A Multicultural Entrapment*, chapter 6.

50 Karayanni, *A Multicultural Entrapment*, chapters 4 and 5; Michael Karayanni, "Multiculturalism as Covering: On the Accommodation of Minority Religions in Israel" (2018) 66 *American Journal of Comparative Law*, 831.

9

West Bank and Gaza Personal Status Law

JONATHAN KUTTAB AND ADRIEN K. WING

Palestinians fall under a dizzying array of laws and courts of differing and sometimes overlapping jurisdictions that adjudicate their personal status matters. The specific court or law that applies depends both on the religious/communal identity of the person and the area in which the person lives.

In the nineteenth and early twentieth century, the entire region was part of the Ottoman Empire. The 1871 Ottoman Civil Code was a major source of law.[1] The 1917 Ottoman Law of Family Rights (OLFR)[2] was the main elaboration on personal status law, primarily influenced by the Hanafi School of Islamic jurisprudence.

9.1 Millet System

The personal status law applicable depends primarily on the religious community or millet to which the person belongs.[3] An understanding of this system is crucial to understanding personal status law not only in Palestine but throughout the region, whose personal status laws evolved from this Ottoman system in varying degrees.

The millet system was introduced during the Ottoman era as a means for the sultan to preside over the numerous religious minorities. The solution was to grant broad autonomous powers to each millet and give it authority over personal status affairs of members of its community.[4] The system consisted of allowing each community to have its own schools, charitable institutions, and religious courts and permission to run its internal affairs, all under the authority of the sultan. In return, the head of each community was directly responsible to the sultan for the behavior of individuals in that community.[5]

At the time, this was a very progressive view, as it granted religious freedom and autonomy to many minorities. The Sunni majority and Shiites would have their own *Shari'a* courts, the Christians, their respective ecclesiastical courts, and the Jews, their rabbinical courts. Eleven

Christian communities were identified, recognized as distinct millets, and authorized to set up their separate ecclesiastical courts.

It should be understood that the principles of freedom of conscience and individual religious liberty, as well as separation of church and state, were not present then, even in Europe.[6] An individual was a Muslim or a Jew or a Greek Orthodox or an Armenian by virtue of being born into and belonging to a particular group. The religious identity was treated as if it were an ethnic issue. It had nothing to do with systems of belief and whether a particular individual worshipped or followed the rituals of his or her religious community.

You were Armenian because you were born of Armenian parents and your name ended with ". . . ian" (son of). It made no difference whether you believed in God or worshiped in the church. The rhythm of your life, your relationships, and identity were fixed and determined at birth. In this sense, religious freedom was a collective and corporate phenomenon, rather than an individual one. The laws of the state were incorporated and reinforced in the community for each minority.[7]

Individuals who chose to disassociate themselves from their religious community, or worshipped or married across religious lines, as well as held religious beliefs that did not fall within one of the recognized religious communities, found themselves in difficult situations.[8] In addition, attempts at evangelism and proselytizing were resisted and fought not only by the majority group but by all the different groups.

During the past century, as the different countries obtained their independence from Ottoman rule and began developing their separate legal systems, and created civil courts, most of them kept the millet system, with respect to family law and personal status matters. This was often viewed as a method of protecting the rights of the minorities, as well as out of respect for the *Shari'a* courts, which were being deprived of authority in all other civil matters, such as contracts and obligations.

This system continues to govern many of the countries of the Middle East today, including Israel, Palestine, Jordan, Syria, Lebanon, and Egypt. Personal status matters in each of these countries continue to be governed by the religious courts of the community to which an individual belongs.

The past century has seen the introduction of many Western concepts into the Middle East, many of which would be enshrined in constitutions as well as pronouncements of modernity. Yet the millet system continued to thrive, in clear contradiction to Western concepts of individual freedoms and secularism.[9]

The millet system described above was canonized in Palestine through a number of laws in the early twentieth century. For instance, the Law of Registering Marriages and Divorces of 1919 authorized the relevant religious persons to record marriages: for Muslims, the ma'zoon; for Christians, the priest or pastor; for Jews, the rabbi; and for Druze, the sheikh of the tribe.[10] After the end of the Ottoman Empire, the area came under the British Mandate from 1920 to 1948.

In the preamble to the Law Regulating Religious Denominations of 1938, it stated:

> Article 83 of the Declaration of the Constitution of Palestine of 1922[11] allowed each religious denomination which is recognized by the government to enjoy autonomous independence with respect to handling its internal affairs, subject to the provisions of any law or Order issued by the high Commissioner.[12]

Appendix 2 of this law lists the following religious denominations as recognized: Eastern Greek Orthodox, Latin (Catholics), Gregorian Armenians, Armenian (Catholics), Assyrian Catholics, Chaldean (Catholics), Jews, Roman Melkite Catholics, Maronites, and Syrian Orthodox.[13] The Lutheran Church and the Arab Episcopal (Anglican) Church were subsequently added to the list.[14]

From 1948 on, when Israel came into being, different additional sources of law came into effect in the various areas.

Geographically, Palestinians today live under several separate juridical systems depending on their place of residence. Those who are residing in the State of Israel as it existed before 1967 are governed by Israeli laws, which are sufficiently confusing and varied in their own right. The Palestinians living in East Jerusalem have also been under Israeli law since the 1967 Occupation. Professor Michael Karayanni has written a chapter in this volume on these Palestinians.[15] This chapter concerns those Palestinians who are living in the two other main areas – the West Bank and Gaza.[16]

The chapter next discusses what happened in the West Bank and then Gaza.

9.2   West Bank

9.2.1   Broad Framework of Law

The West Bank is governed by a combination of Ottoman laws, British Mandate laws, Jordanian laws, Israeli military orders, and Palestinian laws. When Israel was created in 1948, the portions of Palestine that remained in Arab hands were the Gaza Strip, which was administered by Egypt, and the West Bank (including East Jerusalem), which was under Jordanian authority. Jordanian law, which itself was a combination of Ottoman Law and some British mandate regulations, was promulgated in the West Bank. As Jordan developed its law into a more modern system of civil and criminal law, these developments were applicable in the West Bank as well. In 1967, following the Six Day War, the Israeli army occupied all the West Bank and East Jerusalem. Israeli Military Order No. 1 stated that the existing laws would continue in effect, unless changed by the Military Commander, who took on all legislative, executive, and judicial powers.[17]

Between 1967 and 1994, the laws in the West Bank were generally frozen at the level Jordanian law was in 1967. Some of the laws have been changed in several ways. Some laws have been amended by Israeli military orders that applied to most areas of life. There have been over 2,000 of these orders as of 2020.[18] Some of these military orders applied to the functioning of the courts and their procedures, but none directly affected personal status matters. Another major change was the 1980 Knesset law, which effectively annexed East Jerusalem and surrounding areas, some of which includes parts of the West Bank. Israeli law and administration have been applied to those areas and their populations.[19]

Another change occurred in 1994, when the Palestinian National Authority (PA) was created and given civilian authority and some security authority in portions of the West Bank. There are currently three areas of jurisdiction: areas designated under the Clinton Administration-era Oslo Agreements as Areas A and B, which fall under the authority of the PA, and areas designated as Area C, which while subject to the same laws as Areas A and B, face a totally different situation. About 55 percent of Palestinians live in Area A, yet it has only about 18 percent of the territory; 41 percent live in Area B, with 20 percent of the land; and only 1 percent live in Area C, with 62 percent of the territory.[20] Area C, which contained most of the settlements, army bases, and vast areas between them (including most of the Jordan Valley), continued to be governed under direct Israel Military (and Civil) administration.[21] Since Palestinian police and execution departments have no authority in Area C, however, litigants cannot ensure compliance or respect for the writ of Palestinian courts in those areas. This means that they would require, if possible, separate legal steps to give effect to any judicial pronouncements.[22] This chapter will not cover the issue of Jewish settlers residing either in East Jerusalem or the West Bank (usually in areas designated as Area C under the Oslo Agreements) as they use Israeli laws and refuse the jurisdiction of Palestinian courts.

The resulting situation is quite confusing from the legal point of view, especially since some areas shifted from C to B and A in a number of steps, and these changes were expected to continue when negotiations were being conducted between Israel and the PA. Furthermore, Israel often ignored the separate status of the different zones. Where Israeli Jewish persons were involved, Israeli law usually applied regardless of their location. Where Arabs were involved, Israel would sometimes allow Palestinian law to apply or – if it had an interest – refuse to apply Palestinian law and either impose Israeli laws or use the military courts in the West Bank to claim jurisdiction to reach the desired result. To further complicate matters, the Christian Religious courts, which handled exclusively matters of personal status for Christians, were situated in East Jerusalem but continued to apply Jordanian laws, as will be described below . In this, they were assisted by the fact that the millet system, which gave religious courts this jurisdiction, continued to apply in Palestine, Jordan, and Israel itself.

Further complexity occurred after the Palestinian elections of 2007, in which Hamas – which was dominant in Gaza – won against Fatah, the historic dominant party. A schism occurred, which has not been fully resolved as of 2022. A civil war–like situation occurred with the bottom line being that Hamas has controlled Gaza and the PA (under Fatah) has controlled the West Bank ever since. Thus, any PA legislation or presidential edicts have only been able to be applied in the West Bank. There was some movement to unify and coordinate laws between the West Bank and Gaza, but this process ceased with the schism and has not influenced personal status law in any case.

In addition, to complicate things further in the current era, the law is clear as to Palestinians residing in Areas designated as "C" under the Oslo agreements. The Palestinian police are not allowed to enter these areas, and execution of judgments, as well as service of process, requires Israeli participation and involvement. Such participation is not always guaranteed. On the other hand, it may involve Israeli legal participation, even though Israeli courts and laws have no clear jurisdiction. Parallel to that, decisions of courts in East Jerusalem will also involve Israeli law, and parties to litigation there often involve Israeli laws when it is in their interests and frustrate Palestinian courts in East Jerusalem.

With these limitations in mind, we can now proceed to the substance of personal status law.

9.2.2 Sources of Legislation in the West Bank

Jordan passed the Law of Family Rights in 1951 (Law No. 92 of 1951), which specifically stated in its preambular section on Reasons for Passage of the Law, that it continued in the traditional path of the OLFR in declaring that it followed the Hanafi School of Islamic *Shari'a* interpretation, and considered it binding and determinative, where no text in the law existed to contradict it.[23]

9.2.2.1 Personal Status Law of 1976

Jordan passed the Jordanian Law No. 61 Law of Personal Status of 1976 (PSL)[24] to replace the 1951 law, and the West Bank Palestinians applied it as well. Like its predecessor, the PSL stated that it followed the OLFR in declaring the Hanafi School of interpretation to be determinative in all matters where no text to the contrary exists.[25] Yet the law also drew on the other three Sunni Schools of interpretation, as well as the laws in the surrounding Arab countries and *ijtihad* (interpretation).[26] This tradition of following the Hanafi school of *Shari'a* interpretation primarily (while reserving the right of the legislator to draw on other schools), and on *ijtihad* in arriving at texts and interpretations that suit the modern age, is of vital importance.

For the Muslim Palestinians living in the West Bank, the PSL continues to be the governing law. It has 186 articles and governs matters including marriage and engagements, divorce, *khul'* (divorce by women), separation, *idda* (seclusion period after divorce), as well as *nafaka* (alimony), custody, visitation, and other similar matters.[27]

Few amendments have been made to this law as will be described below. The *Shari'a* courts in the West Bank also follow Jordanian *Shari'a* court precedents, since most attorneys practicing before these courts studied in Jordan, Beirut, or Syria and follow the same jurists as Jordanian lawyers. No uniquely Palestinian jurisprudence in this area has developed in the West Bank and is unlikely to arise until the unification of West Bank and Gaza laws occurs at some undetermined time in the future.

This Jordanian law continues to be in effect in the West Bank with no amendments or changes. However, in 2001, a number of amendments were issued, but they were only to come into effect when passed by the

Palestinian legislature (PLC). The PLC had been suspended since 2007, and Palestinian President Mahmoud Abbas dissolved it in 2019.[28] An election scheduled to be held in May 2021 was postponed. It remains to be seen what, if anything, happens to the 2001 proposed amendments if such an election is held and the PLC is reconstituted.

Among the more prominent provisions of the current law are the following:

Age of Competence and Consent to Marry   Under the PSL, regardless of their age, both prospective brides and grooms must consent to the marriage.[29] Forced marriages (*zawaj ijbari*) are not allowed. A Presidential Decree of November 4, 2019, raised the minimum age of marriage to eighteen years in both the West Bank and the Gaza Strip, but allows for exceptions to be made by the court and by the chief justice of *Shari'a* courts.[30] The amendment applied to Christians as well as Muslims.[31] As noted below, it is unclear if the decree is being followed in Gaza. To determine what exceptions might be allowed, we can look at the practice prior to the Decree for potential guidance.

PSL Article 5 specifies that the male needs to be at least sixteen and the female at least fifteeen years of age to be engaged to marry.[32] The proposed 2001 amendment, referred to above, permits the *qadi* (religious judge) to allow a girl over fifteen to get married if the potential husband has financial capacity, it is in the interest of the potential bride, and there is no "legitimate reason" for objections by the guardian. Even if the young woman's father or grandfather objects, and if she was over eighteen, the *qadi* can approve. The proposed amendment mentions that the chief justice will issue regulations to determine if the marriage is "in the interest" of the proposed bride. No such regulations have been issued yet. Article 7 prohibits the marriage of a girl to a male who is more than twenty years older than her, unless the judge ensures that she has consented, and that the marriage is in her interest.[33]

Agency in Marriage   Marriage is a contract[34] made by offer and acceptance in a formal setting, *majlis al 'iqd* (place of contract), between the engaged couple or their agents.[35] The marriage must be done in the presence of witnesses, who shall be either two Muslim men, or one Muslim man and two women.[36] First-time brides need to have a guardian (*wali*), who must be an adult Muslim male. The guardian is usually a male relative of the bride (father, paternal grandfather, brother, uncle, etc.).[37] If she remarries and is over eighteen, she does not require consent of a *wali*.

A woman can claim to have no guardian, and the consent of the guardian is not required, if she had been previously married and she is over eighteen years of age.[38] There are provisions to subsequently cancel her consent, however, if it later appears that the husband lacked capacity.

Various conditions can be put in the marriage contract as long as they are not contrary to the purpose of marriage or prohibited. Article 19(1) provides specific examples, including the following: (a) her husband cannot remove her from her country of origin, (b) her husband cannot take another wife during their marriage, (c) her husband shall delegate to her the power to divorce if she desires, and (d) her husband shall settle her in a certain country.[39]

Although conditions are permitted, it is difficult for women to actually include them because inclusion can be severely frowned upon, and judges often refuse women this right.[40]

The registration of marriages is mandatory. While failure to register a marriage contract is punishable by imprisonment, the marriage is not invalidated.[41]

Article 35 states that a wife will be entitled to a dowry (*mahr*), financial maintenance, and inheritance.[42] Article 36 requires the husband to provide the marital home.[43] Article 37 states that the wife must live with her husband, unless there is a condition in the contract that permits otherwise. If she refuses to live with her husband, she loses her right to support.[44] Article 68 states that a wife forfeits her right to maintenance if she takes a job outside the home without her husband's permission.[45] Article 69 indicates that a wife loses her support, and is considered recalcitrant (*nashez*), if she leaves the home without permission or prevents the husband from entering the home, unless he has injured her.[46]

Polygamy   Polygamy is permitted in the West Bank, in that a Muslim man can marry up to four wives at a time (polygyny). It should be noted that polygamy rates are very low.[47] The deteriorating economic situation in the West Bank and Gaza means that men have difficulty maintaining more than one wife. Yet with the number of widows on the rise, men may be encouraged to enter into polygamous marriages.[48] Article 40 indicates that a polygamous husband has to treat all wives equally and cannot house them all together unless they agree.[49] There is no mechanism that provides a process of verification concerning equal treatment. Consent of other wives or potential wives is not needed, but a judge or deputy must inform a prospective bride that her prospective husband is married and inform the existing wives that the husband intends to marry another woman.[50] In 2018, the *Shari'a* Supreme Council issued a circular on polygamy stating that a man must inform the first wife or previous wives about his intention to take another wife before he does so, and preferably through the court.[51]

If the marriage contract has a condition forbidding polygamy, and the husband violates the condition, the wife can petition a judge to dissolve the marriage. According to various sources, the reality is that most women whose husband takes another wife without permission are probably not able to get a divorce.[52]

Guardianship/Custody   Women do not have equal guardianship rights over children, even if it might be in the best interest of the child/children. In both the West Bank and Gaza Strip, a father has priority right over the guardianship of his children followed by the paternal grandfather and then other male relatives in a prescribed order.[53]

A mother usually can retain custody of a daughter until eleven, and a son until nine.[54] Article 162 permits extension of custody of the minor children to the mother until they reach adulthood as long as she has dedicated herself to their upbringing (by not remarrying or working outside the house),[55] but she loses that right if she remarries.[56] If a mother has custody, the father pays support. The right of custody extends to other appropriate females in the chain of relationship, but ends at nine years for the boys and eleven years for the girls.[57] Prior to March 2018, a custodian mother was not able to obtain a passport or any official documents for the children in her custody; the guardian's signature or written agency letter was required.[58] In March 2018, the Council of Ministers in the West Bank issued a decision to allow women who have custody of their children to open bank accounts for their children, transfer their children to different schools, and apply for their passports.[59]

In both the West Bank and Gaza Strip, a judge may order the continuation of the custody by a mother, whose husband has died and who has brought up and looked after the children, if such custody is deemed to be in the best interest of the children, and subject to the right of access by the paternal relatives.[60] In the West Bank, a mother loses custody if: (a) she is deemed of unsound mind, untrustworthy, or incapable of upbringing or maintaining her children; (b) she is an apostate; (c) she is housing her children where there are persons who are malicious to the children; or (d) she remarries and her new spouse is not a close blood relative of the child (*mahram*).[61]

Under both laws, fathers solely retain all guardianship rights even when the child is officially living with the mother. Where the father is absent or passed away, then the guardianship of his children passes to the paternal grandfather, and then other male relatives in a prescribed order. A woman is not allowed to manage her child's inheritance if her husband dies. Instead, a male relative from the deceased husband's family will take over the management of the child's inheritance, which can impact child maintenance. As guardian, a father can withdraw money from a child's bank account opened by the mother even if the child lives with the mother, but a mother cannot do the same if the child lives with the father.[62] In the West Bank, a woman needs the permission of her child's guardian (usually the father) if she wishes to travel abroad with her child.[63]

Divorce

Divorce by Husband   Under both the PSL and 1954 Egyptian Law on Family Rights (FRL)[64], a husband may use unilateral repudiation known as *talaq* to divorce his wife without much fanfare.[65] He must tell the judge of the repudiation.[66] The PSL provides that the husband register the repudiation before a judge, and if he does not, he must report to the religious court for the registration within fifteen days. A penalty exists for failure to register.[67]

PSL Article 83 *et. seq.* details the right of a husband to divorce his wife.[68] Divorce can be done by a word or agent.[69] There are both revocable and irrevocable divorces. The first two declarations of divorce are revocable and may be revoked with no financial consequences, that is, no new dowry.[70] The third time a husband declares a divorce, however, it is irrevocable. He cannot remarry his divorced wife, unless she has been married to another person and is then divorced by him.[71] Divorce brings on financial consequences concerning the dowry, which is in two portions. While one portion is payable at the marriage, the delayed portion is payable only upon divorce.

Also, the divorced wife is entitled to alimony (*nafaka*), which she may lose under certain circumstances.[72] For example, a divorced wife who works outside the house without permission from her ex-husband is not entitled to alimony.[73] The proposed 2001 law amendment referred to above makes this permission final – once given, or deemed to have been given, either explicitly or implied, it cannot be withdrawn without a legitimate cause.

Under the PSL, a husband may delegate his unilateral right to divorce to his wife (*isma'*) if there is such a stipulation in the marriage contract,[74] thus permitting her to pronounce *talāq* upon herself (*talāq-i-tafwid*).[75]

Divorce by Wife: Khul' – Redemptive Divorce   While it is very easy for men to divorce their wives, it is much more difficult for women to divorce their husbands. Women may have to show evidence, which can result in delays in court. There can be more social stigma against women seeking divorce.[76] Some women may fear losing custody of their children if they seek a divorce.[77]

A wife can seek and obtain a redemptive divorce (*mukhala'ah* or *khul'*), if she pays her husband a mutually agreed price.[78] A *khul'* divorce requires the consent of both parties and does not require a ruling from the court. Additionally, (a) a wife's entitlement to financial maintenance during the waiting period after the divorce (*iddah*) is not forfeited unless the *agreement* states and (b) child custody, support, and maintenance may not be part of a *khul'* agreement.[79]

Divorce by Wife: Fasakh – Judicial Divorce   Under both the PSL and the FRL, valid grounds for a wife seeking a judicial divorce include the following: (a) impotence or inability to consummate a marriage; (b) incurable or contagious and dangerous disease, or madness (a wife may obtain a divorce after one year of the husband's diagnosis); (c) failure to provide maintenance; (d) prolonged and unjustified absence of more than one year; and (e) receiving a prison sentence of over three years (wife may seek divorce after one year).[80]

Other Grounds   The PSL permits a wife to obtain a divorce on the basis of "dispute and discord." The couple must undergo a mandatory mediation process.[81]

Maintenance during *Iddah*   Neither the West Bank nor Gaza recognize the concept of marital assets.[82] During the *iddah* period, wives receive maintenance or alimony.[83] The period is between three months to one year, depending on the woman's condition, such as menstruation or pregnancy.[84] Financial maintenance can be terminated if the ex-wife is deemed disobedient.[85] In the West Bank, an ex-wife can also obtain maintenance for one year beyond the *iddah* period if she claims the husband divorced her in an abusive manner such as without reasonable cause.[86]

9.3   Gaza

9.3.1   Broad Framework of Law and Source of Legislation

The laws in Gaza have some similarities and some differences as compared to those in the West Bank, some of which have been noted above. In 1948, at the time Israel was created, the Gaza Strip was subject to Egyptian control under the Egyptian Governor General. The FRL was applied in Gaza, where it is still the primary source of law. When the Israeli Occupation began in Gaza in 1967, one of the consequences was that the personal status law remained frozen. Advances that were occurring in other Arab countries, including Egypt, were not applied in Gaza.

9.3.1.1   Age of Competence and Consent to Marry

As with the PSL, both spouses must consent to the marriage under the FRL, and forced marriages are not allowed.[87] It is unclear if the Presidential Decree of November 2019 raising the marital age to eighteen for both sexes has been regarded as legal in Gaza, as Hamas has been in charge rather than the PA. Assuming that Gaza is not following the Decree, then FRL Article 5 indicates that the minimum legal age for marriage is seventeen for females and eighteen for males. Although the FRL sets the absolute minimum age of marriage at nine and twelve, a 1996 directive from the Chief Islamic Justice (*Qadi-Al-Quda*) raises the absolute minimum legal age to fifteen for girls and sixteen for boys.[88] Articles 6 and 7 permit a judge to authorize the marriage of a girl under seventeen or a boy under 18, if the boy or girl claim they have reached puberty and they appear to be physically mature; in addition, a minor girl's guardian must agree to the marriage.[89]

9.3.1.2   Agency in Marriage

Regardless of her age, a prospective bride requires the consent of a *wali* to enter into marriage. The guardian must be Muslim and a male relative of the bride (father followed by the paternal grandfather, etc.).[90] Unlike the PSL, the FRL is silent regarding whether a *wali* is required if a woman wants to remarry.

FRL Article 20 indicates marriage is a contract.[91] The registration of marriages is mandatory. While failure to register a marriage contract is punishable by imprisonment, the marriage is not invalidated.[92] Article 38 provides that a wife is entitled to *mahr*, financial maintenance and inheritance, as soon as the marriage is concluded properly.[93] Article 39 requires that the husband obtain a marital home.[94] Article 40 requires a wife to live in her husband's home and to travel with him unless there is a reason to prevent her from traveling and that she should obey her husband. A husband is required to treat her well.[95] Article 66 provides that a wife loses her financial maintenance if she is *nashez*.[96]

9.3.1.3   Polygamy

FRL Article 14 permits a Muslim man to marry up to four wives at one time.[97] Article 42 of the FRL provides that a husband with more than one wife must treat each of his wives equally and fairly.[98] There is no process of verification via *Shari'a* courts to ensure financial and emotional fairness and equality is actually taking place. Consent of wives/potential wives is not required. Article 24 provides that in the event the wife stipulates that her husband cannot take another wife and the latter does so, the wife or her fellow wives may seek a divorce.[99]

Pursuant to the FRL, both spouses may stipulate conditions in their marriage contract, including regarding polygamy. Specific conditions that a wife may stipulate besides limiting her husband from taking another wife during their marriage[100] include, for example, that her husband cannot relocate her without her consent.[101]

9.3.1.4   Guardianship/Custody

As is applicable in the West Bank, fathers control guardianship, but mothers may have custody rights. A mother has priority right over her daughter until she reaches nine and her son until he reaches seven. A judge may extend a mother's right to custody over her children if it is deemed to be in the best interest of the children.[102]

Both in the West Bank and Gaza Strip, a judge may order the continuation of the custody by a mother whose husband has died and who has brought up and looked after the children if such custody is deemed to be in the best interest of the children and subject to the right of access and inspection of the paternal relatives.[103] If a woman remarries, she will generally lose her custody of the children.

9.3.1.5   Divorce

Divorce by Husband   As under the PSL, the FRL permits a husband to unilaterally repudiate his wife.[104] FRL Article 77 requires a husband to inform a judge of the repudiation.[105] The FRL does not indicate whether a husband can delegate *usma'* to the wife as the PSL indicates. Sunni jurisprudence (*fiqh*), which would include the Hanafi School, does permit this delegation.[106]

Divorce by Wife: *Khul'* **– Redemptive Divorce**   The FRL does not specifically address *Khul'* divorce. In practice, where a woman petitions a judge for divorce, a judge may grant a divorce if the couple agree to a specific sum of money that a wife pays to the husband in exchange for his consent.[107]

Divorce by Wife: *Fasakh* **– Judicial Divorce**   As mentioned above regarding the PSL, valid grounds for seeking a judicial divorce in Gaza by a wife include a husband's (a) impotence or inability to consummate a marriage, (b) incurable or contagious and dangerous disease or madness (a wife may obtain a divorce after one year of the husband's diagnosis), (c) failure to provide maintenance, (d) prolonged and unjustified absence of more than one year, and (e) receiving a prison sentence of over three years (wife may seek divorce after one year).[108]

Other Grounds   FLR Article 97 states that a wife may seek divorce on the basis of "harm," and the couple must undergo a mandatory mediation process. A Directive issued by the Gaza Higher *Shari'a* Court Council clarifies that the article covers any harm inflicted by words or actions, where a man's treatment of his wife is contrary to acceptable custom in a manner that a wife cannot endure.[109] Examples provided include *painful* beating, abandonment without reason, penetration that is not natural, or verbal insults to her or her father.[110]

In 2012, the Chief Islamic Justice directed that:

> Judges have the discretion to decide whether the marriage is harmful for the wife rather than the woman having to submit evidence in cases of judicial separation. Divorce proceedings must be completed in three months.[111]

9.3.1.6   Maintenance during *Iddah*

Gaza does not recognize the concept of marital assets.[112] Women receive maintenance for the *iddah* period, which can range from between three months to one year and depends on the woman's situation, for example, whether she is menstruating or pregnant.[113] Unlike the PSL, the FRL does not contain the concept of compensation beyond the *iddah* period.

9.4   Palestinian Authority: Hopes for Reform?

The Palestine Liberation Organization (PLO) passed the Palestinian Declaration of Independence on November 15, 1988. It called for a constitution "based on ... nondiscrimination in public rights on the basis of race, or color, or between men and women."[114] Under the Oslo Accords, a Palestinian government was created not directly of the PLO as a whole, but for those who lived in the Occupied Territories. The Palestinian Legislative Council (PLC) of the PA passed the Basic Law in 1997. PA President Yasser Arafat ratified it in 2002.[115] Article 4 (2) provides that "[t]he principles of Islamic *Shari'a* shall be a principal source of legislation."[116] Article 9 provides that "Palestinians shall be equal before the law and the judiciary, without distinction based upon race, sex, color, religion, political views or disability."[117] The Basic Law was supposed to be a temporary constitution,[118] to be replaced by the permanent constitution upon independence, but remains in effect due to current legal limbo during which independence remains to be achieved.

When the PA began to operate, there were high hopes for creating new personal status laws that were more modern and responsive to modern needs. For one thing, the Palestinians had, for the first time in their history, a PLC that had the authority to make laws, as opposed to following legislation created by others. In addition, the fact that the development of laws in Gaza and the West Bank had followed different paths, because Gaza was under Egyptian administration while the West Bank followed Jordanian law, created an imperative to legislate. This could lead to considering unification of the laws applicable in both segments of the territory, which is now under qualified Palestinian control. In 1994, the Chief Justice Sheikh Muhammad Abu Sardan publicly spoke of the need to unify the provisions of Gaza and West Bank *Shari'a* law. He also spoke of the need to look beyond the four schools of Islamic interpretation and utilize *ijtihad* in preparing modifications that better serve the interests of the Muslim population and reflect modern situations.[119]

Calls for reform and modernization, however, met with considerable resistance from traditionalists, who feared that a modern law may deviate too far from their particular conception of Islamic law. Reformers point out that there is a difference between *Shari'a* (God's divine law) and *Fiqh* (human understanding and elaboration). Reformers argued "... the two terms are deliberately used interchangeably in relation to the rights of women precisely in order to invoke divine sanctity in defense of human understandings of the Qur'an and Sunna."[120]

The fears of traditionalists were well founded since reformers were arguing for greater equality between men and women and new restrictions on marriage by minors, as well as restrictions on polygamy and marriages where the age difference is greater than fifteen years, as well as other elements that they felt were not compatible with human rights in the modern age. They pointed correctly to the huge discrepancies between existing law and the various international instruments and treaties such as the Convention on the Elimination of all Forms of Discrimination Against Women (CEDAW), which provide for full gender equality, and which are inimical to some of the prevailing practices and provisions of traditional *Shari'a* law.[121]

One organized effort that met with great resistance by traditionalists was the Palestinian Parliament for Women and Legislation (also known as the Model Parliament), which was established in 1997. It included nongovernmental organizations, and was active in both the West Bank and Gaza, but was unable to propose changes that were accepted by the PLC.[122] Among the suggestions made by the Model Parliament were that women should not need permission of a guardian to enter into a marriage contract; polygyny should require court permission; divorce should require court permission; if a divorced mother remarries, custody should be determined in the best interests of the child; *nafaqa* should be paid from date of separation; and assets acquired after marriage should be joint property.[123] Other efforts have also been made to draft laws, but none have resulted in legislative change.[124]

Further efforts were also stymied after Hamas won the 2006 PA elections and formed a majority within the PLC. The tensions between the previously ruling party Fatah and Hamas resulted in a civil war where Hamas accomplished a military takeover of Gaza.[125] With its traditionalist views, Hamas was not interested in creating a unified modern personal status law.

Since that time, PA President Abbas has issued presidential decrees that only apply in the West Bank, and the Gaza branch of the PLC issues laws that apply within Gaza.[126]

A National Committee was created, and after many meetings it published a draft Family Law in 2010.[127] This law was not passed by the PLC, which no longer existed, but it certainly pointed in the direction that some reformers hoped to move. A 2013 draft was developed as well under the Supreme Judge Department.[128]

One problem is that the current family law and the conservative interpretations of *Shari'a* are often contrary to the principles of gender equality, as well as other protections for the rights of women and of the child. Reformers argue that family law should be amended to reflect these modern ideals and that international standards and constitutional principles should take precedence over outdated provisions of family law, while conservatives and traditionalists see in those changes a direct attack on Islam and an attempt to substitute human (and Western) values for divine laws.

Palestine acceded to CEDAW in 2014, without any reservations.[129] It is the only Arab state to have done so.[130] It is notable that, as recently as 2018, the PA has acknowledged the need to harmonize personal status laws currently in force in the West Bank (including occupied Jerusalem) and the Gaza Strip. A report submitted to the CEDAW committee noted that the Palestine State party report, as well as State party's Replies to List of Issues and Questions (LOIQ), indicated that a judicial committee was formed in 2015 to review legislation regarding the *Shari'a*-based justice system and drafts of laws were prepared on regulating work of *Shari'a* courts. According to Section 116 of the replies to LOIQ's on matters pertaining to marriage and family relations, "[a]ll legal provisions that are discriminatory against women will be reviewed and brought into line with the (CEDAW) Convention."[131]

A new personal status law radically changing prevailing laws is unlikely in the near future, particularly given the legislative paralysis resulting from the Gaza/West Bank split and the May 2021 violence between Israel and Hamas and between Palestinians living in Israel and their Jewish neighbors. It remains to be seen how much civil society may continue to push for reforms.

Presidential decrees have continued to be issued. For example, in December 2019, Mahmoud Abbas issued a Presidential decree recognizing an Evangelical Council of the Holy Land and granting certain civil rights to evangelical groups that had not been recognized in the existing laws. This decree allows the different churches who are part of this Council to conduct marriages, register church property, and enjoy a minimal "legal" existence that had been effectively denied to them by virtue of their not appearing in the list of recognized churches mentioned in the law.[132]

9.5 Conclusion

The political situation remains bleak. In such conditions, the status quo, that is, the dysfunctional split personal status system that exists today, may remain. Although it seems fairly implausible at this point, the two-state solution could result in some change in personal status law. Perhaps the PA would be able to function once again and a new PLC would be elected. Modern legislation could be passed, and a unified code could occur. Alternatively, perhaps the two parts of Palestine would decide to retain differences, much as states in the United States have done. If one state came about (equally implausible at the moment), each community might decide to retain the millet system as representative of their deeply held beliefs.

Alternatively, under a revitalized two-state or one-state solution, a new possibility could emerge. All the myriad denominations, as well as secular people, will need to learn to coexist together. It may well be possible to dream of a proper, modern civil personal status law that provides an alternative to all who wish to abide by its provisions and escape the religious courts of their respective faith communities.[133] Such a law would solve many problems that are not properly addressed by the millet system.

Most modern societies provide for a separation of religion and state. Nowhere is this more needed than in Palestine, where religion comes in many colors and shapes, and where a number of faith communities do not even have a recognized status and the necessary religious court structure to go with it. Furthermore, many individuals marry across religious lines or have no desire to be governed by the ancient rules of the religious communities in which they were born. A modern, secular civil personal status law can provide a proper framework for regulating personal status matters, while leaving those who wish to abide by the strictures of their religion free to do so.

In many countries there is a civil law that applies to everyone, yet those who choose a Catholic religious wedding, for example, can get one, and the state will recognize that wedding and its consequences. If they later choose to divorce, they can do so, even if their particular religious community does not recognize their divorce and would not allow them to remarry in a religious ceremony. Yet their divorce – just like their marriage – is recognized and effective. Could this ever be in Palestine's future?

Notes

1 Ottoman Civil Code 1871.
2 Ottoman Law of Family Rights (OLFR) 1917.
3 L. Welchman, *Beyond the Code: Muslim Family Law and the Shar'i Judiciary in the Palestinian West Bank* (Kluwer, 2000), p. 33.

4 K. Barkey, "Islam and Toleration: Studying the Ottoman Imperial Model" (2007) 19 *International Journal of Politics, Culture, and Society*, 5–19, 16; B. Aral, "The Idea of Human Rights as Perceived in the Ottoman Empire" (May 2004) 26(2) *Human Rights Quarterly*, 454–82, 465.

5 Aral, "The Idea of Human Rights," 465.

6 Aral, "The Idea of Human Rights," 461.

7 Aral, "The Idea of Human Rights," 473.

8 Barkey, "Islam and toleration," 16.

9 F. Gocek, "Ethnic Segmentation, Western Education, and Political Outcomes: Nineteenth-Century Ottoman Society" (Autumn 1993) 14 (3) *Poetics Today*, 517–525.

10 Law of Registering Marriages and Divorces 1919 article 2.

11 Declaration of the Constitution of Palestine 1922, Palestine Order-in Council, published in the Official Gazette, September 1, 1922, https://unispal.un.org/DPA/DPR/unispal.nsf/0/C7AAE196F41AA055052565F50054E656.

12 The Law Regulating Religious Denominations, British Mandate in Palestine 1938.

13 The Law Regulating Religious Denominations, Appendix 2.

14 The Law of the Directorates (Majalis) of the Non Moslem Religious Denominations (No. 2) 1938.

15 See Chapter 8 in this volume. M. Karayanni, "The Palestinian Minority in Israel." M. Karayanni, *Conflicts in a Conflict: A Conflict of Law Case Study on Israel and the Palestinian Territories* (Oxford, 2014).

16 See A. Wing and H. Kuttab, "Hamas, Constitutionalism, and Palestinian Women" (2007) 50 *Howard Law Journal*, 479–514; N. Shehada, *Applied Family Law in Islamic Courts: Shari'a Courts in Gaza* (Routledge, 2018).

17 Israel Military Order No. 1 (1967).

18 L. Daniele, "ICC and Palestine symposium: Imprisoning' Self-Determination – The Israeli Military Law Enforcement System in the West Bank and Its Relevance for the ICC" (July 2, 2020) *Opinio Juris*, http://opiniojuris.org/2020/02/07/icc-and-pales tine-symposium-imprisoning-self-determination-the-israeli-military-law-enforce ment-system-in-the-west-bank-and-its-relevance-for-the-icc/.

19 I. Lustick, "Has Israel Annexed East Jerusalem?" (1997) 5(1) *Middle East Policy*, 34–45.

20 Dana El Kurd, *Polarized and Demobilized: Legacies of Authoritarianism in Palestine* (Oxford, 2020), p. 8.

21 El Kurd, *Polarized and Demobilized*, p. 8.

22 El Kurd, *Polarized and Demobilized*, p. 8.

23 Jordanian Law of Family Rights preamble (Law No. 92 of 1951).

24 Jordanian Law of Family Rights preamble (Law No. 92 of 1951).

25 PSL Art. 183.

26 L. Welchman, *Islamic Family Law: Text and Practice in Palestine* (Women's Centre for Legal Aid and Counseling, 1999), p. 19.

27 PSL.

28 S. Anabtawi and N. Brown, "Why Mahmoud Abbas Dissolved the Palestinian Parliament – And What It Means for the Future," *Washington Post*, January 18, 2019, www.washingtonpost.com/news/monkey-cage/wp/2019/01/18/heres-what-the-dissol ution-of-the-legislative-council-means-for-the-future-of-palestinian-governance/.

29 PSL Arts. 14, 15.

30 Adam Rasgon, "Abbas Bans Child Marriage, with Some Legal Exemptions," *Times of Israel*, November 6, 2019, www.timesofisrael.com/abbas-bans-child-marriage-with-some-legal-exemptions/.
31 UNDP, "The State of Palestine Gender Justice and the Law," December 2019, p. 2, www.unescwa.org/sites/www.unescwa.org/files/events/files/palestine_country_assessment_-_english.pdf.
32 PSL Art. 5.
33 PSL Art. 7.
34 PSL Art. 2.
35 PSL Art. 14.
36 PSL Art. 16.
37 PSL Arts. 9–11.
38 PSL Art. 13.
39 PSL Art. 19.
40 Musawah, "Thematic Report on Muslim Family Law and Muslim Women's Rights in Palestine," 70th CEDAW Session Geneva, Switzerland, July 2018, p. 18, https://tbinternet.ohchr.org/Treaties/CEDAW/Shared%20Documents/PSE/INT_CEDAW_NGO_PSE_31669_E.pdf.
41 PSL Art. 17; Jordanian Penal Code Article 279(1)(1960), www.files.ethz.ch/isn/152932/Legal_Analysis_EN.pdf; Palestine Cabinet Website (West Bank), "Issuance of Marriage Contract," http://palestinecabinet.gov.ps/GovService/ViewService?ID=567.
42 PSL Art. 35.
43 PSL Art. 36.
44 PSL Art. 37.
45 PSL Art. 68.
46 PSL Art. 69.
47 As per Palestine's 2014 Multiple Cluster Indicator Survey, about 4 percent of marriages in Palestine are polygamous (3 percent in West Bank and 6 percent in Gaza Strip). Musawah, "Thematic Report on Muslim Family Law and Muslim Women's Rights in Palestine," p. 17.
48 A. Al-Ghoul, "Gaza's Unhappy Sister Wives," *ALMONITOR*, March 18, 2015, www.almonitor.com/pulse/originals/2015/03/gaza-hamas-conservative-rise-of-polygamy.html; Zeina Jallad, "Palestinian Women and Security: A Legal Analysis' (Geneva Centre for the Democratic Control of Armed Forces, 2012), p. 12 n. 12, www.files.ethz.ch/isn/152932/Legal_Analysis_EN.pdf.
49 PSL Art. 40.
50 Supreme Judge Department Directive No. 48/2011, Upper Council of Sharia Jurisdiction (West Bank), www.kudah.pna.ps/userfiles/image/ الزوجة 20 %غابلا% 20 .jpg; P. Johnson and R. Hammami, "Change and Conservation: Family Law Reform in Court Practice and Public Perceptions in the Occupied Palestinian Territory," 2013, p. 40, http://iws.birzeit.edu/sites/default/files/2016-12/Family%20Law%20Survey%20FINAL%20WEB_Penny%20and%20Rema_0.pdf.
51 UNDP, p. 19.
52 Musawah, "Thematic Report on Muslim Family Law and Muslim Women's Rights in Palestine," p. 18.
53 Musawah, "Thematic Report on Muslim Family Law and Muslim Women's Rights in Palestine," p. 31.

54 PSL Arts. 154, 161.
55 PSL Art. 162.
56 PSL Art. 156.
57 PSL Art. 161.
58 Musawah, "Thematic Report on Muslim Family Law and Muslim Women's Rights in Palestine," p. 31.
59 "Video: Hamdallh Announces a Package of Measures for women," *Maan News Agency*, March 5, 2018, www.maannews.net/Content.aspx?id=941467.
60 Article 1 of Law No. 1/2009 amending the Personal Status Law.
61 PSL Arts. 155–156, 166.
62 Human Rights Watch interview with Sabah Salameh, coordinator of the Muntada Forum to Combat Violence against Women – representing a coalition of seventeen nongovernmental organizations, Ramallah, April 11, 2018.
63 www.hrw.org/news/2018/06/11/human-rights-watch-womens-centre-legal-aid-and-counselling-and-equality-now-joint; PSL Art. 166.
64 FRL, www.plc.gov.ps/menu_plc/arab/files/ ./الوقائع02%الفلسطينية/0/قانون02%حقوق02%العائلة فلسطينhtm.
65 PSL Arts. 83–101; FRL Arts. 67–77.
66 PSL Art. 101; FRL Art. 77.
67 Jordanian Penal Code Art. 281.
68 PSL Art. 83.
69 PSL Art. 87.
70 PSL Art. 93.
71 PSL Art 100.
72 PSL Art. 67.
73 PSL Art. 68.
74 PSL Art. 19.
75 PSL Art 87.
76 Musawah, "Thematic Report on Muslim Family Law and Muslim Women's Rights in Palestine," p. 24.
77 CBS News, "Divorced Women in Gaza Denied Child Custody', April 27, 2015, www.marsad.ps/en/2015/04/27/divorced-women-in-gaza-denied-custody-rights/.
78 I. Schneider, *Debating the Law, Creating Gender, Sharia Law Making and Palestine, 2012–18* (Brill 2020).
79 PSL Arts. 102–109.
80 PSL Arts. 113–131.
81 PSL Art. 132.
82 Musawah, "Thematic Report on Muslim Family Law and Muslim Women's Rights in Palestine," p. 26.
83 PSL Art. 79.
84 PSL Art. 80.
85 PSL Art 81.
86 PSL Art. 134.
87 FRL Arts. 21, 22.
88 Welchman, *Beyond the Code*, pp. 120–121.
89 FRL Arts. 6, 7.
90 FRL Arts. 11, 12.
91 FRL Art. 20.

92 Gaza Council of Ministers Order No. 4/269/11 of 2012, www.ljc.gov.ps/images/ stories/pdf/mazon.pdf.
93 FRL Art. 38.
94 FRL Art. 39.
95 FRL Art. 40.
96 FRL Art. 66.
97 FRL Art. 14.
98 FRL Art. 42.
99 FRL Art 24.
100 FRL Art 24.
101 FRL Art 40.
102 FRL Art. 118 as amended by Art. 1 of Law No. 1/2009 amending the Personal Status Law.
103 Art. 1 of Law No. 1/2009.
104 PSL Arts. 83–101; FRL Arts. 67–77.
105 PSL Art. 101; FRL Art. 77.
106 Musawah, "Thematic Report on Muslim Family Law and Muslim Women's Rights in Palestine," p. 22; al-Fatawi al-Mu'asira fi al-Talaq, http://arabicmegalibrary .com/pages-5582-10-1359-0.html.
107 Information obtained from *Palestinian Advocate*, February 2017; Al-Hayat Al-Jadida, "'*Khul'* in Gaza between Personal Freedom and Societal and Legal Complications," *Al-Hayat Al-Jadida*, May 10, 2016, www.alhaya.ps/ar_page.php? id=14bbd0by21740811Y14bbd0b; M. Othman, "'*Khul'* in Gaza: By Mutual Consent in Courts and Judicial on Paper," *Al-Monitor*, April 13, 2015, www.almonitor.com/ pulse/ar/originals/2015/04/gaza-divorce-sharia-courts-khul-wealthy-women.html.
108 FRL Arts. 84–102.
109 FRL Art. 97.
110 State of Palestine Judicial Authority, Higher Shari'ah Court Council (Gaza), "Cases of *Tarfriq* between Reality and Hope," www.ljc.gov.ps/index.php?option=com_ content&view=article&id=670.
111 Johnson and Hammami, "Change and Conservation," pp. 19–20.
112 Musawah, "Thematic Report on Muslim Family Law and Muslim Women's Rights in Palestine," p. 26.
113 FRL Arts. 57, 112.
114 Palestinian Declaration of Independence (November 15, 1988), www.mideastweb .org/plc1988.htm.
115 For discussion of the Basic Law, see A. Wing, "The Palestinian Basic Law: Embryonic Constitutionalism" (1999) 31 *Case Western Reserve Journal of International Law*, 383–426; Palestinian Basic Law, Amended Basic Law 2003, www.palestinianbasiclaw.org/basic-law/2003-amended-basic-law. Basic Law 2003, amended 2005 (*al-Qānūn al-Asāsī*).
116 Basic Law Art. 4.
117 Basic Law Art. 9.
118 See comments at www.palestinianbasiclaw.org/basic-law/2003-amended-basic-law.
119 Welchman, *Islamic Family Law*, p. 21.
120 Welchman, *Islamic Family Law*, p. 13.

121 See Convention on the Elimination of All Forms of Discrimination Against Women (CEDAW), December 18, 1979, United Nations, Treaty Series, vol. 1249, p. 13, www.refworld.org/docid/3ae6b3970.html.

122 D. Scheindlin, "Palestinian Women's Model Parliament," *Middle East Review of Internatioal Affairs* (September 1998), https://ciaotest.cc.columbia.edu/olj/meria/meria98_scheindlin.html; Welchman, *Beyond the Code*, p. 361.

123 Scheindlin, "Palestinian Women's Model Parliament"; Shehada, *Applied Family Law in Islamic Courts*, p. 145.

124 L. Goudarzi-Gereke, "Perspectives on Palestinian Family Law: Divorce Regulations in the Qadi al-Qudat's Draft Law of 2013 in the Context of Current Legislation and Demanded Reforms," in I. Schneider and N. Edres (ed.) *Uses of the Past: Shari'a and Gender in Legal Theory and Practice in Palestine and Israel* (Harrassowitz Verlag, 2018), pp. 52–53.

125 S. Anabtawi and N. Brown, "Why Mahmoud Abbas Dissolved the Palestinian parliament – and What It Means for the Future,"*Washington Post*, January 18, 2019, www.washingtonpost.com/news/monkey-cage/wp/2019/01/18/heres-what-the-dissolution-of-the-legislative-council-means-for-the-future-of-palestinian-governance/.

126 Goudarzi-Gereke, "Perspectives on Palestinian Family Law," p. 49.

127 Palestine draft Family Law (2010).

128 Goudarzi-Gereke, "Perspectives on Palestinian Family Law," p. 53.

129 https://tbinternet.ohchr.org/_layouts/15/TreatyBodyExternal/Treaty.aspx?CountryID=217&Lang=en; see M. Qafisheh, "Without Reservation: Reforming Palestinian Family Laws in Light of CEDAW," in I. Schneider and N. Edres (eds.) *Uses of the Past: Shari'a and Gender in Legal Theory and Practice in Palestine and Israel* (Harrassowitz Verlag, 2018), (ed.) p. 29.

130 Qafisheh, "Without Reservation," p. 29.

131 List of issues and questions in relation to the initial report of the State of Palestine, February 19, 2018. Replies of the State of Palestine CEDAW/C/PSE/Q/1/Add.1.

132 Daoud Kuttab, "Palestinian Evangelicals Celebrate Abbas Decree," *Arab News*, December 17, 2019, www.arabnews.com/node/1599981/middle-east.

133 Such proposals have been objected to in the past by the religious establishments. Welchman, *Beyond the Code*, p. 374; Qafisheh, "Without Reservation," p. 35.

Qatari Family Law, When Custom Meets *Shari'a*

LINA M. KASSEM

10.1 Introduction

Qatar, a small state in the Persian Gulf, that declared its independence in 1971, has undergone major political and economic developments in a relatively short time period. Perhaps because Qatar made so many gains in terms of economic development, observers assumed that it was also on the path to a more liberal and progressive political system. Of course, the rule of law is an instrumental part of any movement toward progressive reforms. Most of the recent legal reforms have taken place under the leadership of the former emir of Qatar, Sheikh Hamad bin Khalifa Al-Thani, who is now referred to as the father emir. Sheikh Hamad's tenure (1995–2013) can be characterized as one that promoted legal reform, while still maintaining the religious and traditional values of Qatari society. Navigating legal and political reform, while still preserving cultural customs and traditions, has been a difficult balancing act at times for the state and its ruler.

The balancing act continues under the current emir, Sheikh Tamim bin Hamad Al-Thani, who became the head of state on June 25, 2013. In an unexpected and extraordinary move, especially for the region, the father emir, handed power over to his son. The transition was seen by some as a way of ushering in a younger generation of leadership in Qatar. The struggle to reconcile progressive legal reforms with the entrenched religious authority has continued under the young emir's leadership. The leadership's ability to introduce just enough reforms, while seemingly maintaining traditional Islamic values is arguably one of the reasons why Qatar remained relatively stable during the tumultuous period of the Arab Spring.

It is worth mentioning that Qatar, much like other GCC states,[1] has historically had a symbiotic relationship with the Ulema or religious scholars. While some significant progress has been made under the new leadership, especially in appointing women in leadership positions,[2] the pace of change remains incremental. One of the main remaining obstacles is the lack of an effective national mechanism to deal with issues resulting from gender inequality. Recent changes indicate that women's affairs have been delegated to the Ministry of Administrative Development, Labor and Social Affairs, signifying a downgrading in their status in the overall political structure. In the past, it could be argued that women's issues held more prominence under the Qatar Supreme Council for the family, which in fact was much more dedicated to women's issues. Qatar remains a state where any legal reforms concerning women's rights are almost entirely driven by state feminism, which in this case depends on the will and eagerness of the current political leadership.

10.2   History of Legal Reforms

In 2004, a new constitution was introduced that Qataris overwhelmingly approved of in a nationwide referendum held the following year.[3] The new constitution, still in effect today, defines the state of Qatar as a democratic Arab state with Islamic *Shari'a* as the main source of legislation. It also allows for greater individual rights. The most important rights guaranteed under the new constitution are contained in several articles. Article 34 stipulates equal rights for all Qatari citizens.[4] Article 35 affirms that, "All people are equal before the law. There shall be no discrimination on account of sex, origin, language, or religion."[5] However, the constitution also asserts in Article 21 the importance of the family as "the foundation of the society" and therefore it should have "religion, morals, and love" as its pillars. The article emphasizes the role of the state in protecting the family by "supporting its principles, bolstering its ties, and preserving ideals of matrimony, childhood and the elderly."[6]

What could potentially be open to less than an optimal interpretation regarding women's rights appears in Article 37, which affirms the right of an individual to protect his or her privacy from any outside intervention, by stating that "no interference be allowed in his or her privacy or family affairs or residence or correspondence or any interference affecting his or her honor or reputation."[7] What is implicit in this articulation is that the state should stay out of familial conflicts, including those between a husband and wife. This article coupled with societal norms, that the male head of the family is the ultimate arbitrator when it comes to issues of "family affairs," including the implicit right for a husband to "discipline" his wife, without outside intervention, could be regarded as allowing, if not condoning domestic violence.

The seeming contradiction in Qatari Law was highlighted by a former law professor at Qatar University, Dr. Abdel Hamid Alansari.[8] In an interview with a local Qatari newspaper, when asked whether Qatari law protects women, Dr. Alansari alluded to the contradictions in Qatari law and argued that while the constitution grants Qatari women equal rights, the law still allows a husband to use violence under the pretext that he has a right to discipline her. Alansari claims that in cases of domestic violence, Article 47 of the Penal Code stipulates that no crime is committed if an act was done in good faith, or if the act is considered a right according to law or Islamic *Shari'a*.[9]

Qatar's judicial system uses both civil law and Islamic law. When it comes to all aspects of family law, *Shari'a* or the interpretation of Islamic law,[10] is the main source of Qatari legislation. The official *madhhab* (school of thought) for the state of Qatar is the Hanbali school of *fiqh* (Islamic jurisprudence), which is applied to all personal status matters.

Until 2006, Qatar's *Shari'a* courts applied the "Muscat Document of the GCC Common Law of Personal Status" adopted at the 7th Session of the Supreme Council of the GCC in October 1996.[11] The Muscat Document was drafted as a reference law for all the members of the Gulf Cooperation Council. The law is divided into 282 articles that deal with issues that commonly fall under the jurisdiction of family law or *Shari'a* courts, such as inheritance, marriage, divorce and custody.

In 1997, Qatar began drafting its own personal status law. A panel of judges drafted a preliminary Qatari personal status law that was tested in certain courts to gauge the public's reaction, as well as to obtain feedback from lawyers and judges. This process was in fact the leadership's attempt at ensuring that the traditional sensibilities of the religious establishment were not disturbed. This "trial run" in fact made it more difficult to eliminate practices and traditions that did not conform to Islamic law, yet were part of the established traditions and customs, further enforcing the power and legitimacy of these customs.

One example of this is the continuation of the traditional practice of arranged marriages by parents, sometimes without the consent of the daughter and less frequently even a son. Islamic *Shari'a* is unambiguous regarding the requirement that the consent of both parties, including the bride, is necessary for the marriage to be valid.

What is perhaps more troubling is that the majority of judges were not and still are not Qatari.[12] The fact that Qatar suffers from a dearth of qualified Qatari judges continues to be problematic for several reasons. One of these reasons is clearly the threat to the independence of expatriate judges.

On the other extreme, there has been an apparent overdependence on Egyptian *Shari'a* judges.[13] Beginning in the late 1950s, many members of the Muslim brotherhood, especially ones from Egypt escaping political persecution, ended up in the Persian Gulf. Several settled in Qatar and went on to have influential positions there. This dependence was mutually beneficial in that it not only provided Qatar with needed expertise but also some religious legitimacy. However, this meant that Qatar relied on a more literal and often more conservative interpretation of *Shari'a* from prominent scholars such as Dr. Yusuf Al-Qaradawi. It is also interesting to note that Dr. Al-Qaradawi established the first College of *Shari'a* at Qatar University and became its inaugural dean.

David Roberts provides a detailed historical analysis of the relationship between Qatar and the Muslim Brotherhood, providing examples of how influential members of the brotherhood were in establishing the Qatari bureaucracy.[14] Roberts argues that members of the brotherhood were especially influential in educational institutions. This trend was beginning to change as evident by an initiative led by Sheikha Moza to establish educational institutions, especially through the Qatar Foundation, of promoting educational institutions allowing for more inclusive and progressive interpretations of Islamic *Shari'a*. One such example is the establishment of the College of Islamic Studies in 2007.[15]

Sheikh Hamad came to power in 1995, with the vision of promoting Qatar as a modern and progressive beacon in the Persian Gulf. Many of these projects, especially those aimed at empowering women, were led by his wife Sheikha Moza. Having Sheikha Moza spearhead projects aimed at providing more rights to women allowed Sheikh Hamad to take the credit for the farsighted and progressive initiatives, while having a lightning rod to detract criticism coming from the more conservative religious establishment. As mentioned earlier, the religious establishment was strengthened by the considerable influence of mostly Islamic brotherhood clerics who found a safe haven in Doha starting in the late 1950s.

In 1998, an Emiri decree (No. 53) established the Qatar Supreme Council for Family Affairs (QSCFA), headed by Sheikha Moza.[16] The QSCFA was established to study and propose solutions to the different issues and problems concerning Qatar family law and to build on the draft law proposed by a panel of judges. A sub-committee was formed by the QSCFA that worked on the draft law for five years. Similarly, to the first panel of judges, this committee included a task force made up of *Shari'a* judges[17] in order to work out the remaining obstacles in the draft Family Law. The draft law was revised, and the panel organized a public seminar in October 2000 that included lawyers, jurists, and academics.

The QSCFA committee task force also held several meetings with members from the National Committee for Women's Affairs (NCWA)[18] to obtain feedback and reach consensus. The NCWA was, for the most part, a civic society organization made up mostly of prominent Qatari women. Some of the leaders of this group would eventually be recruited to serve at the QSCFA. It is important to note that the members of the NCWA were not only able to have some influence over the new family law, they also submitted some amendments for the task force of judges to consider. For example, one of the issues they lobbied for was a minimum age for marriage, and they succeeded in establishing a minimum age of sixteen for females, when the original draft had stated that puberty is the minimum age of marriage for females. The current law states that the marriage age is eighteen for males and sixteen for females.[19]

10.3   Qatari Family Law

The Qatari Family Law (QFL), which was the result of all the efforts discussed above, officially came into effect on August 28, 2006.[20] The QFL reflects the importance placed on the family by Qatar. The law is meant to stabilize, reform, and protect the family from any possible fragmentation as well as settling any potential disputes that arise between family members. Having said that, the collective rights of the family can, and often do, conflict with the individual rights of women. When such conflicts arise, QFL is primarily used to empower the collective right of the family at the expense of the individual rights of women. The laws enshrined in the QFL are not only a reflection of religious tenets, but they also reflect the social, historical, and cultural experience of the people of Qatar.

QFL incorporates 301 articles that deal with marriage, the different obligations and rights of the husband and the wife,[21] child custody, kinship, alimony, child support, inheritance, and guardianship.

Article 3 states that courts are to interpret the QFL according to the Hanbali school's interpretations of *Shari'a*.[22] In cases where there is no clear interpretation or mandate from the Hanbali perspective, the court may turn to interpretations from the other Sunni Islamic schools of thought such as the Maliki, Hanafi, or Shafi'.[23] The court however does not have to follow the dictates of the other schools of thought and may issue its own ruling based on its own justifications. If the court chooses to do so, the court's ruling must be clearly articulated, and it must provide its justification for deviating from one of the Islamic schools of law. There is also an allowance for the court to use its powers of *ijtihad* (*the exercise of judge's reason to interpret*), when there is a unique case with no clear articulation or interpretations from any of the Islamic schools of law. However, it is understood that these judgments would be based on the general rules of jurisprudence in Islamic law. Several scholars have pointed to the potential problems that could arise from the *ijtihad* of individual judges.[24] What makes this potentially more troubling in Qatar's case is the overwhelming presence of expatriate judges as mentioned earlier.[25]

It is important to note that, while in certain circumstances, the majority of Qataris follow the Hanbali school, the QFL does allow for those who follow other schools of thought, along with non-Muslims, to follow their own religious code. However, non-Muslims can also choose to be under the jurisdiction of the QFL.[26]

Although the main foundation of the QFL is based on an interpretation of Islamic *Shari'a*, the law also relies on societal customs or what is referred to as *Urf*, which then becomes an important reference for the settlement of disputes within the family. There are numerous references to customs in the QFL, including Article 5, which deals with the definition of engagement, which can occur through a clear offer and acceptance of a marriage proposal by the spouses.[27] Engagement can also occur according to the requirements deemed acceptable according to Qatari customs. This allows for the common practice of arranged marriages, whereby a father or a male guardian can arrange the marriage of his daughter (or female relative) without necessarily consulting the bride to be. Even though this practice has been common for years and continues even to this day, it is contrary to Islamic principles. Islamic *Shari'a* dictates that marriage cannot be entered into without the consent of both the bride and the groom.[28]

Article 36 requires that a male guardian conclude the contract on behalf of the bride in the presence of two male witnesses.[29] The bride's presence is not necessary and often not preferred at the conclusion of the marriage contract. It is assumed, however, that her guardian has consulted her and has received her agreement. The Sheikh who is conducting the marriage contract is normally expected to ask the bride directly, however this is sometimes frowned upon. Often the Sheikh will ask the bride from behind a barrier.

Another example is Article 45, which requires that Qatari customs be taken into consideration when resolving conflicts over the dowry.[30] For example, in cases where there is a dispute regarding the nature of any amount given by the husband to the wife (whether the amount given was dower or a gift) and no conclusive evidence was presented, the law requires the judge to resolve the dispute according to the norms and customs of Qatari society.

Article 61 stipulates that a wife's alimony be dependent on what is customary in Qatar,[31] while Article 76 makes a similar statement regarding child support. The father is responsible for providing the following specified items: food, clothes, housing, medical expenses, education, and any necessary travel, in addition to what is customary in Qatari society.[32]

10.4 Marriage

The main component of QFL deals with the definition of family. It provides laws and guidelines for the marriage contract, including imposing restrictions on possible marriage partners. Article 9 states that marriage is between a man and a woman and entered into with the intention of it being of permanent status, for the provision of the security of home and stability.[33] This definition is another important example of NCWA's influence and how they lobbied not only to ensure that marriages are officially registered to combat the possibility of *urfi* (unregistered marriage) but also insisted on permanency as a requirement of marriage to combat the recent phenomena of *misyar*, or traveler's marriage in Saudi Arabia.[34] The *misyar* marriage is similar to the *muta* or temporary marriages that are permissible for Shi'a Muslims.[35] Even though the majority of Sunni Muslim scholars frown upon the practice, prominent legal scholars, such as Dr. Yusuf Al-Qaradawi, agrees that *misyar* constitutes a legal marriage because it fulfills the main principles of Islamic marriages.[36] Consequently, the QFL definition of marriage is an attempt at curbing the temporary marriages.

As mentioned above, another issue that was the subject of intense debate was the minimum age of marriage for females. The original draft suggested a minimum age of fourteen for girls, however, after intense pressure, supported by a survey of Qataris, the minimum age was raised to sixteen. Article 10 states that the registration of the marriage according to the law is required, but the law does allow for the discretion of the judge to authorize the marriage even if the bride does not meet the age requirement.[37] Allowing the individual judge to grant the marriage of a female under sixteen is again an instance where Qatari customs are given priority over laws. As stated previously, QFL Article 17 sets a minimum age of sixteen years for females and eighteen years for males. However, the minimum age requirements may be waived by court approval if the guardian and the couple agree. Judges can use the justification of *urf*, or Qatari traditions that only require that the couple should have reached puberty as a condition for marriage.

Another requirement for marriage is found in Article 18,[38] which requires the couple to undertake certain medical tests before they can get married.[39] What is interesting here is that even though the medical tests are mandatory, if the couple insist on getting married, the official cannot refuse to complete the registration process of the marriage based on the results of the medical exam. This example of Qatari law is unique when compared to other codified family laws in GCC countries. Qatari law seems to be relying on the couple's judgment to make an informed decision without attempting to dictate to them the consequences.

Concerning polygyny, Article 14 of the QFL stipulates that a man must notify his current wife (or wives) after he has married a new wife.[40] According to Lynn Welchman, there was extensive debate regarding the requirement of the husband to inform his existing wife (or wives) with opponents arguing that they "could find no Shari basis for this requirement, that it was not local practice, and such a requirement could lead to problems."[41] However, the proponents of the requirement, mostly the NCWA, prevailed and were also able to provide some form of financial protection to the new wife.

Article 14 stipulates that the new wife must be notified of the husband's financial status.[42] Nevertheless, even with this stipulation, Qatari law again takes a less intrusive role and allows the wife to make her own informed decision. The official registering the marriage cannot refuse to register it, if the couple consents to the marriage even though there may be doubts regarding the husband's ability to meet his financial responsibilities to his new wife.

Article 67 stipulates that a man cannot force his second wife to live in the same house as the first, unless both wives agree.[43] Either wife, however, can change her mind and refuse to live in the same house as a co-wife, if she can convince the judge that this living arrangement would cause her harm.

Articles 55–58 deal with the rights of the husband and wife to each other.[44] Article 56 stipulates that both the husband and wife have the same right to enjoy lawful sexual relations with each other.[45] They are supposed to be faithful to each other, live in the same place together, be kind to each other, and must be able to show one another mutual respect, mercy, and love. They are both required to protect their family. Both are also required to care for their children and raise them to have good morals. Finally, the last part of the Article 56, which is mostly derived from custom, is the stipulation that both have to respect each other's parents and relatives.

While Article 57 prohibits a husband from "hurting her (his wife) physically or morally,"[46] Article 58 discusses the obligation of a wife to her husband.[47] She is to take care of him and obey him. The Article also stipulates that the wife should supervise the household, taking care of her children from the marriage and breastfeed them according to *Shari'a*.

As mentioned earlier in the chapter, if a wife disobeys her husband, some judges have ruled that it is within the husband's rights to discipline his wife according to the interpretation of *Shari'a* principles as applied to the Penal Code.[48]   It is important to note that to date, Qatar has not passed any legislation on domestic violence, and so there is no systematic approach to the problem of domestic violence. This is again an issue where traditions dictate that the victim, more often than not a female, put the interest of the family and its reputation ahead of her own personal safety. Blaming the victim is also used to preempt the victim from contacting law enforcement. In the rare instances where victims do contact law enforcement, they are often told that they should try and resolve these issues within the family.[49]

Article 57 also dictates the financial obligation of the husband to his wife, which includes the *maher*, or dowry, in addition to providing for her financially and allowing her to visit her family and relatives (according to custom).[50] A husband is prohibited from taking his wife's personal savings and cannot harm her emotionally or financially. If he has more than one wife, he must treat them all equally. Article 68 expands on the rights of the wife by stipulating that the husband must allow the wife to continue her education until she finishes grade 12.[51] The husband is also required to arrange for his wife to pursue, if she desires, higher education, in Qatar, so long as her studies do not interfere with her family obligations.

10.5   Guardianship

Articles 26–30 cover the role of guardians during the marriage contract.[52] The law stipulates that a bride be required to have a male guardian complete the marriage contract on her behalf and with her consent. The woman's guardian is usually her father.[53] The guardian must be male, of sound mind, and have reached puberty. He must be a Muslim if he is to act as a guardian over a Muslim woman. Article 28 states that the woman must enlist her guardian to carry out the marriage contract.[54]

According to Article 29: "Marriage is concluded with the permission of the *qadi* by the guardianship of the more distant guardian in the following two cases: 1) If the closer guardian obstructs the woman, or there are a number of guardians with the same level of relationship, and they all veto or they differ. 2) If the closer guardian is absent, and the judge considers that waiting for his opinion will result in the loss of a benefit in the marriage."[55]

According to Article 30, the law also stipulates that if the woman does not have a male guardian, then the judge will act as her guardian.[56] Women, even if they reach adulthood, may not enter into marriage contracts without the involvement of a guardian. However, the judge or whomever is designated as a guardian is not allowed to forcibly use his authority to marry the woman under his guardianship to himself.

10.6   Divorce

There are several circumstances in which a wife is considered *nashez*, or disobedient. These include:

(1) If she does not give herself to her husband (sexually) and if she refuses to move with him when he moves the household.
(2) If she leaves the house without his permission or without a legitimate purpose according to the interpretation of *Shari'a*. (It is interesting to note, that the interpretation of *Shari'a* here is left open. It is assumed, however, that whatever is traditionally thought of as a legitimate reason is acceptable.)
(3) If she does not allow her husband entry into their home, again, unless she has a legitimate excuse according to interpretation of *Shari'a*.
(4) If a wife leaves the country or goes to work without her husband's permission, assuming that he is being reasonable.

Again, the standard applied is the predominant practice in Qatari society. When a wife is considered *nashez*, she forfeits some of her rights, including her husband's financial support.

However, Article 53 does allow the parties to mitigate the default rules contained in the QFL by amending their marriage contract.[57] For example, a woman might include a condition that her husband cannot forbid her from going to work, unless her work contradicts Islamic *Shari'a*. This stipulation is based on the long historical practice that marriage contracts can be negotiated ahead of time and the wife can impose certain conditions, as long as these conditions do not violate Islamic *Shari'a*.[58] Another possible amendment is for the wife to limit the number of wives her husband may marry.

While amending the marriage contract is possible, it should be noted that very few women in Qatar include conditions in their marriage contracts. Judith Tucker explains that

> the jurists also held out the possibility of including voluntary conditions, or stipulations, in the marriage contract. Although a stipulation might not always work in the favor of the bride – the Hanbalis thought, for example, that the father of an under-age girl could stipulate in the contract that part payment of the mahr be reserved to him – most of the stipulations anticipated by the jurists expanded the rights of the wife. Other possible stipulations entertained by Hanbalis, who devoted the most attention to the subject, included prohibiting the husband from taking a second wife or a concubine, preventing him from removing his wife from her native city or even from her own house, and requiring him to accept to house and maintain his wife's children from a previous marriage.[59]

However, new marriage certificates seldom include a section for these stipulations, and they must be added manually. When women do include a stipulation, it is usually to limit the number of wives the husband may marry if any, and in that case, the condition would be that she would be granted a divorce, in case her husband decides to marry a second wife.

The QFL has eighty-seven articles that deal with the consequences of ending a marriage.[60] Article 101 defines the different categories of divorce.[61] If it is due to the wishes of the husband, it is called *talaq*. If both desire a divorce, it is called *mukhala*. If the divorce is ordered by a judge, it is called *faskh*.

The *talaq* is further divided into two categories: one that is revocable and one that is not. A revocable *talaq* involves making the pronouncement of divorce only once. Normally, the former takes place during the *aida*, or waiting period, which is a time period not exceeding three months, to make sure that the wife is not pregnant.[62] During that period, the husband can reconsider and continue to be married to his wife. If the *aida* period passes before the husband has decided to return his wife, he must enter into a new contract, where the wife can get another *maher*.[63]

The second category of *talaq* is a non-revocable *talaq* in which the husband makes the divorce pronouncement three times. In that case, the woman must be married to another man first, with the intention of a lasting marriage and have the marriage consummated. Only if the woman gets a divorce from the second husband can the first husband marry the woman again. Article 113 stipulates that in all divorce cases, the man must pronounce "I divorce you"[64] to his wife in front of a judge for it to be formally recognized. The judge is required to try to reconcile the couple. As a result of the dramatic rise in divorce rates recently,[65] there has been an attempt through governmental organizations such as the Family Consulting Center to try to lower the cases of divorce.

In most situations in Qatar, before they can finalize their divorce, couples who want a divorce are ordered to see a family counselor[66] to try to see if there is any possibility of reconciliation. In the case of *talaq*, if the court sees that the wife is not at fault, the judge will order some financial compensation.

Article 115 specifies that every divorced woman, who was not at fault for the divorce, shall be granted *mut'a* (an agreed upon sum of money that the husband has to pay in the event that he asks for divorce), unless the financial condition of the husband prevents him from doing so.[67] The amount of the *mut'a* is also related to the financial ability of the husband and maintenance usually cannot exceed three years. Article 72 stipulates that a divorced woman during her *aida*, or waiting period, will forfeit the *nafaqa*, or maintenance, if she leaves her husband's house.[68]

The QFL allows the woman to be granted a divorce by petitioning a court. The first type of petition is called a *faskh* divorce. For a *faskh* divorce, a woman has to prove that the continuation of the marriage would cause her harm or injury. These conditions include the husband's failure to provide financial support or maintenance or if he deserted his wife for a period of at least a year.[69] The wife can also ask for a divorce when the husband has breached the marriage contract or in cases when the mental or physical condition of the husband would cause her harm. This includes the cases when the man is infertile, and thus he would be causing his wife the harm of not being able to have her own children.

As for *khul*, or redemptive divorce, a husband can agree to divorce his wife provided that she returns an agreed amount of the *maher* and gives up her right to the *muakhar*, or the agreed upon sum of money that is the right of the wife upon divorce. Article 122 gives the court the right to rule for *khul* even without the consent of the husband, if the attempt at reaching an agreement between the couple failed after a period of six months.[70] In that case, the wife will have to forgo her financial rights and return the *maher*. The justification for the law is that neither party has the intent in continuing the marriage, and the husband has been delaying the divorce proceedings in the hopes of gaining a larger financial concession from his wife.

10.7   Child Custody/Guardianship

According to the QFL, the husband and wife have different responsibilities with regard to the care and upbringing of their children. The father is designated as the guardian, while the mother is defined as the custodian. As such, the father is financially responsible for the children, while the mother is responsible for their upbringing. As stated above, the role of the mother is stipulated in Article 58, where the woman's obligation to the husband and family during the marriage is to take care of the children and raise them to be good Muslims.[71]

Article 120 specifies that the right to the custody of children, and any of the rights that the children have to be negotiated, is part of the divorce decree between the couple.[72] When dealing with issues of child custody, in general the QFL grants custody of the children to the mother because it is believed to be in the best interest of the child.

The QFL goes to great lengths to provide an ordered hierarchy of who is to be the children's custodian. After the mother, custodial preference is followed by the father, then the paternal grandmother, and then the maternal grandmother. Article 170 specifies the conditions the judge must take into consideration when determining who to grant custody over the children. The judge must consider the best interest of the child, including the emotional tie between the child and the custodian, and the custodian's ability to care for the child.[73]

The general spirit of the QFL is that the best interest of the child is above the rights of both parents, and Article 166 states that the mother's custody is preferred for a young child, unless the judge determines otherwise.[74] Article 173 stipulates that the mother should have custody of her son until the age of thirteen and a daughter until the age of fifteen. However, the best interest of the child principle has been used by judges to extend the mother's custodial period to fifteen years of age for boys and until the girls are married.[75] Article 125 uses the best interest of the child principle to justify the mother's permanent custody of a mentally or physically handicapped child.[76]

Article 180 specifies the location of custody as the place where the guardian resides.[77] However, if the marriage contract took place in Qatar, the judge could decide that it is to the benefit of the child that the mother can retain custody of the child, even if she lives abroad or in a different city than the guardian. However, Article 185 specifies that the law does require that in cases in which the mother is non-Qatari, and she intends to take the children out of Qatar, the court will rule in favor of the Qatari husband retaining custody of the children.[78] However, if the non-Qatari mother wants to remain in Qatar, she will retain custody of the children. According to Article 168, the mother could also lose custody of her child if she remarries someone who is not a close relative to the child's father.[79] There is some bias against mothers, since the father's custody is unaffected by the nationality or religion of the woman, if he remarries. A mother's custody can be limited if she is non-Muslim, or if the judge has doubts that she will raise the child to be a good Muslim. In that case, the non-Muslim mother's custody is shortened until the child reaches seven years of age. Women who are atheist or from a non-monotheistic religion are rarely if ever granted custody over their children.[80]

10.8   Paternity

When it comes to paternity or *nasab* and establishing the lineage from the father to the child, the QFL does not allow for adoption. According to *fiqh*, all laws dealing with *nasab* mandate that the child can only be linked by lineage to their biological father. The child can have a *wali* or a guardian who would take care of the child, educate the child, and make sure the child receives proper guidance and act as any parent is required to act toward their children. The lineage of the child, however, will only follow his biological father. The child will also retain the name of his father.

10.9   Citizenship Rights

The law governing citizenship rights in Qatar stipulates that a Qatari male can pass on Qatari citizenship to his children and to his wife.[81] The law does not offer Qatari women the same rights; therefore, Qatari women cannot pass their citizenship to their spouse or to their children.

While this has been very problematic for years, it became much more so during the 2017 blockade imposed on Qatar by some of the GCC states, Saudi Arabia, Bahrain, and the United Arab Emirates. At the beginning of the blockade, participating states ordered their citizens out of Qatar within fourteen days.[82] What made this especially devastating was the large numbers of marriages between Qataris and GCC nationals. According to the Doha International Family Institute, approximately 7 percent of all registered marriages in Qatar were those between Qatari women and GCC nationals.[83]

The blockade was especially traumatic on families residing in Qatar with a Qatari mother and a Gulf Arab father. The children were born and raised in Qatar and were for the most part unfamiliar with their father's national home. It also raised a much more harrowing predicament for the Qatari mother. To its credit, Qatar did not force any GCC citizens out of the country; and in 2018, a new law was passed to try and mitigate the effect of the blockade on non-citizen children of Qatari mothers by granting them permanent residency. While this permanent residency provided many entitlements to non-citizen children of Qatari mothers, including free health care and access to public schooling, it stopped short of providing them with full citizenship.[84] This issue continues to be a major focus of activists and NGOs calling for complete gender equality in Qatar.

10.10   Conclusion

This close examination of Qatar's efforts to develop a family law code that seeks to ameliorate some of the vulnerabilities faced by women living in traditional Qatari society shows both the extent to which these efforts have been successful, as well as highlighting some of its shortcomings. There is still much work that needs to be done. Reconciling the need for progressive legal reforms, while upholding long-held customs and traditions has proven difficult. While Qatar has sought to strengthen the rights of women through the ratification of international conventions such as CEDAW, it continues to have reservations on certain articles, which, according to the state's interpretation, is "inconsistent with the provisions of Islamic law and family law.[85] Perhaps more telling is the extended clarification from the state that argues that the state of Qatar considers legislation that is mostly meant to be "conducive to the interest of promoting social solidarity." Again, here the emphasis is placed on the collective right of the family at the expense of the individual rights of women.

While government attempts at promoting real and progressive legal reform cannot be completely dismissed, there needs to be a parallel movement among civil society groups to further encourage the government in the direction of more progressive reforms. The work done by independent groups such as the one that drafted a CEDAW "shadow report" are essential to help further the progress made so far.[86]

Notes

1 This is much more evident in Saudi Arabia and the alliance between the ruling Al Saud family and Muhammad ibn Abd al Wahhab, the founder of the Wahhabism. The founder of the state of Saudi Arabia entered into a power sharing alliance with ibn Abd al Wahhab, in which Al Saud would control the state politically, while Ibn Abd al Wahhab would provide the religious guidelines for the new state. This alliance, albeit difficult at times, continues to the present day. The alliance provides the ruling family the legitimacy to rule over the state, while allowing the religious establishment to dictate the religious principles and laws to which society must conform.

2 An example of recent measures include the appointment of four women to the Shura Council, along with the appointment of a woman to be the deputy foreign minister and official spokesperson for the Ministry of Foreign Affairs in 2017.

3 Qatar Constitution (2004), www.constituteproject.org/constitution/Qatar_2003 .pdf?lang=en.

4 Qatar Constitution Article 34.

5 Qatar Constitution Article 35.

6 Qatar Constitution Article 21.

7 Qatar Constitution Article 37.

8 Qatar University College of Sharia and Islamic studies publication, http://qspace.qu .edu.qa/bitstream/handle/10576/9499/038202-0008-fulltext.pdf?sequence=10.

9 Qatar Penal Code Article 47.

10 It should be noted that states rely on human understanding (that of mostly male Jurists) to interpret the divine laws as revealed in the holy Quran.

11 The Muscat document was a consultative document adopted at the 7th session of the Supreme Council of the GCC in accordance with a recommendation from the GCC Justice Ministers, in October 1996, www.gccsg.org/eng/index.php?action=Sec-Show&ID=51.

12 Based on interviews conducted by the author. It is interesting to note that there have been recent attempts by the Qatari government to recruit more Qataris as Judges. One recent example is an initiative by the Supreme Judiciary Council at Qatar University, entitled "Judges of Tomorrow," which "contributes to achieving the vision of the Supreme Judiciary Council relevant to the Qatarisation of the judiciary sector with national cadres that are qualified to carry out their duties and perform them fully," www.thepeninsulaqatar.com/article/17/12/2020/Supreme-Judiciary-Council,-QU-launch-%E2%80%98Judges-of-Tomorrow%E2%80%99-ini

tiative. For a discussion on the specific influence of members of the Islamic brotherhood on the GCC, see C. Freer, *Rentier Islamism: The Influence of the Muslim Brotherhood in Gulf Monarchies* (Oxford University Press, 2018).

13 D. Roberts, *Reflecting on Qatar's Islamist Soft Power* (Brookings, 2019), p. 6, www .brookings.edu/wp-content/uploads/2019/04/FP_20190408_qatar_roberts.pdf#:~: text=While%20Yusuf%20Al%20Qaradawi%20played%20a%20role%20in,in% 20Qatar%2C%20the%20majority%20are%20not%20even%20Qatari. For a discussion on the influence of the Islamic Brotherhood on the GCC, see Freer, *Rentier Islamism* and B. Haykel, "Qatar and Islamism," in *Policy Brief* (Norwegian Peacebuilding Resource Centre, February 2013).

14 D. Roberts, "Qatar and the Muslim Brotherhood: Pragmatism or Preference?" (Fall 2014) 21(3) *Middle East Policy*, www.mepc.org/qatar-and-muslim-brotherhood-pragmatism-or-preference.

15 See www.hbku.edu.qa/en/cis.

16 Emiri Decree No. 53 (1998).

17 There are only male judges on Shari'a Court. It is interesting to note that the first female judge was appointed in 2010, Judge Maha Al Thani became the first female judge in Qatar and the GCC.

18 R. Maktabi, "Female Citizenship and Family Law in Kuwait and Qatar: Globalization and Pressures for Reform in Two Rentier States" (2016) 1 *Nidaba*, 20–34, https://journals.lub.lu.se/nidaba/article/view/15846/14335.

19 Qatar Family Law (QFL) Article 17, www.almeezan.qa/LawPage.aspx?id=2558& language=en.

20 QFL Article 17.

21 The fact that husbands and wives have different rights and obligations has been highlighted by scholars as an example of inequality in the marriage. The argument centers on the interpretation of verse 4:34 of the Quran. The debate is often referred to as the maintenance obedience exchange, where the husband is expected to provide the maintenance and the wife is obligated to obey. There has been several attempts especially by Islamic Feminist scholars to reinterpret the verse through a feminist lens in order to arrive at a more equitable relationship between a husband and wife. For additional information see Ayesha Chaudhry, Lynn Welchman And Marwa Sharafeldin. Morocco is the only Arab state that has the same rights and obligations for the husband and wife in family law.

22 QFL Article 3.

23 These schools of thought are not listed in any particular order of priority.

24 Wael Hallaq argues: "If legal pluralism was there to stay – a fact which the jurists never questioned – then it had to be somehow curbed or at least controlled, for, as a matter of consistency and judicial process, doctrinal uncertainty was detrimental. Which of the two, three, or four opinions available should the judge adopt in deciding cases or the jurisconsult opt for in issuing fatwas? The discourse of the jurists, in hundreds of major works that we have at our disposal, is overwhelmingly preoccupied by this problem: Which is the most authoritative opinion?" W. Hallaq, *Authority, Continuity, and Change in Islamic Law* (Cambridge University Press, 2001), p. 126. Judith Tucker argued that while Ijtihad can be used by jurists for a more progressive interpretation, however, they also, "had the power of their respective states behind them. Theirs was not simply an intellectual exercise in reviewing the law, but also a state project geared to specific agendas: in every case

legal reform entailed the assertion of state power over religious courts and person-nel as well as basic questions of identity implicit in marriage practices." J. Tucker, *Women, Family, and Gender in Islamic Law* (Cambridge University Press, 2008), p. 76.

25 The state of Qatar has initiated a Qatarization initiative, such as the one mentioned earlier, in conjunction with Qatar University and the Supreme Judiciary Council to recruit qualified Qatari students and train them to become judges. In its overview of the Supreme Judicial Council, MENAFN details the priority the council places on Qatarization.   https://menafn.com/1101091111/Qatar-Supreme-Judicial-Council-creates-new-specialized-departments#:~:text=The%20Supreme%20Judicial%20Council%20is%20implementing%20a%20plan,the%20level%20of%20Qatari%20courts%20to%20ensure%20.

26 QFL Article 4.

27 QFL Article 5.

28 QFL Article 13.

29 QFL Article 36.

30 QFL Article 45.

31 QFL Article 61.

32 QFL Article 76.

33 QFL Article 9.

34 It is interesting to note that this relatively recent phenomenon in Saudia Arabia, the only other state aside from Qatar that follows the Hanbali school of thought, contradicts the teachings of Ibn Hanbal. He took a very firm stance on the illegitimacy of any sort of temporary marriage. A. Ibn Hanbal, *Chapters on Marriage and Divorce: Responses of Ibn Hanbal and Ibn Rahwayh*, trans. Susan A. Spectorsky (University of Texas Press, 1993).

35 Karen Ruffle explains that "*mut'a* is a form of temporary marriage . . . a man and a woman agree to be married for a set period of time, and the husband pays the wife a form of wage (*ajr*) in exchange for lawful sexual relations with her during the contract period. When the contract expires, the temporary marriage is complete, and the woman is free to enter into another *mut'a* after a forty-five-day waiting period (*'idda*). Any children born from a temporary marriage are legally considered legitimate and have the right to inherit, though in practice some fathers reject the paternity of offspring born from *mut'a*. The principal purpose of *mut'a* is the fulfillment of sexual pleasure, and procreation is typically not the couple's objective. *Mut'a* is distinctive to Shi'ism and is permitted by the Ja'fari school of law. The schools of Sunni law prohibit *mut'a*," www.oxfordbibliographies.com/view/document/obo-9780195390155/obo-9780195390155-0055.xml?rskey=0mBLTN&result=77&q=

36 www.islamopediaonline.org/fatwa/muta-marriage-marriage-sunni-view.   Karen Ruffle argues: "Although mut'a is prohibited by Sunni schools of law, several types of nonpermanent marriage exist, including misyar (ambulant) marriage, which has gained official state sanction in Saudi Arabia, and 'urfi (customary) marriage, which is becoming increasingly popular in Egypt," www.oxfordbibliographies.com/view/document/obo-9780195390155/obo-9780195390155-0055.xml?rskey=0mBLTN&result=77&q=.

37 QFL Article 10.

38 QFL Article 18.

39 The medical exam is to diagnose any existing or potential mental or physical disorders. The probability of genetic diseases is very common due to so much intermarriage. For example, both parents could be carriers of thalassemia (a genetic blood disorder).

40 QFL Article 14.

41 L. Welchman, "Bahrain, Qatar, UAE: First Time Family Codification in Three Gulf States," in Bill Atkin (ed.) *The International Survey of Family Law* (July 2010), pp. 167.

42 QFL Article 14.

43 QFL Article 67.

44 QFL Articles 55–58.

45 QFL Article 56.

46 QFL Article 57.

47 QFL Article 58.

48 Penal Code Article 47.

49 Based on interviews by the author conducted with victims of domestic violence, 2013.

50 QFL Article 57.

51 QFL Article 68.

52 QFL Articles 26–30.

53 If the father is deceased, then the women's guardian would be her paternal grandfather, son, brother (from her father's side if she only has half-brothers), and lastly her paternal uncle, in that order.

54 QFL Article 28.

55 QFL Article 29. Translation by Lynn Welchman.

56 QFL Article 30.

57 QFL Article 53.

58 Amira Sonbol has written extensively about these marriage contracts, showing that they allowed the wife to gain much more rights, as stipulated by *Shari'a*, as opposed to the mostly standard forms of marriage contracts that are used in Islamic states. A. Sonbol, *Women, the Family, and Divorce Laws in Islamic History* (Syracuse University Press, 2007); A. Sonbol, *Gulf Women* (Syracuse University Press, 2012); A. Sonbol, "A History of Marriage Contracts in Egypt," in *The Islamic Marriage Contract: Case Studies in Islamic Family Law* (Islamic Legal Studies Program, Harvard Law School, 2008).

59 Tucker, *Women, Family, and Gender in Islamic Law*, p. 49.

60 QFL Articles 101–188.

61 QFL Article 101.

62 QFL Article 111.

63 QFL

64 QFL Article 113. The Qatari law stipulates that a man can make this unilateral declaration to his wife at any point, however, it is not accepted as divorce if the emotional and physical status of the husband is under duress or if the husband makes the divorce pronouncement in a moment or instance of anger, or when he has been drinking alcohol. The recognized divorce is when a husband has reached the conclusion with premeditation. QFL Articles 108–110.

65 QFL Article 129.

66 Going to see a counselor is mainly an attempt at reducing the divorce rate and to ensure that the couple has a chance to reconsider getting a divorce.

67 QFL Article 115.
68 QFL Article 72.
69 QFL Article 144.
70 QFL Article 122.
71 QFL Article 58.
72 QFL Article 120.
73 QFL Article 170.
74 QFL Article 166.
75 QFL Article 173.
76 QFL Article 125.
77 QFL Article 180.
78 QFL Article 185. If the mother is Qatari, there are no legal limitations for her to travel with her child. Until 2012, all Qatari women needed the permission of a male guardian to leave the country.
79 QFL Article 168.
80 QFL Article 175.
81 Law No. 38 of 2005 on the acquisition of Qatari nationality, www.refworld.org/pdfid/542975124.pdf.
82 www.aljazeera.com/features/2020/6/5/qatar-gulf-crisis-your-questions-answered.
83 S. Alharahsheh and F. Almeer, "Cross-National Marriage in Qatar" (2018) 16 (1–3) *Hawwa*, pp. 170–204, doi.org/10.1163/15692086-12341336.
84 Law No. 10 of 2018 on permanent residency (September 4, 2018). For additional information, see Z. Babar, "The Cost of Belonging: Citizenship Construction in the State of Qatar" (2014) 68(3) *The Middle East Journal*, 403–420.
85 For Qatar reservations, see www.bayefsky.com/html/qatar_t2_cedaw.php.CEDAW; www.ohchr.org/EN/HRBodies/CEDAW/Pages/Introduction.aspx.
86 https://tbinternet.ohchr.org/Treaties/CEDAW/Shared%20Documents/QAT/INT_CEDAW_NGO_QAT_16177_E.pdf.

GLOSSARY

There are many spellings of words. We have standardized them to a large degree. A country may be listed that uses the term, but other countries may use it as well.

adoul	religious notaries acting in their capacity as civil servants, traditionally responsible for drawing up personal status acts (Morocco)
El Ahkam El Shariya	*Shari'a* rulings
al-'arāḍī al-'amīrīyya	state-owned lands (Iraq)
Al-Azhar	Islamic university in Cairo
Al-sha'ab yurīd iṣqāṭ al-niẓām	the people want the fall of the regime (Iraq)
al-wasiya al-wajiba	obligatory bequest (Jordan).
athmeen	sinning
Baath party	political party that exists in Iraq and Syria
bāṭil	unconsummated marriages invalid (Iraq)
CEDAW	Convention on the Elimination of Discrimination against Women
chiqaq	irreconcilable differences divorce
CPS	Tunisia code of personal status Jasmine Revolution – Arab Spring revolution in Tunisia 2010–2011
Dairat Qadi al Quda'	Jordanian Supreme Justice Department (SJD)
dower	bride price where husband gives resources to his future wife (Egypt), *mohar* (Israel)
Druze	minority ethnic group in Lebanon, Syria, Israel, and elsewhere
faskh	the divorce is ordered by a judge (Qatar)
fatiha	a verbal marriage without a written contract whereby two persons are declared married after the reading of the Koranic verses from the *Surah* of the *fatiha* (Algeria)
fatwa	Islamic opinion
fiqh	noncodified Islamic jurisprudence
haḍāna	right to raise the child (Iraq)

GCC	Gulf Cooperation Council
hadith	saying of the prophet Mohamed
Hanafi	one of four schools of Sunni Islam
Hanbali	one of four schools of Sunni Islam
'*idda/ aida*	waiting period following divorce or widowhood during which a woman may not remarry (Egypt, Qatar)
ijab	an offer of one of the parties
ijbar	guardianship with the right of compulsion (Lebanon)
ijtihad	juridical reasoning, legal interpretation
Islam	religion of over one billion people
isma	right of married woman to repudiate herself (Egypt)
Ja'fari/Jafaree	one of schools of Shi'a Islam
JPSL	Jordanian Personal Status Law
kafa'a	financial compatibility (Jordan)
el-khitba	engagement to be married
khol'à	*same as khul'* (Algeria, Morocco)
khul'/khulu'	no fault divorce where wife can divorce her husband without cause (Egypt)
Knesset	Israeli parliament
lex patriae	law of their nationality
li'an	when a husband accuses his wife of adultery and that a child is not his own
Madhab	Islamic school of thought such as Hanafi (Qatar)
Ma'dhun	an official with authority to perform civil marriages (Egypt)
Majalla	Code of Personal Status (Tunisia)
Maliki	one of four schools of Sunni Islam
maṣlaḥa mashrū'a	legitimate interest (Iraq)
mahr al mithel/ maher	dowry
mahram	a member of one's family with whom marriage would be considered haram (illegal) in Islam (Jordan)
majlis al 'iqd	place of contract (West Bank)
ma'ruf	good way, decent
MENA	Middle East/North Africa region
millet	concept of having religious jurisdiction and personal religious law govern matters of family law; religious community
misyar	traveler's marriage in the Persian Gulf states
Moudawana	Morocco Personal Status Code
moujahidat	women who fought in the Algerian war of independence
mubah	allowed
mukhala	if both desire a divorce (Qatar)

mukhbirin	appointing informants by a *Shari'a* court to assess alimony payments for Muslim women (Israel)
musawegh shar'i	religiously legal reason (Jordan)
Muslim	person who practices Islam
mut'a	financial compensation (Egypt), temporary marriage in Shi'a countries
nafaqa al	*'idda* alimony (Egypt)
nasel	lineage (Jordan)
nashez	disobedient wife
nassab	paternity, literally family lineage (Israel)
NCWA	National Committee for Women's Affairs (Qatar)
NGO	nongovernmental organization
nushuz	disobedience
OFRL	Ottoman Family Rights Law
Personal Status Law	codified family law in many countries
PNA	Palestinian National Authority
Qadi/qaddi	*Shari'a* court judge (Israel)
QFL	Qatari Family Law
qiwamah	men have financial responsibility for women
QSCFA	Qatar Supreme Council for Family Affairs
Qur'an or Koran	Holy book for Muslims
rahmah wa muwadah	compassion and love
Réforme et Renouveau	Islamic movement in Morocco
rida'ah	two persons connected through the relationship of suckling, that is, the wet nurse and her family are forbidden to marry the baby and members of the baby's family (Lebanon)
sadaq el mithl	"proper" dower (Algeria)
Shafi'	one of four schools of Sunni Islam
Shari'a	Islamic law
sheikh	religious figure
Shi'a	type of Islam practiced by a minority of Muslims as opposed to Sunni Islam practiced by the majority of Muslims
shiqāq	discord (Iraq)
sunnah	sayings of the Prophet Muhamed
Sunni	type of Islam practiced by majority of Muslims as opposed to Shi'a Islam practiced by a minority
surah	verse in the Koran
ta'ah	duty of obedience that women have
tafreeq	separation or repudiation, often referred to as women's divorce (Jordan)

takhayyur	selection of rulings without restriction to a particular madhhab (Egypt)
talfīq	"patching" of rules from various Islamic sources
ṭalāq	the right of a husband to repudiate the marriage (Iraq)
tamlik	A wife may repudiate herself if her husband has granted her that right (Morocco)
tasarruf	economize, thrift, successorship in the right of transacting over real property, control or disposition (Iraq)
udda	separation (West Bank)
ulema/ oulema	body of Muslim scholars recognized as having specialist knowledge of Islamic law and theology
'urfi/orfi	customary marriage (Egypt)
wajeb	required
wali	guardian for a minor or a woman
wilāya	guardianship over the child

BIBLIOGRAPHY

Ababneh, S. "Do You Know Who Governs Us? The Damned Monetary Fund, Jordan's June 2018 Rising." (2018) *Middle East Report* (June 29), https://merip.org/2018/06/do-you-know-who-governs-us-the-damned-monetary-fund/.

"Islamic Political Parties as a Means to Women's Empowerment? The Case of Hamas and the Islamic Action Front." DPhil Thesis, University of Oxford (2010).

"The Time to Question, Rethink and Popularize the Notion of 'Women's Issues': Lessons from Jordan's Popular and Labor Movements from 2006 to Now." (2020) 21(1) *Journal of International Women's Studies*, 271–288, https://vc.bridgew.edu/jiws/vol21/iss1/21.

"Troubling the Political: Women in the Jordanian Day-Wage Labor Movement." (2016) 48(1) *International Journal of Middle East Studies*, http://journals.cambridge.org/action/displayAbstract?fromPage=online& aid=10117205.

Abbott, P., and A. Teti "Why Women's Rights Have Made Little Progress since the Arab Spring." *Newsweek*, April 21, 2017, www.newsweek.com/arab-spring-gender-equality-women-rights-progress-egypt-tunisia-587317.

Abi-Mershed, O. (ed.) *Social Currents in North Africa: Culture and Government after the Arab Spring* (Oxford University Press, 2018).

Abu-Odeh, L. "Egyptian Feminism: Trapped in the Identity Debate." (2004) 16 *Yale Journal of Law and Feminism*, 145–191.

"Heads of Family Are Mother and Father: Why New Saudi Law Amendments Are Important." Egyptian Streets, December 6, 2019, https://egyptianstreets .com/2019/12/06/heads-of-family-are-mother-and-father-why-new-saudi-law-amendments-are-important/.

"Modernizing Muslim Family Law: The Case of Egypt." (2004) 37 *Vanderbilt Journal of Transnational Law*, 1043–1146.

Adnan, G. *Women and the Glorious Qu'ran: An Analytical Study of Women Related Verses of Sura An-Nisa* (University of Gottingen Press, 2004).

A/HRC/36/6 Add.1 Human Rights Council Report of the Working Group on the Universal Periodic Review, Morocco, August 2017.

A/HRC/36/13, 19 July 2017, Human Rights Council Report of the Working Group on the Universal Periodic Review, Algeria. Rapport du Groupe de travail sur l'Examen périodique universel Algérie, Additif Observations sur les conclusions et/ou recommandations, engagements et réponses de l'État examine.

A/HRC/36/13/Add.1 19 Septembre 2017, Conseil des droits de l'homme (Algeria).

Ait-Zai, N. "Le divorce dans le droit de la famille algérien." www.cicade.org (2016) (Algeria).

adala.justice.gov.ma/production/statistiques/Tribunaux/FR/Mar_&_Div_pour_Site_FR.pdf; http://adala.justice.gov.ma/production/statistiques/SJF/FR/30-10-12%20VR%20Finale%20Statistique%20Francais.pdf. (Morocco).

al Ali, Z. "Libya's Final Draft Constitution: A Contextual Analysis." International Institute for Democracy and Electoral Assistance (2020), https://constitutionnet.org/sites/default/files/2020-12/Libya%20analysis%20-%20Zaid%20Al-Ali%20%28December%202020%29%20%28English%29.pdf, 16.

Al Hawamda, M. *The Historical Development of Personal Status Law in Jordan* (original in Arabic: *Al tatawour al tareekhi liqanoon al ahwal al shakhsiya fil urdun*), Markaz al Rayi Lil Dirasat (Al Rayi Center for Research, 2003), www.alraicenter.com.

Al Ra'i. "'Solidarity' Welcomes Parliaments Approval to Change Articles (62) and (98) of the Penal Code" (Tadamun turaheb bimuwafaqat al Nuwwab a'la ta'dil al-Madatayin 62 wa 98 Auqubat), *Al Ra'i*, July 30, 2017 (Jordan).

Al-Sharmani, M. *Gender Justice and Legal Reform in Egypt: Negotiating Muslim Family Law* (American University in Cairo, 2017).

Recent Reforms in Personal Status Laws and Women's Empowerment. Family Courts in Egypt (AUC Social Research Center, 2008), www.pathwaysofempowerment.org/Familycourts.pdf.

Al-Ulum, M. B. *Shedding Light on the Iraqi Personal Status Code* (Nu'man, 1963).

"Algeria: Bouteflika Announces a Reform of the Family Code." *Le Monde* (March 9, 2015), www.lemonde.fr/afrique/article/2015/03/09/algerie-bouteflika-annonce-une-reforme-du-code-de-la-famille_4590103_3212.html.

Alghurair, D. H. "Family Law in the United Arab Emirates: Overview." Thomson Reuters, November 1, 2020, https://uk.practicallaw.thomsonreuters.com/4-612-5426?transitionType=Default&contextData=(sc.Default)&firstPage=true#co_pageContainer.

Alhibri, A. "Islam, Law and Custom: Redefining Muslim Women's Rights." (1997) 12 *American University Journal of International Law and Policy*, 1–44.

Ali, K. *Marriage and Slavery in Early Islam* (Harvard University Press, 2014).

Amara, T. "Arab Spring Beacon Tunisia Signs New Constitution." Reuters, January 27, 2014, www.reuters.com/article/us-tunisia-constitution/arab-spring-beacon-tunisia-signs-new-constitution-idUSBREA0Q0OU20140127.

Amawi, A. "Gender and Citizenship in Jordan." In S. Joseph (ed.) *Gender and Citizenship in the Middle East* (Syracuse University Press, 2000), pp. 158–184.

Ammoumou, Z. "Les droits matériels de la femme divorcée." In *Regard sur le droit de la famille dans les pays du Maghreb* (CIDEAL, 2008), pp. 85–92.

Amnesty International. "Algeria: Briefing to the Committee on the Elimination of Discrimination against Women" (December 2004).

"Palestine (State of) 2019" (2019).

Anderson, J. N. D. "A Law of Personal Status for Iraq." (1960) 9 *The International and Comparative Law Quarterly*, 542–563.

An-Na'im, A. A. "Algeria, Democratic and Popular Republic of." Emory University School of Law (2015), https://scholarblogs.emory.edu/islamic-family-law/home/research/legal-profiles/algeria-democratic-and-popular-republic-of/.

"Iraq, Republic of." Emory University School of Law (2015), https://scholarblogs.emory.edu/islamic-family-law/home/research/legal-profiles/iraq-republic-of/.

An-Nai'im, A. A. *Islamic Family Law in a Changing World: A Global Resource Book* (Zed Books, 2002), vol. 2.

"Lebanon (Lebanese Republic)." Emory University School of Law (2015), https://scholarblogs.emory.edu/islamic-family-law/home/research/legal-pro files/lebanon-lebanese-republic/.

"Morocco, Kingdom of (& Western Sahara)." Emory University School of Law (2015), https://scholarblogs.emory.edu/islamic-family-law/home/research/legal-profiles/morocco-kingdom-of-western-sahara/.

"Palestine/Palestinian Territories of West Bank and Gaza Strip." Emory University School of Law (2015), https://scholarblogs.emory.edu/islamic-family-law/home/research/legal-profiles/palestinepalestinian-territories-of-west-bank-and-gaza-strip/.

"Qatar, State of." Emory University School of Law (2015), https://scholarblogs.emory.edu/islamic-family-law/home/research/legal-profiles/qatar-state-of/.

"Tunisia, Republic of (Draft: Under Review)." Emory University School of Law (2015), https://scholarblogs.emory.edu/islamic-family-law/home/research/legal-profiles/tunisia-republic-of%EF%BF%BD%EF%BF%BD-draft-under-review/.

"Yemen, Republic of." Emory University School of Law (2015), https://scholarblogs.emory.edu/islamic-family-law/home/research/legal-profiles/yemen-republic-of/.

Antoci, I. P., R. S. Gatina, and A. Elnaggar "Women's Rights in Marriage and Divorce Based on Sharia Regulations and the UAE Personal Status Law (Part 1 – Women's Rights in Marriage and the Marriage Contract)." *The UAE Jurist*, February 4, 2021, https://theuaejurist.com/womens-rights-in-mar riage-and-divorce-based-on-sharia-regulations-and-the-uae-personal-status-law-part-1-womens-rights-in-marriage-and-the-marriage-contract/.

ArabNews. "UAE Amends Laws on Personal Status, Civil Transactions and Criminal Procedures." ArabNews.com (November 7, 2020), www.arabnews .com/node/1759656/middle-east.

Aral, B. "The Idea of Human Rights as Perceived in the Ottoman Empire." (May 2004) 26(2) *Human Rights Quarterly*, 454–482.

Arrott, E., L. Bryant, and H. Ridgwell, "Tunisians Mourn Losses in Jasmine Revolution." *Voice of America*, January 21, 2011, www.voanews.com/learnin genglish/home/world/Tunisians-Mourn-Loses-in-Jasmine-Revolution-114390324.html.

Association Démocratique des Femmes du Maroc (ADFM). "Rapport des ONG de Défense des Droits des Femmes au Maroc au Titre du 2e Examen Périodique Universel (EPU)" (November 2011).

Association Démocratique des Femmes du Maroc (ADFM), LDDF. "Droits des femmes; Implementation of the CEDAW Convention: Non-Governmental Organisations' Shadow Report to the Third and the Fourth Periodic Report of the Moroccan Government" (November 2007).

Avi-Guy, O. "New Order, Same Rules." *Sydney Morning Herald*, December 27, 2011, www.smh.com.au/opinion/politics/new-order-same-rules-20111226-1paf2.html#ixzz1kx11wnXn.

Bahrain Center for Human Rights. "The Legal Status of Women in Bahrain" (2017), http://bahrainrights.org/sites/default/files/NEW%20BCHR%20Legal %20Status%20of%20Women%20in%20Bahrain.pdf.

Bains, I. "Day of Shame in the Middle East: Female Protesters Beaten with Metal Poles as Vicious Soldiers Drag Girls through Streets." *Daily Mail Online*, December 19, 2011, www.dailymail.co.uk/news/article-2075683/Egypt-vio lence-Female-protesters-brutally-beaten-metal-poles-vicious-soldiers.html.

Baker, C. *The Women's Movement against Sexual Harassment* (Cambridge University Press, 2007).

Barkey, K. "Islam and Toleration: Studying the Ottoman Imperial Model." (2007) 19(1/2) *International Journal of Politics, Culture, and Society*, 5–19.

Barlas, A. *Believing Women in Islam: Unreading Patriarchal Interpretations of the Qu'ran* (University of Texas Press, 2002).

Barzilai, G. *Communities and the Law, Politics and Cultures of Legal Identities* (University of Michigan Press, 2003).

"Fantasies of Liberalism and Liberal Jurisprudence: State Law, Politics and the Israeli Arab-Palestinian Community." (2000) 34 *Israel Law Review*, 425–450.

Bayat, A. *Revolution without Revolutionaries: Making Sense of the Arab Spring* (Stanford University Press, 2017).

Revolutionary Life: The Everyday of the Arab Spring (Harvard University Press, 2021).

Beaugé, F. "En Algérie, le code de la famille récemment reformé maintient la femme sous tutelle." *Le Monde* (February 24, 2005).

Ben Maḥmūd, F., H. Ben Sulaymah, and S. Dawlah, *Majallat al-aḥwāl al-shakhṣīyah* (M. Borrmans, *Personal Status Law* (Markaz al-Dirāsāt al-Qānūnīyah wa al-Qaḍāʾīyah, 2010) (in Arabic, English, and French).

Bernard-Maugiron, N. "Egyptian Family Law Reform: Between Law in the Books and Law in Action." In N. Nassari (ed.) *Changing God's Law: the Dynamics of Middle Eastern Family Law* (Ashgate, 2016), pp. 181–203.

"The Judicial Construction of the Facts and the Law: The Egyptian Supreme Constitutional Court and the Constitutionality of the Law on the Khul." In B. Dupret et al. (eds.) *Narratives of Truth in Islamic Law* (CEDEJ-I. B. Tauris, 2007), pp. 243–264.

Bernard-Maugiron, N., and B. Dupret. "Breaking-off the Family: Divorce in Egyptian Law and Practice." (2008) *Hawwa: Journal of Women in the Middle East and the Islamic World*, 52–74.

"From Jihan to Suzanne: Twenty Years of Personal Status in Egypt." (2002) 19 *Recht van de Islam*, 1–19.

Bhaumik, G. "An Expat Guide to Getting a Divorce in Qatar." *Expatica* (August 10, 2020), www.expatica.com/qa/living/love/getting-a-divorce-in-qatar-72159/.

Bordat, S. W. "Difficultés pratiques d'accès des femmes à la justice." Colloque "Droits des femmes et révolutions arabes." Le Mans, Université du Maine (June 29, 2012).

Bordat, S. W., and S. Kouzzi, "Legal Empowerment of Unwed Mothers: Experiences of Moroccan NGOs." In Legal Empowerment working Paper No. 14 (International Development Law Organization, 2010).

Borrmans, M. *Statut personnel et famille au Maghreb: de 1940 à nos jours* (Mouton, 1977), p. 335 (in French).

Bostanji, S. "Turbulence in the Legal Application of the Tunisian Code of the Personal Status: Conflict in Reference Frames in Work." (2009) 61 *Revue Internationale De Droit Comparé*, 7–47 (in French).

"Bothaina Kamel says She Has No Regrets on Dropping Out of Race." *Egypt Independent*, April 8, 2012, www.egyptindependent.com/news/bothaina-kamel-says-she-has-no-regrets-over-dropping-out-race.

Bouazza, B. "Tunisian Women Demonstrate to Protect Their Rights." *Associated Press*, November 2, 2011, www.google.com/hostednews/ap/article/ALeqM5iBwopsJzONk0IPtzGReBdjjCK9PA?docId=3b92f6a715784eccb490d4a50e24b7be.

Brand, L. *Women, the State and Political Liberalization: Middle Eastern and North African Experiences* (Columbia University Press, 1998).

Bras, J. "La Réforme du Code de la Famille au Maroc et en Algérie: Quelles avancées pour la Démocratie?" (2007) 37(4) *Critique Internationale*, 93–125.

Brown, N., and M. Dunne, "Egypt's Draft Constitutional Amendments Answer Some Questions and Raise Others." *Carnegie*, http://egyptelections

.carnegieendowment.org/2011/03/03/egypt%E2%80%99s-draft-constitutional-amendments-answer-some-questions-and-raise-others.

Brownson, E. *Palestinian Women and Muslim Family Law in the Mandate Period* (Syracuse University Press, 2019).

Byrne, E. "The Women MPs Tipped to Play Leading Roles in Tunisia's New Assembly." *The Guardian,* October 28, 2011, www.guardian.co.uk/world/2011/oct/29/women-mps-tunisia-government.

CA 245/81, 38(3) P.D. 169 (1984) (Israel).

CA 3077/90, 49(2) PD 578 (1995) (Israel).

CEDAW/C/MAR/5–6, Committee on the Elimination of Discrimination against Women, "Combined Fifth and Sixth Periodic Reports Submitted by Morocco under Article 18 of the Convention. Due in 2014." February 19, 2020.

Center for History and New Media. "Law, Code of Personal Status." Imperialism in North Africa, February 1, 2021, https://chnm.gmu.edu/wwh/modules/lesson9/lesson9.php?s=11.

Chafi, M. Code de Statut Personnel Annoté (1996) (Morocco).

Chambers, V., and C. Cummings. "Building Momentum: Women's Empowerment in Tunisia." Case Study Report. Overseas Development Institute (2014).

"Charbel Urged to Approve Lebanon Civil Marriage." *Daily Star*, February 15, 2013, www.dailystar.com.lb/News/Politics/2013/Feb-15/206602-charbel-urged-to-approve-lebanon-civil-marriage.ashx#ixzz2P5Ay8nEJ.

Charrad, M. M. "Becoming a Citizen: Lineage versus Individual in Morocco and Tunisia." In S. Joseph (ed.) *Gender and Citizenship in the Middle East* (Syracuse University Press, 2000), pp. 70–87.

"Contexts, Concepts and Contentions: Gender Legislation in the Middle East." (2007) 5 *Hawwa: Journal of Women in the Middle East and the Islamic World*, 55–72.

"Cultural Diversity within Islam: Veils and Laws in Tunisia." In H. L. Bodman and N. Tohidi (eds.) *Women in Muslim Societies: Diversity within Unity* (Lynne Rienner Press, 1998), pp. 63–79.

"Gender in the Middle East: Islam, States, Agency." (2011) 37 *Annual Review of Sociology*, 417–437.

"Policy Shifts: State, Islam and Gender in Tunisia, 1930s–1990s." (Summer 1997) 4 *Social Politics*, 284–319.

"Progressive Family Law: How It Came About in Tunisia." (2016) 24 *Transnational Law & Contemporary Problems*, 18; *Journal of Gender, Race & Justice*, 351–360.

"Repudiation versus Divorce: Responses to State Policy in Tunisia." In E. N. Chow and C. W. Berheide (eds.) *Women, the Family and Policy: A Global Perspective* (State University of New York Press, 1994), pp. 51–69.

"State and Gender in the Maghrib." (March–April 1990) *Middle East Report*, 19–24.

States and Women's Rights: The Making of Postcolonial Tunisia, Algeria, and Morocco (University of California Press, 2001).

"Tunisia at the Forefront of the Arab World: Two Waves of Gender Legislation." (2007) 64 *Washington and Lee Law Review*, 1513–1527.

"Unequal Citizenship: Issues of Gender Justice in the Middle East and North Africa." In M. Mukhopadhyay (ed.) *Gender Justice, Citizenship and Development* (International Development Research Centre, 2007), pp. 233–262.

Charrad, M. M., and A. Zarrugh. "Constructing Citizenship: Gender and Changing Discourses in Tunisia." In H. Danielson, K. Jegerstedt, R. L. Muriaas, and B. Ytre-Arne (eds.) *Gendered Citizenship: The Challenges of Representation* (Palgrave Press, 2016), pp. 137–158.

"Equal or Complementary? Women in the New Tunisian Constitution after the Arab Spring." (2014) 19 *The Journal of North African Studies*, 230–243.

"From Colonialism to the Arab Spring: Gender, Religion and State." In R. A. Scott and S. M. Kosslyn (eds.) *Emerging Trends in the Social and Behavioral Sciences* (John Wiley and Sons, 2015), doi.org/10.1002/9781118900772.etrds0135.

Chatelard, G. "The Constitution of Christian Communal Boundaries and Spheres in Jordan." (2010) 52(3) *Journal of Church and State*, 476–502.

Chemais, A. "Divorced from Justice: Women's Unequal Access to Divorce in Egypt." (December 2004) 16(8) *Human Rights Watch Report*, 1–68.

Cheriet, B. *"Le Cas Algérien" Femmes, Droit de la Famille et Système Judiciaire en Algérie, au Maroc et en Tunisie* (UNESCO, 2010), pp. 17–60.

Cherland, K., "The Development of Personal Status Law in Jordan & Iraq." Claremont McKenna College Senior Theses 865 (2014), https://scholarship.claremont.edu/cgi/viewcontent.cgi?referer=https://www.google.com/&httpsredir=1&article=1926&context=cmc_theses.

Chigier, M. *Husband and Wife in Israeli Law* (Harry Fischel Institute for Research in Talmud and Jurisprudence, 1985).

Clark, J., and A. Young. "Islamism and Family Law Reform in Morocco and Jordan." (2008) 13(3) *Mediterranean Politics*, 333–352.

Coleman, I. "Are the Mideast Revolutions Bad for Women's Rights?" *Washington Post*, February 20, 2011, www.washingtonpost.com/wpdyn/content/article/2011/02/18/AR2011021806962.html.

"Blue Bra Girl' Rallies Egypt's Women vs. Oppression." CNN, December 22, 2011, www.cnn.com/2011/12/22/opinion/coleman-women-egypt-protest/index.html.

Colombo, S., and D. Huber (eds.) *Ten Years of Protests in the Middle East and North Africa: Dynamics of Mobilisation in a Complex (Geo) Political Environment* (Peter Lang, 2022).

Commission of the European Communities. "Country Report 'Palestinian Authority' of the West Bank and Gaza." (December 5, 2004), www .refworld.org/pdfid/4153e6d54.pdf.

Committee on the Elimination of Discrimination against Women. "Combined Third and Fourth Periodic Report of States Parties: Morocco." (September 18, 2006) CEDAW/C/MAR/4.

"Combined Fifth and Sixth Periodic Reports Submitted by Morocco under Article 18 of the Convention." (January 16, 2020) CEDAW/C/MAR/5–6.

Communiqué du Collectif 20 Ans Barakat. "Une Nouvelle Fois les Droits des Femmes sont Bafoués." (March 8, 2005) (Algeria).

Conditions, Not Conflict: Promoting Women's Rights in the Maghreb through Strategic Use of the Marriage Contract (Global Rights, 2008).

"Concluding Comments of the Committee on the Elimination of Discrimination against Women." (April 8, 2008) CEDAW/C/MAR/CO/4.

Connors, J. O., and C. Mallat. *Islamic Family Law.* Arab and Islamic Laws Series, Centre of Islamic & Middle East Law (CIMEL) (School of Oriental and African Studies, 1990).

Conseil des Droits de l'homme. "Rapport du Groupe de Travail sur l'examen Périodique Universel Algérie, Additif Observations sur les Conclusions et/ ou Recommandations, Engagements et Réponses de l'État Examine." (September 19, 2017) A/HRC/36/13/Add.1.

Conseil Economique. "Social et Environnemental." (2019) (Morocco).

Constitution de la République Algérienne Démocratique et Populaire. JORADP N° 76 du 8 décembre 1996 modifiée par: Loi n°02-03 du 10 avril 2002 JORADP N°25 du 14 avril 2002; Loi n°08-19 du 15 novembre 2008 JORADP N.

Convention on the Elimination of All Forms of Discrimination Against Women. G.A. Res. 34/180, U.N. GAOR, 34th Session 107th plenary meeting, U.N. Doc. A/Res/34/180 (December 18, 1979).

Cuno, K. M. *Modernizing Marriage: Family, Ideology, and Law in Nineteenth and Early Twentieth-Century Egypt* (Syracuse University Press, 2015).

Dabaas, F. "The Impact of the Corona Pandemic on issues of Personal Status" (Ta'theer Jaihat al Corona ala qadaya al-Ahwal al-Shakhsiyya). Solidarity is Global Institute (SIGI), Zoom Round Table, May 19, 2020.

Dabbous, D. "Legal Reform and Women's Rights in Lebanese Personal Status Laws." Chr. Michelsen Institute (September 2017), www.researchgate.net/ publication/320558138_Legal_Reform_and_Women's_Rights_in_ Lebanese_Personal_Status_Laws.

David, H. "Women's Divorce Rights in Jordan: Legal Rights and Cultural Challenges." Thesis, SIT Graduate Institute/SIT Study Abroad (2018), https://digitalcollections.sit.edu/cgi/viewcontent.cgi?article=3990&context= isp_collection.

Davies, C. "The Woman Who Wants to be Egypt's First Female President." CNN, September 16, 2011, www.cnn.com/2011/09/13/world/meast/egypt-both aina-kamel/index.html.

Decisions of Tyre Shari'a Court, judgement 259, record 11 (February 9, 2000) and of the Supreme Ja'fari Shari'a Court, judgement 59/466, record 116 (June 18, 2002).

Decree No.15 on Lebanese Nationality (and amendments), January 19, 1925, www .refworld.org/pdfid/44a24c6c4.pdf.

Deeks, A. S., and M. D. Burton, "Iraq's Constitution: A Drafting History." (2007) 40 *Cornell International Law Journal*, 1–87.

Dehnert, E. "As Lebanon, Jordan, Tunisia End 'Marry-Your-Rapist' Laws, Where Next?" *Huffington Post*, September 1, 2017, www.huffingtonpost.com/entry/ as-lebanon-jordan-tunisia-end-marry-your-rapist-laws-where-next_us_ 59a986c8e4b0b5e530fe49e1.

Dessi, A. "Popular Mobilisation and Authoritarian Reconstitution in the Middle East and North Africa: Ten Years of Arab Uprisings." In S. Colombo and D. Huber (eds.) *Ten Years of Protests in the Middle East and North Africa: Dynamics of Mobilisation in a Complex Ggeo) political Environment* (Peter Lang, 2022), pp. 191–206.

Deveaux, M. *Gender and Justice in Multicultural Liberal States* (Oxford University Press, 2006).

Diamond, L. *Squandered Victory: The American Occupation and the Bungled Effort to Bring Democracy to Iraq* (Owl Books, 2005).

Democratic Association of Women of Morocco (ADFM), https:// learningpartnership.org/who-we-are/partnership/democratic-association-moroccan-women.

Dib, G. *Law and Population in Lebanon* (Law and Population Programme, 1975).

Doi, A. "Marriage," www.usc.edu/dept/MSA/humanrelations/womeninislam/ marriage.html.

Draft report of the Working Group on the Universal Periodic Review, Morocco, 25 May 2012, A/HRC/WG.6/13/L.1; CCPR/C/MAR/CO/6 Human Rights Committee, Concluding Observations on the sixth periodic report of Morocco, December 1, 2016.

Dridi, H. "Tunisian Women Demonstrate to Preserve Their Rights following Islamist Election Victory." *Associated Press*, November 2, 2011, www .washingtonpost.com/world/africa/tunisian-women-demonstrate-to-preserve-their-rights-following-islamist-election-victory/2011/11/02/gIQAJnh4fM_story.html.

Edelman, M. *Courts, Politics, and Culture in Israel* (University of Virginia Press, 1994).

"EGYPT: Government Defends Military Trials, 'Virginity Tests' to Human Rights Advocates." *Los Angeles Times*, June 7, 2011, http://latimesblogs.latimes.com/

babylonbeyond/2011/06/egypt-government-justifies-military-trials-virginity-tests-to-human-rights-advocates.html.

"Egypt's Quiet Gender Revolution." *Think Africa Press*, August 24, 2011, http://thinkafricapress.com/egypt/egypt-quiet-gender-revolution.

Eighth Amendment to the Personal Status Code, No. 34 of 1983, issued April 18, 1983 (Iraq).

Eisenman, R. H. *Islamic Law in Palestine and Israel: A History of the Survival of Tanzimat and Shari'a in the British Mandate and the Jewish State* (Brill, 1978), pp. 196–223.

El Alami, D. S. "Law No. 100 of 1985 Amending Certain Provisions of Egypt's Personal Status Laws." (1994) 1(1) *Islamic Law and Society*, 116–130.

El Alami, D., and D. Hinchcliffe. *Islamic Marriage and Divorce Laws of the Arab World* (Kluwer Law International, 1996).

El Cheikh, N. M. "The 1998 Proposed Civil Marriage Law in Lebanon: The Reaction of Muslim Communities." (1998–1999) 5 *Yearbook of Islamic Studies & Middle East Law*, 147–161.

Elhais, H. "New Amendments in UAE Family Law." (2020), www.hg.org/legal-articles/new-amendments-in-uae-family-law-54636.

El Gemayel, A. E. *The Lebanese Legal System* (International Law Institute in cooperation with Georgetown University, 1985), vol. I.

El Khazen, F. *The Communal Pact of National Identities: The Making and Politics of the 1943 National Pact*. Centre for Lebanese Studies (Oxford University Press, October 1991).

Engelcke, D. "Establishing Filiation (Nasab) and the Placement of Destitute Children into New Families: What Role Does the State Play?" (2019) 34(3) *Journal of Law and Religion*, 408–432.

"Jordan." In N. Yassari, L. Moeller, I. Gallala-Arndt (eds.) *Parental Care and the Best Interests of the Child in Muslim Countries* (Asser Press Den Haag, 2017), pp. 121–143.

"Law-Making in Jordan: Family Law Reform and the Supreme Justice Department." (2018) 25(3) *Islamic Law and Society*, 274–309.

Reforming Family Law: Social and Political Change in Jordan and Morocco (Cambridge University Press, 2019).

Engelcke, D., and N. Yassari. "Child Law in Muslim Jurisdictions: The Role of the State in Establishing Filiation (Nasab) and Protecting Parentless Children – Symposium Introduction." (2019) 34(3) *Journal of Law and Religion*, 332–335.

Equality Now. "Jordan – Personal Status Law No. 36 of 2010." *Equality Now*, www.equalitynow.org/jordan_-_personal_status_law_no_36_of_2010.

"Tunisia – Personal Status Code of 1956." *Equality Now*, www.equalitynow.org/tunisia_personal_status_code_of_1956.

"Yemen – The Personal Status Act No. 20 of 1992." *Equality Now*, www
.equalitynow.org/yemen_the_personal_status_act_no_20_of_1992.

Evans, S. M. *Tidal Wave: How Women Changed America at Century's End* (Free
Press, 2004).

Esposito, J. L., and N. J. DeLong-Bas, *Women in Muslim Family Law*, 2nd ed.
(Syracuse University Press, 2001).

Fawzy, L. E. "Muslim Personal Status Law in Egypt: The Current Situation and
Possibilities of Reform through Internal Initiative." In L. Welchman (ed.)
Women's Rights and Islamic Family Law: Perspectives on Reform (Zed
Books, 2004), pp. 15–94.

Federal Court of Cassation, First Personal Status Panel, Case 2289/2010, decided
March 4, 2010 (Iraq).

Federal Court of Cassation, First Personal Status Panel, Case 2076/2010, decided
April 22, 2010 (Iraq).

Federal Court of Cassation, First Personal Status Panel, Case 2964/2010, decided
November 7, 2010 (Iraq).

Federal Supreme Court of Iraq, Decision 59 of 2011.

First Instance Court in Meknes, Family Division, Number 1783, July 9, 2009,
Number 1931/8/ 5M (Morocco).

Fisk, R. "Bonfire of the Dictator." *The Independent*, December 31, 2011, www
.independent.co.uk/news/world/middle-east/bonfire-of-the-dictators-6283351
.html.

Freeman, J. *The Politics of Women's Liberation: A Case Study of an Emerging Social
Movement and Its Relation to the Policy Process* (McKay Press, 1975).

"Gaddafi Dead: Bodies of Leader, Son, Aide Taken from Misrata Freezer."
Huffington Post, October 24, 2011, www.huffingtonpost.com/2011/10/24/
gaddafi-dead-body_n_1029418.html.

Ghandour, Z. "Religious Law in a Secular State: The Jurisdiction of the Shari'a
Courts of Palestine and Israel." (1990) 5 *Arab Law Quarterly*, 25–48.

Ghezali, S., L. Hanoune, and K. Messaoudi. "Engendering or Endangering
Politics in Algeria?" (Spring 2006) 2(2) *Journal of Middle East Woman
Studies*, 64.

Giunchi, E. (ed.) *Adjudicating Family Law in Muslim Courts* (Routledge, 2014).

Glendon, M. *Abortion and Divorce in Western Law* (Harvard University Press,
1987).

*State, Law and Family: Family Law in Transition in the United States and
Western Europe* (North Holland, 1977).

Global Rights, "Promoting Women's Human Rights in Morocco, Algeria and
Tunisia through Strategic Use of the Marriage Contract." (2011).

Goadby, F. M. *International and Inter-Religious Private Law in Palestine*
(Hamadpis Press, 1926).

Gocek, F. "Ethnic Segmentation, Western Education, and Political Outcomes: Nineteenth-Century Ottoman Society." (Autumn 1993) 14(3) *Poetics Today*, 507–538.

Gomaa, A. "In Egypt's Democracy, Room for Islam." *New York Times*, April 1, 2011, www.nytimes.com/2011/04/02/opinion/02gomaa.html.

Gómez-Rivas, C. "Women, Shari'a, and Personal Status Law Reform in Egypt after the Revolution." (October 1, 2011), www.mei.edu/publications/women-sharia-and-personal-status-law-reform-egypt-after-revolution.

Gordon, M. S. "Ben Ali, Zayn al-Abidine." In P. Mattar (ed.) *Encyclopedia of the Modern Middle East and North Africa*, 2nd ed. (Macmillan Reference USA, 2004), vol. 1, p. 439, www.britannica.com/biography/Zine-al-Abidine-Ben-Ali.

Gottschalk, R. "Personal Status and Religious Law in Israel." (1951) 4 *International Law Quarterly*, 454–461.

Greenblatt, A. "In Arab States, It's Good to Be the King." NPR, November 12, 2011, www.npr.org/2011/11/10/142218146/in-arab-states-its-good-to-be-the-king.

Guide to Jaafaree (Ja'fari) Justice (1994) (Lebanon).

Gunay, C. "Mubarak's Egypt: Bad Paternalism, and the Army's Interest in Managed Transition." *OpenDemocracy*, February 3, 2011, www.opendemocracy.net/cengiz-g%C3%BCnay/mubaraks-egypt-bad-paternalism-and-armys-interest-in-managed transition.

Hallaq, W. B. *Authority, Continuity, and Change in Islamic Law* (Cambridge University Press, 2001).

Hamoudi, H. A. "Decolonizing the Legal Centralist Mind: Legal Pluralism and the Rule of Law." In D. Marshall (ed.) *The International Rule of Law Movement: A Crisis of Legitimacy and the Way Forward* (Harvard University Press, 2014), pp. 135–166.

Islamic Law in a Nutshell (West Academic, 2020).

"Notes in Defense of the Iraq Constitution." (2012) 33 *University of Pennsylvania Journal of International Law*, 1277–1301.

"The Political Codification of Islamic Law." (2016) 33 *Arizona Journal of International & Comparative Law*, 329–382.

"Sex and the Shari'a: Defining Gender Norms and Sexual Deviancy in Shi'i Islam." (2015) 39 *Fordham International Law Journal*, 26–97.

Hamoudi, H. A., and M. Cammack. *Islamic Law in Modern Courts* (Aspen, 2019).

Hamzeh, A. N. "Qatar: The Duality of the Legal System." (1994) 30(1) *Middle Eastern Studies*, 79–90.

Hanafi, L. "Moudawana and Women's Rights in Morocco: Balancing National and International Law." (2012) 18 *ILSA Journal of International and Comparative Law*, 515.

Harris, K. M. "Personal Status Law Reform in Jordan: State Bargains and Women's Right in the Law." MA Thesis, Georgetown University (2015).

Hashem, S. "Personal Status Law, Identity Politics and Gender Rhetoric in Bahrain." University of Bristol (December 2015), https://research-information.bris.ac.uk/ws/portalfiles/portal/198917726/Final_Copy_2018_11_06_Hashem_S_MPhil.pdf.

Hassan, F., and A. Rubin, "Iraq's New Election Law Draws Much Criticism and Few Cheers." *New York Times*, December 24, 2019, www.nytimes.com/2019/12/24/world/middleeast/iraq-election-law.html.

Hayden, S. "Tunisian Muslim Women Allowed to Marry Non-Muslims for First Time in Decades."*Independent*, September 15, 2017, www.independent.co.uk/news/world/africa/tunisia-muslim-women-marry-non-muslims-first-time-decades-islamic-sharia-religion-a7948916.html.

HCJ 187/54 *Biriah* v. *Qadi of Muslim Shari'a Court*, 9 P.D. 1193 (1955) (Israel).

HCJ 2820/03 *Plonit* v. *Druze Appellate Court in Acre* (2006) (Israel).

HCJ 3856/11 (27.6.2013) (Israel).

Hechaime, A. "Actualites du Statut Personnel des Communautes Musulmanes au Liban." Droit et Cultures, droitcultures.revues.org/1992.

Hefner, R. "Rewriting Divorce in Egypt: Reclaiming Islam, Legal Activism and Coalition Politics." In R. Hefner (ed.) *Remaking Muslim Politics: Pluralism, Contestation, Democratization* (Princeton University Press, 2005), pp. 161–188.

Hlayel, A. "An Introduction of the Jordanian Personal Status Law." (2011), aliftaa.jo/index.php/ar/articels/show/id/109.

The Holy Qur'an. Translated by Abdullah Yusuf Ali (Wordsworth Classics, 2000).

Hoodfar, H. *Shifting Boundaries in Marriage and Divorce in Muslim Communities* (Women Living Under Muslim Laws, 1996).

Human Rights Council. "Report of the Working Group on the Universal Periodic Review, Algeria." (July 19, 2017) A/HRC/36/13.

Human Rights Watch. "Jordan: End Child Marriage in Status Talks." (April 3, 2019), hrw.org/news/2019/04/03/jordan-end-child-marriage-status-talks.

"Lebanon: Discriminatory Nationality Law." (October 3, 2018), www.hrw.org/news/2018/10/03/lebanon-discriminatory-nationality-law.

"Tunisia: A Step Forward for Women's Rights: Free to Travel with Their Children." (2015), www.hrw.org/news/2015/11/12/tunisia-step-forward-womens-rights.

"Tunisia: Landmark Action on Women's Rights: First in Region to Lift Key Restrictions on International Treaty." (2014), www.hrw.org/news/2014/04/30/tunisia-landmark-action-womens-rights.

"Unequal and Unprotected: Women's Rights under Lebanese Personal Status Laws." (2015).

"Women's Centre for Legal Aid and Counselling, and Equality Now, Joint Submission to the CEDAW Committee on the State of Palestine, 70th session." (2018), www.hrw.org/news/2018/06/11/human-rights-watch-womens-centre-legal-aid-and-counselling-and-equality-now-joint.

Huntington, S. *Class of Civilizations and Remaking of the World Order* (Simon & Shuster, 1996).

Hussein, A. "Egyptian Army Doctor Cleared over 'Virginity Tests' on Women Activists." *GuardianUK*, March 20, 2012, www.guardian.co.uk/world/2012/mar/11/egypt-doctor-cleared-virginity-tests.

Husseini, R. "Female MPs to Lobby Colleagues for Personal Status Law Amendments." *Jordan Times*, December 26, 2018, www.jordantimes.com/news/local/female-mps-lobby-colleagues-personal-status-law-amendments.

Ibáñez Prieto, A. V. "JNCW Urges Amendments to Women's Rights Legislation." *Jordan Times*, February 26, 2018, www.jordantimes.com/news/local/jncw-urges-amendments-women's-rights-legislation.

Ibn Hanbal, A. *Chapters on Marriage and Divorce: Responses of Ibn Hanbal and Ibn Rahwayh*, trans. S. A. Spectorsky (University of Texas Press, 1993).

Ibn Ishaq, M. *The Life of Muhammad*, trans. A. Guillaume (Oxford University Press, 1967).

Ibn Sa'd, M. *The Women of Medina*, trans. A. Bewley (Ta-Ha, 1995).

Immigration and Refugee Board of Canada. "Yemen: Women's Ability (in Practice) to Obtain a Divorce Because Her Husband Has Married a Second Wife Without Her Consent or Because of Spousal Abuse; Whether She Would Retain Custody of Younger Children; Whether Shelters for Battered Women Exist; Whether Battered Women have Access to Legal Advice; Woman's Ability to Take Her Children out of the Country Without Her Husband's Consent; if She Does So, Penalty." *Refworld*, March 7, 2001, www.refworld.org/docid/3df4bec74.html.

Ingerman, D. "Rewriting Divorce in Egypt: Reclaiming Islam, Legal Activism and Coalition Politics." In Robert Hefner (ed.) *Remaking Muslim Politics: Pluralism, Contestation Democratization* (Princeton University Press, 2005), pp. 161–188.

International Civil Society Action Network. "What Women Say: The Arab Spring and Implications for Women." Brief One, December 2011, www.icanpeacework.org/wp-content/uploads/2011/12/ICAN17.pdf.

International Labour Organization. "Libya – Basic Laws in Natlex." ILO, www.ilo.org/dyn/natlex/country_profiles.nationalLaw?p_lang=en&p_country=LBY.

Iraq Court of Cassation, *Shari'a* Panel, Case 520/1963, decided December 26, 1963.

Shari'a Panel, Case 527/1969, decided June 29, 1969.

Shari'a Panel, Case 539/1968, decided October 3, 1968.

Shari'a Panel, Case 708/1968, decided November 24, 1968.

Iraq Federal Court of Cassation, Personal Status Panel I, Case 3888/2010, decided November 2, 2010.

Iraq Federal Court of Cassation, Personal Status I Panel, Case 4765/2011, decided September 25, 2011.

Iraq Personal Status Court of Kadhmiyya, Case 2601/2001, decided September 5, 2001.

Iraq Personal Status Court of Hayy al-Sha'ab, decided September 14, 2009.

Iraq Personal Status Court of Baya' (Sitting in Cassation), Case 5145/186, decided January 14, 2009.

Iraq Personal Status Law of 1959. Retrieved January 30, 2021. www.refworld.org/pdfid/5c7664947.pdf.

Shari'a Panel, Case 385/1968, decided August 22, 1968.

Personal Status I Panel, Case 899/2011.

Iraq Federal Court of Cassation, Personal Status Court I, Case 3356/2011.

Jaafaree/Jafari Legal Manual (1994).

Jeppie, S., E. Moosa, and R. L. Roberts. *Muslim Family Law in Sub Saharan Africa and Post colonial Challenges* (Amsterdam University Press, 2010).

Jo24. Net. "Parliament's Session Settling the Controversy over Inheritance and Marriage" (Original in Arabic). April 8, 2019, www.jo24.net/post.php?id=315190.

Jordanian Personal Status Law, Law 61/1976, Official Gazette no. 2668, published December 1, 1976.

Jordanian Personal Status Law, Law 15/2019, Official Gazette no. 5578, published June 2, 2019.

Jordan Penal Code No. 18/2011, Official Gazette no. 5090, published May 2, 2011.

Jordan Temporary Personal Status Law, Law 82/2001, Official Gazette no.4524, published December 21, 2001.

Jordan 2010 Temporary Personal Status Law, Law 36/2010, Official Gazette no.5061, published October 17, 2010.

Jordanian National Commission for Women (JNCW). The Comments of the JNCW on the Decisions of the Legal Committee of the House of Representatives on the Temporary Personal Status number 36 for the year 2010 [Mulahadat al Lajneh al Wataniyya li Shu'oon al Mar'a a'la qararat a'la Qararat al-Lajneh al Qanooniyya fi Majles al Nuwwab h'awl Qanoon al Ahwal al Shakhsieyya al Mu'aqat Raqam 36 lisanat 2010] Presented to the committee on December 4, 2018.

Jordan Times, "Family Council Seeks Mother's Right to Approve Medical Intervention for Children." *Jordan Times*, May 16, 2015, www.jordantimes.com/news/local/family-council-seeks-mother%E2%80%99s-right-approve-medical-intervention-children.

Kahn-Freund, O. "On Uses and Misuses of Comparative Law." (1974) 37 *Modern Law Review*, 1–27.

Kail, C. E. *Lebanon Second Republic, Prospects for the Twentieth Century* (Florida University Press, 2009).

Kandar, A. "Refusing the Backseat: Women as Drivers of the Yemeni Uprisings."
    In R. Stephan and M. Charrad (eds.) *Women Rising: In and Beyond the Arab
    Spring* (New York University Press, 2020), p. 68.

Karasapan, O., and Volk, M., "Ten Years After Morocco's Family Code
    Reforms: Are Gender Gaps Closing?" World Bank (April 2014), https://
    openknowledge.worldbank.org/bitstream/handle/10986/20550/901480BRI0
    Box30coll0KNOWLEDGE0NOTES.pdf?sequence=1&isAllowed=y.

Karayanni, M. M. *A Multicultural Entrapment: Religion and State among the
    Palestinian-Arabs in Israel* (Cambridge University Press, 2020).

    "In the Best Interests of the Group: Religious Matching under Israeli Adoption
    Law." (2010) 3 *Berkeley Journal Middle East & Islamic Law*, 1–80.

    "Living in a Group of One's Own: Normative Implications Related to the Private
    Nature of the Religious Accommodations for the Palestinian-Arab Minority
    in Israel." (2007) 6 *UCLA Journal Islamic & Near Eastern Law*, 1–46.

    "Multiculturalism as Covering: On the Accommodation of Minority Religions
    in Israel." (2018) 66 *American Journal of Comparative Law*, 831.

    "Multiculture Me No More! On Multicultural Qualifications and the
    Palestinian-Arab Minority of Israel." (2007) 54 *Diogenes*, 1–46.

    "The Separate Nature of the Religious Accommodations for the Palestinian-
    Arab Minority in Israel." (2006) 5 *Northwestern University Journal
    International Human Rights*, 41–71.

    "Two Concepts of Group Rights for the Palestinian-Arab Minority under
    Israel's Constitutional Definition as a 'Jewish and Democratic' State."
    (2012) 10 *I•CON. – International Journal Constitutional Law*, 304–339.

Kasim, R. "The Personal Status Law and Political Tensions in Iraq." 1001 Iraqi
    Thoughts (February 14, 2019), https://1001iraqithoughts.com/2019/02/14/
    the-personal-status-law-and-political-tensions-in-iraq/.

Katja, Ž. E. *Modernizing Patriarchy: The Politics of Women's Rights in Morocco*
    (University of Texas Press, 2015).

Kelly S., and J. Breslin (eds.) *Women's Rights in the Middle East and North Africa:
    Progress amid Resistance* (Freedom House, 2010).

Khader, A. "Jordanian Legal System." (2012), www.asmakhader.com.

Khalife, N. "Tunisia on Board with Women's Rights." *Huffington Post*, September
    29, 2011, www.huffingtonpost.com/nadya-khalife/tunisia-on-board-with-
    wom_b_981689.html.

Khalil, A. (ed.) *Gender, Women and the Arab Spring* (Routledge, 2015).

Khedher, R., "Tracing the Development of the Tunisian 1956 Code of Personal
    Status." (2017) *Journal of International Women's Studies*, https://vc.bridgew
    .edu/jiws/vol18/iss4/3/.

Kostas, S. "Tunisia, Political Participation and Ideology." *Mediterranean Affairs*,
    February 22, 2016, http://mediterraneanaffairs.com/tunisia-political-partici
    pation-and-ideological-compromise/.

Krajeski, J. "Rebellion." *The New Yorker*, March 14, 2012, www.newyorker.com/talk/2011/03/14/110314ta_talk_krajeski.

Kubaisi, A. *Personal Status in the Fiqh, the Courts and the Law*, vol. 1, rev. ed. (Legal Bookstore, 2007).

Kuwait Law No. 51 of 1984 Concerning Personal Status (1984), www.gcc-legal.org/LawAsPDF.aspx?opt&country=1&LawID=1018#Section_1360.

"La Répudiation Représente 49% des Divorces, le khol'â 11%." *El Watan*, February 20, 2018, www.elwatan.com/archives/actualites/la-repudiation-represente-49-des-divorces-le-khola-11-2-20-02-2018 (Algeria).

LandInfo, "Algeria: Marriage and Divorce." LandInfo Country of Origin Information Centre (March 12, 2018), www.justice.gov/eoir/page/file/1296526/download.

LandInfo, "Libya: Nationality, Registration and Documents." LandInfo Country of Origin Information Centre (December 19, 2014), www.justice.gov/eoir/page/file/989516/download.

Langhi, Z. "Gender and State-Building in Libya: Towards a Politics of Inclusion." In Andrea Khalil (ed.) *Gender, Women and the Arab Spring* (Routledge, 2015).

Lapidot-Firilla, A., and R. Elhadad. *Forbidden Yet Practiced: Polygamy and the Cyclical Making of Israeli Policy* (The Center for Strategic and Policy Studies, 2006).

Latrech, B. "Divorce Under Tunisian Law." HG.org, www.hg.org/legal-articles/divorce-under-tunisian-law-35027.

Law No. 462/1955 on the Abolition of *Shari'a* Courts and Community Councils and Transferring Pending Cases to the National Courts. (Egypt) (1955).

Law 1/2000 organizing certain Conditions and Procedures of Litigation in Matters of Personal Status (Egypt) (2000).

Law 25/1929 (Egypt) (1929).

Law 100/1985 (Egypt)(1985).

Law No. 15 of 2008 (Kurdistan). The Amendment of the Implementation of the Personal Status Code, No. 188 of 1959 in the Region of Kurdistan (2008).

Law of the Right of the Divorced Wife to Housing, No. 77 of 1983 (Iraq).

Law of the *Shari'a* Courts (not numbered), issued by King Feysal I, June 30, 1923. (Iraq).

Law No. 25 of 1920 regarding Maintenance and some Questions of Personal Status and Decree-Law No. 25 of 1929 regarding certain Personal Status Provisions (Egypt).

The Law Office of Jeremy D. Morley. "Basics of Saudi Arabian Legal System." Basics of Saudi Law System, www.international-divorce.com/Basics-of-Saudi-Family-Law-System.htm.

The Law Office of Jeremy D. Morley. "Family Law: United Arab Emirates." UAE: Family Law, www.international-divorce.com/uae_family_law.

The Law Office of Jeremy D. Morley. "Qatar's Child Custody Law." Qatar: Family
    Law, www.international-divorce.com/qatar_child_custody#:~:text=Qatar's
    %20law%20as%20to%20child,22%20of%202006.&text=Qatari%20law%
    20applies%20the%20Sharia,legal%20guardianship%20of%20a%20child.
Layish, A. *Marriage, Divorce and Succession in the Druze Family: A Study based on
    Druze Arbitrators and Religious Courts in Israel and the Golan Heights* (Brill,
    1982).
    *Women and Islamic Law in a Non-Muslim State: A Study Based on the Shari'a
    Courts in Israel* (Wiley, Israel Universities Press, 1975).
"Lebanon National Development Report: Toward's a Citizen State." UNDP Report,
    Lebanon (2008–2009).
Lebanon Texts of the draft optional civil laws, www.civil-marriage-lebanon.com.
Leila, R. "Compromising Women's Rights?" Ahramonline (November 7, 2019),
    http://english.ahram.org.eg/NewsContentP/50/355408/AlAhram-Weekly/
    Compromising-women%E2%80%99s-rights.aspx.
Library of Congress. "Legal Provisions on Gender Equality: Arab Countries."
    (2020), www.loc.gov/law/help/gender-equality/arab.php#_ftn15.
Libya Draft Constitutional Charter for the Transitional Stage 2011, www.al-bab
    .com/arab/docs/libya/Libya-Draft-Constitutional-Charter-for-the-
    Transitional-Stage.pdf.
"Libya Drops Election Quota for Women: New Assembly to Be Elected in June." *Al
    Arabiya*, January 20, 2012, http://english.alarabiya.net/articles/2012/01/20/
    189513.html.
Ligue Démocratique des Droits des Femmes. "Rapport de la Fédération de la Ligue
    Démocratique des Droits des Femmes." Examen Périodique Universel
    Maroc (June 2012) (Morocco).
Ligue Démocratique de Défense des Droits des Femmes. "Droits des Femmes et
    Code de la Famille après 4 ans d'application." (2007) (Morocco).
Lindbekk, M. "Inscribing Islamic Shari'a in Egyptian Divorce." (2016) 3(2) *Oslo
    Law Review*, 103–135.
Loi n° 84-11 du 9 juin 1984 portant code de la famille (Algeria).
Loi n° 15-01 du 13 Rabie El Aouel 1436 correspondant au 4 janvier 2015 portant
    création d'un fonds de la pension alimentaire (Algeria).
Loi n° 15-19 du 18 Rabie El Aouel 1437 correspondant au 30 Décembre 2015
    modifiant et complétant l'ordonnance n° 66-156 du 8 juin 1966 portant code
    penal (Algeria).
Lombardi, C. *State Law as Islamic Law in Modern Egypt: The Incorporation of the
    Shari'a into Egyptian Constitutional Law* (Brill, 2006).
Luck, T. "Across the Arab World, a Women's Spring Comes into View." *Christian
    Science Monitor*, August 9, 2017, www.csmonitor.com/World/Middle-East/
    2017/0809/Across-the-Arab-world-a-Women-s-Spring-comes-into-view.

Lustick, I. *Arabs in the Jewish State: Israel's Control of a National Minority* (University of Texas Press, 1980).

Lynch, S. "Muslim Brotherhood Top Winner in Egypt." *USA Today*, November 4, 2011, www.usatoday.com/news/world/story/2011-12-04/israel-egypt-elections/51641978/1.

MacFarquhar, N. "Saudi Monarch Grants Women Right to Vote." *New York Times*, September 26, 2011, www.nytimes.com/2011/09/26/world/middleeast/women-to-vote-in-saudi-arabia-king-says.html?pagewanted=all.

Mahmassani, M., and I. Messara, *Statut Personnel: Textes en Vigueur au Liban*, Documents Huvelin, FDSP (Beyrouth-Liban, 1971) (in French).

Malki, H. "The Kad o Saiya System: Examples from Moroccan Jurisprudence." (1999).

Mamdani, M. *Define and Rule: Native as Political Identity* (Harvard University Press, 2012).

Marr, P. *The Modern History of Iraq*, 3rd ed. (Westview Press, 2012).

Marzouki, N. "Algeria." In S. Kelly and J. Breslin (ed.) *Women's Rights in the Middle East and North Africa: Progress Amid Resistance* (Freedom House, 2010), pp. 29–58.

M'chichi, A. "Changement Social et Perceptions du Nouveau Code de la Famille." In *Le Code de la Famille: Perceptions et Pratique Judiciaire* (Friedrich Ebert Stiftung, 2007), pp. 27–88 (Morocco).

Ministère de la Justice, "Guide Pratique du code de la famille." (2005) (Morocco).

Ministre de la Solidarité, de la Femme, de la Famille et du Développment Social. "10 ans d'Application du Code de la Famille: Quels Changements dans les Perceptions, les Attitudes et les Comportements des Marocains et des Marocaines?" (2016) (Morocco).

Mir-Hosseini, Z. "Decoding the 'DNA of Patriarchy' in Muslim Family Laws." *Open Democracy*, May 21, 2012, www.opendemocracy.net/print/65974.

Marriage on Trial: A Study of Islamic Family Law: Islamic Family Law in Iran and Morocco (I. B. Tauris, 2000).

Mir-Hosseini, Z., M. Al-Sharmani, and J. Rumminger (eds.) *Men in Charge? Rethinking Authority in the Muslim Legal Tradition* (One World Press, 2014).

Moghadam, V. M., and F. Roudi-Fahimi. *Reforming Family Laws to Promote Progress in the Middle East and North Africa* (Population Reference Bureau, 2000).

Moore, H. "Experts Weigh in on Low Female Representation in Parliament." *The Daily News Egypt*, January 27, 2012, www.thedailynewsegypt.com/experts-weigh-in-on-low-female-representation-in-parliament.html.

Moors, A. "Debating Islamic Family Law: Legal Texts and Social Practices." In M. Meriwether and J. Tucker (eds.) *History of Women and Gender in the Modern Middle East* (Westview Press, 1999), pp. 141–175.

Moroccan Family Code (Moudawana) of February 5, 2004. Human Rights Education Associates (HERA) (2005), www.hrea.org/wp-content/uploads/2015/02/Moudawana.pdf.

Moussavi, A. K. and Voss, C. (eds.) "Guide to Equality in the Family in the Maghreb." Women's Learning Partnership Translation Series (2005), https://learningpartnership.org/sites/default/files/resources/pdfs/Final%20Guide%20to%20Equality%20-%20English.pdf.

Musawah. "Bahrain Overview of Muslim Family Laws & Practices." (August 31, 2017), www.musawah.org/wp-content/uploads/2019/03/Bahrain-Overview-Table.pdf.

"Joint Report on Article 16, Muslim Family Law and Muslim Women's Rights in Kuwait." 68th CEDAW Session (November 2017), https://tbinternet.ohchr.org/Treaties/CEDAW/Shared%20Documents/KWT/INT_CEDAW_NGO_KWT_29225_E.pdf.

"Jordan Overview of Muslim Family Laws & Practices." (May 31, 2017), www.musawah.org/wp-content/uploads/2019/03/Jordan-Overview-Table.pdf.

"Lebanon Overview of Muslim Family Laws & Practices." (May 31, 2017), http://arabic.musawah.org/sites/default/files/Lebanon%20-%20Overview%20Table%2003.18.pdf.

"Oman Overview of Muslim Family Laws & Practices." (May 31, 2017), http://arabic.musawah.org/sites/default/files/Oman%20-%20Overview%20Table%2003.18.pdf.

"Thematic Report on Article 16, Muslim Family Law and Muslim Women's Rights in Oman." 68th CEDAW Session. (October 2017), https://tbinternet.ohchr.org/Treaties/CEDAW/Shared%20Documents/OMN/INT_CEDAW_NGO_OMN_29224_E.pdf.

"Thematic Report on Muslim Family Law and Muslim Women's Rights in Palestine." 70th CEDAW Session (July 2018), https://tbinternet.ohchr.org/Treaties/CEDAW/Shared%20Documents/PSE/INT_CEDAW_NGO_PSE_31669_E.pdf.

"Thematic Report on Muslim Family Law and Muslim Women's Rights in Saudi Arabia." 69th CEDAW Session (February 2018), https://tbinternet.ohchr.org/Treaties/CEDAW/Shared%20Documents/SAU/INT_CEDAW_NGO_SAU_30191_E.pdf.

Nakash, Y. *The Shi'is of Iraq*, 2nd ed. (Princeton University Press, 2003).

Nasir, J. *The Islamic Law of Personal Status*, vol. 23. Arab and Islamic Laws Series, 3rd ed. (Kluwer Law International Press, 2001).

The Status of Women under Islamic Law and Modern Islamic Legislation, 3rd ed. (Brill, 2009).

Nazir, S., and L. Tomppert (eds.) *Women's Rights in the Middle East and North Africa: Citizenship and Justice* (Freedom House Press, 2005).

Norwegian Refugee Council. "The Shari'a Courts and Personal Status Laws in the Gaza Strip." (January 2011), www.nrc.no/globalassets/pdf/reports/the-sharia-courts-and-personal-status-laws-in-the-gaza-strip.pdf.

Nossiter, A. "Hinting at an End to a Curb on Polygamy, Interim Libyan Leader Stirs Anger." *New York Times*, October 29, 2011, www.nytimes.com/2011/10/30/world/africa/libyan-leaders-remark-favoring-polygamy-stirs-anger.html?pagewanted=all.

Okin, S. M. "Is Multiculturalism Bad for Women?" In J. Cohen and M. Nussbaum (eds.) *Is Multiculturalism Bad for Women?* (Princeton University Press, 1999), pp. 7–26.

Order of Recognition of a Religious Community (Evangelical Episcopal Church in Israel), 1970, K.T. 2557, p. 1564.

Order of Religious Community (The Bahai Faith), 1971, K.T. 2673, p. 628.

Ordonnance no. 75-58 du Ramadhan 1395 correspondant au 26 septembre 1975 portant code civil, modifié et complétée. (Algeria).

Ordonnance n° 05-02 du 18 moharram 1426 correspondant au 27 février 2005 modifiant et complétant la loi n° 84-11 du 9 juin 1984 portant code de la famille (Algeria).

Otto, J. *Sharia Incorporated: A Comparative Overview of the Legal System of Twelve Muslim Countries in Past and Present* (Leiden University Press, 2010).

Ounnir, A. "Les Justiciables dans le Circuit Judiciaire Relatif au Contentieux de la Famille." In *Le Code de la Famille: Perceptions et Pratique Judiciaire* (Friedrich Ebert Stiftung, 2007), pp. 89–140 (Morocco).

Paciello, M. C. "Tunisia: Changes and Challenges of Political Transition." Mediterranean Prospects Technical Report No. 3. The Center for European Studies 14, (2011), www.ceps.eu/ceps/download/5632.

Palestinian Basic Law (2005), https://constitutions.unwomen.org/en/countries/asia/palestine.

Pargeter, A., "Libya." *Women's Rights in the Middle East and North Africa* (NY Freedom House, 2010), https://freedomhouse.org/sites/default/files/inline_images/Libya.pdf.

Perego, E. "The Veil or a Brother's Life: French Manipulations of Muslim Women's Images during the Algerian War 1954–62." (2015) 20(3) *Journal of North African Studies*, 349–373.

Personal Status Code of Iraq, No. 188 of 1959, enacted December 30, 1959.

Personal Status Court of Hay Al-Sha'ab, decided August 5, 2009.

Personal Status Code, Art. 3(2), as amended by Article 1 of the Kurdistan Personal Status Code Amendment.

Présidence du Ministère Public, "Public Prosecution Activity in Family Cases in Courts." (2018), www.hcp.ma/Mariage-et-divorce-de-la-femme-marocaine-Tendances-d-evolution_a1261.html.

Prettitore, P. S. "Family Law Reform, Gender Equality, and Underage Marriage: A View from Morocco and Jordan." (2015) 13(3) *The Review of Faith & International Affairs*, 32–40.

"Promoting Women's Human Rights in Morocco, Algeria and Tunisia through Strategic Use of the Marriage Contract: Researching and Documenting the Use of Marriage Contracts among Local Authorities." Global Rights (2011).

"Public Prosecution Activity in Family Cases in Courts." (2018) (Morocco).

Qatar Constitution (2004), www.constituteproject.org/constitution/Qatar_2003.pdf?lang=en.

Qatar Family Law, www.almeezan.qa/LawPage.aspx?id=2558&language=en.

Rachid, A. M. *La Condition de la Femme au Maroc* (Faculté des sciences, 1985) (Morocco).

Ramadan, M. A. "Judicial Activism of the Shari'a Appeals Court in Israel (1994–2001): Rise and Crises." (2003) 27 *Fordham International Law Journal*, 254–298.

Reinkowski, M. *Ottoman "Multiculturalism"? The Example of the Confessional System in Lebanon* (Orient Institute of the Deutsche Morgenlandische Gesellschaft, 1997), https://freidok.uni-freiburg.de/fedora/objects/freidok:4403/datastreams/FILE1/content.

Rekik, S. "Le Code Algérien de la Famille: Pourquoi a-t-il Relégué la Femme Algérienne au Statut de 'Deuxième Sexe ?'" *El Watan*, March 27, 2007.

"Report of the Special Rapporteur on Violence against Women, Its Causes and Consequences, Mission to Algeria." May 19, 2011, A/HRC/17/26/Add.3.

"Report of the Working Group on the Issue of Discrimination against Women in Law and in Practice, Addendum Mission to Morocco." June 19, 2012, A/HRC/20/28/Add.1.

République Tunisienne, *Code de la Nationalité Tunisienne, Code of Tunisian Citizenship* (Imprimerie Officielle, 1983).

Roberts, D. "Qatar and the Muslim Brotherhood: Pragmatism or Preference?" Middle East Policy Council, September 3, 2014, www.mepc.org/qatar-and-muslim-brotherhood-pragmatism-or-preference.

Roberts, R. "Tunisia: 'Landmark' New Law Gives Women Protection from Rape and Domestic Violence." *Independent*, July 28, 2017, www.independent.co.uk/news/world/tunisia-law-women-protect-rape-domestic-violence-north-africa-landmark-rights-abuse-sexual-a7864846.html.

Rogers, A. "Revolutionary Nuns or Totalitarian Pawns: Evaluating Libyan State Feminism after Mu'ammar al-Gaddafi." In F. Sadiqi (ed.) *Women's Movements in Post-'Arab Spring' North Africa* (Palgrave, 2016) p. 177.

Rouhana, N. *Palestinian Citizens in an Ethnic Jewish State: Identities in Conflict* (Yale University Press, 1997).

Russell, M. L. "Competing, Overlapping, and Contradictory Agendas: Egyptian Education Under British Occupation, 1882–1922." (2001) 21(1–2) *Comparative Studies of South Asia, Africa and the Middle East*, 50–60.

Ryan, Y. "Ennahda Claims Victory in Tunisia Poll." *Aljazeera English*, October 26, 2011, www.aljazeera.com/news/africa/2011/10/2011102421511587304.html.

"Tunisia's Election through the Eyes of Women." *AlJazeera*, October 23, 2011, http://english.aljazeera.net/indepth/spotlight/2011tunisiaelection/2011/10/20111022104341755235.html.

Sabbagh, A. "A Critical Assessment of NWMs: The Case of Jordan." (2006).

Sadiqi, F. ed. *Women's Movements in Post-"Arab Spring" North Africa* (Palgrave MacMillan, 2016).

Saghieh, N. *Beyond Civil Marriage: Freedom Is the Principle* (Legal Agenda 2013), https://english.legal-agenda.com/beyond-civil-marriage-freedom-is-the-principle/ (Lebanon).

Saleh, H. "Egyptian Women Fear Regression on Rights." *Financial Times*, October 1, 2012, www.ft.com/content/b203c126-06f5-11e2-92ef-00144feabdc0.

Saleh, Y. "Rewrite Egypt Constitution from Scratch, say Critics." *Reuters*, February 16, 2011, http://af.reuters.com/article/topNews/idAFJOE71F0N620110216.

Salem, N. *The Impact of the Convention on the Elimination of All Forms of Discrimination against Women on the Domestic Legislation in Egypt* (Brill Nijhoff, 2018).

Sally, H. "Tunisian Muslim Women Allowed to Marry Non-Muslims for First Time in Decades." *Independent*, September 15, 2017, www.independent.co.uk/news/world/africa/tunisia-muslim-women-marry-non-muslims-first-time-decades-islamic-sharia-religion-a7948916.html.

Salman, I. *History of Tafileh from the End of the Ottoman Empire to the Independence of the Hashemite Kingdom of Jordan (1892–1946)* [*Tarikh al-Tafileh min awakher al-Dawlah al-Uthmaniyya h'ta Istiqlal al-Malaka al-Urduniyya al-Hashimiyya 1892/1309H–1946/1365H*] (Ministry of Culture, 2009).

Sandy, M. "Saudi Arabia Giving Citizens a 15 Percent Raise to Avoid Becoming the Next Libya." *AOL News*, February 23, 2011, www.aolnews.com/2011/02/23/saudi arabia giving citizens a 15 percent raise to avoid becoming the next libya/.

Sarayrah, R. "Chief Islamic Justice Department Hands over Personal Status Law to Cabinet Today." (Original in Arabic: "Da'irat Qadi Al Quda tarfa' al yaoum ta'leemat khasa bi qanoon al ahwal al shakhsiah limajles al wisara' li'iqrar-iha"), *Al Ghad News*paper, November 21, 2010, www.alghad.jo.

Schemm, P. "This Arab Country Is Allowing Muslim Women to Marry Non-Muslim Men. That's the Good News." *The Washington Post*, September 22, 2017, www.washingtonpost.com/news/worldviews/wp/2017/09/22/this-arab-country-is-allowing-muslim-women-to-marry-non-muslim-men-thats-the-good-news/?utm_term=.d419c4c60f58.

Schneider, I., and N. Edres (eds.) *Uses of the Past: Shari'a and Gender in Legal Theory and Practice in Palestine and Israel* (Harrassowitz Verlag, 2018).

Sebti, F. "Décryptage du nouveau code de la famille." (2007), https://jurismaroc .vraiforum.com/t255-Decryptage-du-nouveau-code-de-la-famille.htm (Morocco).

Second Amendment to the Personal Status Code, No. 21 of 1978, enacted February 20, 1978. (Iraq) (on file with editor).

Serehane, F. "Décryptage du Nouveau Code de la Famille." (March 2004) *Femmes du Maroc Supplément*, https://jurismaroc.vraiforum.com/t255-Decryptage-du-nouveau-code-de-la-famille.htm.

Sezgin, Y. "The Israeli Millet System: Examining Legal Pluralism through the Lens of Nation Building and Human Rights." (2010) 43 *Israel Law Review*, 631–654.

"Women's Rights in the Triangle of State, Law and Religion: A Comparison of Egypt and India." (2011) 25 *Emory International Law Review*, 1007–1028.

Sfeir, G. N. "The Tunisian Code of Personal Status." (1957) 11 *Middle East Journal*, 309–318.

Shachar, A. *Multicultural Jurisdictions: Cultural Differences and Women's Rights* (Cambridge University Press, 2001).

Shahawy, S. "The Unique Landscape of Abortion Law and Access in the Occupied Palestinian Territories." *Health and Human Rights Journal*, December 9, 2019, www.hhrjournal.org/2019/12/the-unique-landscape-of-abortion-law-and-access-in-the-occupied-palestinian-territories/.

Shalaby, M., and A. Marnicio. "Women's Political Participation in Bahrain." In R. Stephan and M. Charrad (eds.) *Women Rising: In and Beyond the Arab Spring* (New York University Press, 2020), p. 321.

Shamleh, M. "Important Changes in the new Jordanian JPSL: The Need to Inform the First Wife When Her Husband Marries Another after the Marriage Contract Is Conducted and Prohibiting Beating Using the Excuse of Nushooz." (Original in Arabic), April 20, 2010, www.sahafi.jo/files/ 51f89b17d8f0daddce0720efe087acd5a3c1b057.html.

Shava, M. "Civil Marriage Celebrated Abroad: Validity in Israel." (1989) 9 *Tel Aviv University Studies Law*, 11–46.

Ha-Din ha-Ishi be-Yisra'el [*The Personal Law in Israel*], 3rd enlarged ed., 2 vols. (Masada, 1991), vol. I (in Hebrew).

"The Nature and Scope of Jewish Law in Israel as Applied in the Civil Courts as Compared with its Application in the Rabbinical Courts." (1985) *Jewish Law Annual*, 3–24.

Shehada, N. *Applied Family Law in Islamic Courts: Shari'a Courts in Gaza* (Routledge, 2018).

Sistani, A. *Minhaj al-Saliheen* (Dar Al-Muwazza' al-Arabi, 2008) (Iraq).

Sonbol, A. A. "A History of Marriage Contracts in Egypt." In *The Islamic Marriage Contract: Case Studies in Islamic Family Law* (Islamic Legal Studies Program, Harvard Law School, 2008), pp. 87–122.

Women of Jordan: Islam, Labour and the Law (Syracuse University Press, 2003).

Women, the Family, and Divorce Laws in Islamic History (Syracuse University Press, 2007).

Sonneveld, N. "Divorce Reform in Egypt and Morocco: Men and Women Navigating Rights and Duties." (2019) 26 *Islamic Law and Society*, 149–178.

"From the Liberation of Women to the Liberation of Men? A Century of Family Law Reform in Egypt." (2017) 7(1) *Religion and Gender*, 88–104.

Khul' Divorce in Egypt: Public Debates, Judicial Practices, and Everyday Life (American University in Cairo Press, 2012).

"Rethinking the Difference between Formal and Informal Marriages in Egypt." In Maaike Voorhoeve (ed.) *Family Law in Islam: Divorce, Marriage and Women in the Muslim World.* New Middle Eastern Studies 5 (I. B. Tauris, 2012), 77–107.

Sonneveld, N., and M. Lindbekk. "A Revolution in Muslim Family Law? Egypt's Pre and Post-Revolutionary Period (2011–2013) Compared." (2015) 5 *New Middle Eastern Studies*, www.brismes.ac.uk/nmes/archives/1409.

Spencer, R. "Egypt: Islamist Judge to Head New Constitution Committee." *Telegraph*, February 15, 2011, www.telegraph.co.uk/news/worldnews/afri caandindianocean/egypt/8326469/Egypt-amist-judge-to-head-new-constitu tion-committee.html.

St. John, R. "Libya's Gender Wars: The Revolution within the Revolution." (2017) 22(5) *Journal of North African Studies*, 888–906.

State of Kuwait. "Law No. 51 of 1984 Concerning Personal Status (51/1984)." Gulf Cooperation Council, www.gcc-legal.org/LawAsPDF.aspx?opt&country=1& LawID=1018#Section_1357.

"Statistiques des Sections de la Justice de la Famille Année." 2011, adala.justice.gov .ma/production/statistiques/SJF/FR/30-10-12%20VR%20Finale% 20Statistique%20Francais.pdf. (Morocco).

Stendel, O. "The Minorities in Israel: Trends in the Development of the Arab and Druze Communities 1948–1973." *The Israel Economist* (1973), 52.

Stephan, R., and M. Charrad. "Introduction: Advancing Women's Rights in the Arab World." In R. Stephan and M. Charrad (eds.) *Women Rising: In and Beyond the Arab Spring* (New York University Press, 2020), p. 1.

Stephan. R., and M. Charrad (eds.) *Women Rising: In and Beyond the Arab Spring* (New York University Press, 2020).

Stilt, K. "Islamic Law and the Making and Remaking of the Iraqi Legal System." (2004) 36 *George Washington International Law Review*, 695–756.

Stopler, G. "Countenancing the Oppression of Women: How Liberals Tolerate Religious and Cultural Practices that Discriminate against Women." (2003) 12 *Columbia Journal Gender & Law*, 154–221.

"The Free Exercise of Discrimination: Religious Liberty, Civic Community and Women's Equality." (2004) 10 *William & Mary Journal Women & Law*, 459–532.

"'A Rank Usurpation of Power': The Role of Patriarchal Religion and Culture in the Subordination of Women." (2008) 15 *Duke Journal Gender Law & Policy*, 365–397.

Stowasser, B. F. *Women in the Qur'an, Traditions, and Interpretation* (Oxford University Press, 1994).

Supreme Council for Family Affairs. "Youth Attitudes towards the Issues of Marriage." (2010) (Qatar).

Sutter, J. "The Faces of Egypt's 'Revolution 2.0.'" CNN World, February 21, 2011, www.cnn.com/2011/TECH/innovation/02/21/egypt.internet.revolution/index.html.

Tabazah, S. "Jordan's Civil Society Fights for More Rights in Personal Status Law." *Al-MONITOR*, December 26, 2018, www.al-monitor.com/pulse/originals/2018/12/jordan-civil-status-code-women-marriage-divorce-children.html.

Tabet, G., *Women in Personal Status Laws: Iraq, Jordan* (Gender Equality and Development Section, UNESCO, 2005).

Tarabey, L. *Family Law in Lebanon: Marriage and Divorce among the Druze* (I. B. Tauris, 2013).

"Tawakkul Karman Says Yemenis Will Continue with Their Peaceful Revolution." *Al Arabiya*, November 10, 2011, http://english.alarabiya.net/articles/2011/11/10/176398.html.

The 1931 Regulations for *Shari'a* courts, Part. 4 of the Code of Civil and Criminal Procedure that was dealing with personal status cases and Law No 162 of 1955 Law No. 462/1955 on the Abolition of *Shari'a* Courts and Community Councils and Transferring Pending Cases to the National Courts (Egypt).

The Message of the Qur'an. Translated by Muhammad Asad (The Book Foundation England, 2003).

The World Bank Group. "Urban Population." (2016), data.worldbank.org/indicator/SP.URB.TOTL.IN.ZS?end=2016&start=1960.

Toledano, H. *Judicial Practice and Family Law in Morocco* (Columbia University Press, 1982).

Touchent, D. "Features: A Guide to the Tunisian legal system." *Legal and Technology Resources for Legal Professionals* (2002), www.llrx.com/node/870/print.

Treitel, A. "Conflicting Traditions: Muslim Shari'a Courts and Marriage Age Regulation in Israel." (1995) 26 *Columbia Human Rights Law Review*, 403–438.

Tucker, J. "Revisiting Reform: Women and the Ottoman Law of Family Rights, 1917." (1996) 4(2) *The Arab Studies Journal*, 4–17.

    Women, Family, and Gender in Islamic Law (Cambridge University Press, 2008).

Tunisia Code of Personal Status (CPS). See "Appendix: English Translation of the Tunisian Personal Status Code." In Voorhoeve, Maaike. *Gender and Divorce*

Law in North Africa: Sharia, Custom and the Personal Status Code of Tunisia (I. B. Tauris, 2014).

"Tunisia's Islamist Ennahda Party Wins Historic Poll." BBC, October 27, 2011, www.bbc.co.uk/news/world-africa-15487647.

Ulrichsen, K. "The Uprising in Bahrain: Regional Dimensions and International Consequences." L. Sadiki (ed.) *Routledge Handbook of the Arab Spring* (Routledge, 2015), p. 133.

UN Committee on the Elimination of Discrimination against Women. "Third Periodic Report of State Parties: Lebanon." (July 7, 2006).

UN Committee on the Elimination of Discrimination against Women. "Concluding Observations of the Committee, 51st session, 13 February–2 March 2012." CEDAW/C/DZA/CO/3–4.

UNDP. "National Human Development Report 2008–2009."

UN Women. "Revisiting Rwanda Five Years after Record-breaking Parliamentary Elections." August 13, 2018, www.unwomen.org/en/news/stories/2018/8/fea ture-rwanda-women-in-parliament.

"Tunisia's New Constitution: A Breakthrough for Women's Rights." February 11, 2014, www.unwomen.org/en/news/stories/2014/2/tunisias-new-constitution.

UNICEF. "The State of the World's Children." (2016), www.unicef.org/publica tions/files/UNICEF_SOWC_2016.pdf, p. 151.

"Tunisia: Statistics." (2013), www.unicef.org/infobycountry/Tunisia_statistics .html.

United Nations, Human Rights Council. "Report of the Working Group on the Issue of Discrimination against Women in Law and in Practice." (June 19, 2012), A/HRC/20/28/Add.1.

United Nations Human Rights Office of the High Commissioner. "On Mechanisms for Parity between Men and Women: 'No Delays!': The Working Group Ends Its Visit to Morocco (February 13–20, 2012), www .ohchr.org/EN/NewsEvents/Pages/DisplayNews.aspx?NewsID=11842&LangID=E.

United States Department of State. "2017 Country Reports on Human Rights Practices: Saudi Arabia." (2017), www.state.gov/reports/2017-country-reports-on-human-rights-practices/saudi-arabia/.

United States Department of State Office of International Religious Freedom. "West Bank and Gaza 2019 International Religious Freedom Report." (2019), www.state.gov/wp-content/uploads/2020/06/WEST-BANK-AND-GAZA-2019-INTERNATIONAL-RELIGIOUS-FREEDOM-REPORT.pdf.

United States Embassy in Kuwait. "Family Law in Kuwait." https://kw.usembassy .gov/u-s-citizen-services/local-resources-of-u-s-citizens/family-law-kuwait/.

Vitta, E. "Codification of Private International Law in Israel?" *Israel Law Review* 12 (2), 129–154.

The Conflict of Laws in Matters of Personal Status in Palestine (Bursi, 1947).

"The Conflict of Personal Laws." (1970) 5 *Israel Law Review*, 170–202.

Volpp, L. "Blaming Culture for Bad Behavior." (2000) 12 *Yale Journal of Law & the Humanities*, 89–118.

Voorhoeve, M. (ed.) *Family Law in Islam: Divorce, Marriage and Women in the Muslim World* (I. B. Tauris, 2012).

Wadud, A. *Inside the Gender Jihad: Women's Reform in Islam* (One World, 2006).

Warga, J., "Has Morocco's 'Family Code' Shown How Gender Equality Can Coexist with Islam in the Courts?" *The World*, May 18, 2015, www.pri.org/stories/2015-05-18/has-moroccos-family-code-shown-how-gender-equality-can-coexist-islam-courts.

Warrick, C. *Law in the Service of Legitimacy: Gender and Politics in Jordan* (Ashgate, 2009).

Watts, S., "The Impact on Women of Changes in Personal Status Law in Tunisia." World Health Organization (June 2007), www.who.int/social_determinants/resources/changes_personal_status_tunisia_wgkn_2007.pdf.

Weiss, M. *In the Shadow of Sectarianism: Law, Shi'ism and the Making of Modern of Lebanon* (Harvard University Press, 2010).

Welchman, L. "Bahrain, Qatar, UAE: First time Family Codification in Three Gulf States." in B. Atkin (ed.) *International Survey of Family Law 2010* (Family Law, 2010), pp 163–178.

Beyond the Code: Muslim Family Law and the Shari Judiciary in the Palestinian West Bank (Kluwer, 2000).

"The Development of Islamic Family Law in the Legal System of Jordan." (October 1988) 37(4) *The International and Comparative Law Quarterly*, 868–886.

"Gulf Women and the Codification of Muslim Family Law." In A. A. Sonbol (ed.) *Gulf Women* (Bloomsbury Qatar Foundation, 2010).

"In the Interim: Civil Society, the Shar'i Judiciary and Palestinian Personal Status Law in the Transitional Period." (2003) 10(1) *Islamic Law and Society*, 34–69.

Women and Muslim Family Laws in Arab States: A Comparative Overview of Textual Development and Advocacy (Amsterdam University Press, 2007).

Whitaker, B. "Tunisia Is Leading the Way on Women's Rights in the Middle East." *The Guardian*, September 20, 2011, www.guardian.co.uk/commentisfree/2011/sep/10/tunisia-un-human-rights-women.

Wing, A. K. "The Arab Fall: The Future of Women's Rights." (2012) 18 *University of California Davis Journal of International Law & Policy*, 445–469.

"Constitutionalism, Legal Reform, and the Economic Development of Palestinian Women." (2006) 15 *Transnational Law & Contemporary Problems*, 655–716.

"Critical Race Feminist Conceptualization of Violence: South African and Palestinian Women." (1997) 60 *Albany Law Review*, 943–976.

"Critical Race Feminist Conceptualization of Violence: South African and Palestinian Women." In A. K. Wing (ed.) *Global Critical Race Feminism: An International Reader* (New York University Press, 2000), pp. 332–347.

"Critical Race Feminism and the International Human Rights of Women in Bosnia, Palestine, and South Africa: Issues for Lat-Crit Theory." (1997) 28 *Miami Inter-American Law Review*, 337–360.

"Custom, Religion and Rights: The Future Legal Status of Palestinian Women." (1994) 35 *Harvard Journal of International Law*, 149–200.

Democracy, Constitutionalism & the Future State of Palestine: With a Case Study of Women's Rights (PASSIA Institute, 1994).

"Foreword." In K. McKanders (ed.) *Arabs at Home and in the World: Human Rights, Gender Politics, and Identity* (Taylor & Francis Routledge, 2019), pp. vii–ix.

"Global Critical Race Feminism: A Perspective on Gender, War and Peace in the Age of the War on Terror." (2007) 15 *Michigan State Journal of International Law*, 1–20.

"Global Critical Race Feminism Post 9-11: Afghanistan." (2002) 6 *Washington University Journal of Law & Policy*, 19–36.

"Healing Spirit Injuries: Human Rights in the Palestinian Basic Law." (2002) 54 *Rutgers Law Review*, 1087–1100.

"Introduction to the Symposium: Women in the Revolution: Gender and Social Justice after the Arab Spring." (2015) 24 *Transnational Law & Contemporary Problems*, 293–302.

"Introduction: Toward Gender Equality in Palestine." In H. Ludsin (ed.) *Women and the Draft Constitution of Palestine* (Women's Centre for Legal Aid and Counselling, 2012), pp. 12–27.

"Liberation to State Building in South Africa: Some Constitutional Considerations for Palestine." In S. Silverburg (ed.) *Palestine and International Law: Essays on Politics and Economics* (Mc Farland & Co., 2002), pp. 199–213.

"The New South African Constitution: An Example for Palestinian Consideration." (1992–1994) 7 *Palestine Yearbook of International Law*, 105–30.

"The Palestinian Basic Law: Embryonic Constitutionalism." (1999) 31 *Case Western Reserve Journal of International Law*, 383–426.

"Palestinian Women and Human Rights." In D. Koenig and K. Asken (eds.) *Women's International Human Rights: A Reference Guide* (Transnational, 2001), pp. 567–612.

"Palestinian Women and Human Rights in the Post 9-11 World." (2002) 24 *Michigan Journal of International Law*, 421–430.

"Palestinian Women: Their Future Legal Status." (1994) 16(1) *Arab Studies Quarterly*, 55–73.

"A Truth and Reconciliation Commission for Palestine/Israel: Healing Spirit Injuries." (2008) 17 *Transnational Law & Contemporary Problems Journal*, 139–164.

"Tunisian Constitutionalism and Women's Rights." (November 27, 2012), www .iconnectblog.com/2012/11/tunisian-constitutionalism-and-womens-rights.

"Twenty-First Century Loving: Gender Equality in the Muslim World." (2008) 76 *Fordham Law Review*, 2895–2906.

"The War against Terror: Religion, Clothing, and the Human Right to Peace." In B. Goh, B. Offord, and R. Garbutt et al. (eds.) *Activating Human Rights and Peace* (Ashgate, 2012), pp. 189–199.

"Women, Gender and International Conventions." In S. Joseph (ed.) *Encyclopedia of Women and Islamic Cultures, Family Law, & Politics* (Brill, 2005), pp. 306–309.

"'Women in the Revolution: Gender and Social Justice After the Arab Spring: Roundtable Discussion (Symposium: Women in the Revolution: Gender and Social Justice After the Arab Spring)." with A. Souaiaia, M. Charrad, K. Bennoune, S. Ahmadi, S. F. Aziz, S. Yildirim, and S. Ghadiri (2015) 24 *Transnational Law & Contemporary Problems*, 391 410; and (2016) 18 *Journal of Gender, Race & Justice*, 437.

Wing, A. K., and H. A. Kassim. "After the Last Judgment: The Future of the Egyptian Constitution." (2011) 52 *Harvard International Law Journal Online*, 301, www.harvardilj.org/2011/04/online_52_wing_kassim.

"Founding Mothers for a Palestinian Constitution." In S. H. Williams (ed.) *Constituting Equality* (Cambridge University Press, 2009), pp. 290–311.

"The Future of Palestinian Women's Rights: Lessons from a Half Century of Tunisian Progress." (2007) 64 *Washington & Lee Law Journal*, 1551–1570.

"Hamas, Constitutionalism, and Palestinian Women." (2007) 50 *Howard Law Journal*, 479–514.

Wing, A. K., and S. Merchan. "Rape, Ethnicity and Culture: Spirit Injury from Bosnia to Black America." (1993) 25 *Columbia Human Rights. Law Review*, 1.

"Spirit Injury, Exile, and the State of Palestine." In A. Haebich and B. Offord (eds.) *Landscapes of Exile* (Peter Lang, 2008) pp. 249–262.

Wing, A. K., and P. Nadimi. "Muslim Women's Rights in the Age of Obama." (2011) 20 *Transnational Law & Contemporary Problems Journal*, 431–464.

Wing, A. K., and S. Nielson. "Gaza, Gender, and the Age of Obama." (2009) 36 *Rutgers Law Record*, 150–164.

Wing, A. K., and N. Shalhoub-Kevorkian. "Violence against Palestinian Women in the West Bank." In R. Goel and L. Goodmark (eds.) *Comparative Perspectives on Domestic Violence: Lessons from Efforts Worldwide* (Oxford University Press, 2015), pp. 59–70.

Wing, A. K., and M. Smith. "Critical Race Feminism Lifting the Veil? Muslim Women, France and the Headscarf Ban." (2006) 39 *University of California at Davis Law Review*, 743–786.

Wing, A. K., and O. Varol. "Is Secularism Possible in a Majority-Muslim Country in the Post 9/11 World? The Turkish Example." (2007) 42 *Texas Journal of International Law*, 1–54.

World Intellectual Property Organization. "Tunisia: The Constitution of Tunisia, 1959." (2011), www.wipo.int/wipolex/en/details.jsp?id=7201.

Worrall, J. "Protest and Reform: The Arab Spring in Oman." In L. Sadiki (ed.) *Routledge Handbook of the Arab Spring* (Routledge, 2015), p. 480.

Yehia, K., "On Tunisia's Elections." *Al Ahram*, http://weekly.ahram.org.eg/2011/1071/re4.htm.

Zeidguy, R. *Analyse de la jurisprudence, Le Code de la Famille: Perceptions et Pratique Judiciaire'* (Friedrich Ebert Stiftung, 2007), pp. 217–271 (Morocco).

Zuhur, S. "Empowering Women or Dislodging Sectarianism: Civil Marriage in Lebanon." (2002) 14 *Yale Journal of Law & Feminism*, 177–208.

Zulficar, M. "The Islamic Marriage Contract in Egypt." In A. Quraishi and F. E. Vogel (eds.) *The Islamic Marriage Contract: Case Studies in Islamic Family Law*. Harvard Series in Islamic Law, 6 (Harvard University Press, 2008), pp. 231–274.

INDEX

For EU product safety concerns, contact us at Calle de José Abascal, 56–1°,
28003 Madrid, Spain or eugpsr@cambridge.org.

www.ingramcontent.com/pod-product-compliance
Ingram Content Group UK Ltd.
Pitfield, Milton Keynes, MK11 3LW, UK
UKHW020354140625
459647UK00020B/2471